The School of
Restoration

The School of Restoration

The story of one Ugandan woman who has
given hope to hundreds of female survivors of
war and violence

Alice Achan
and Philippa Tyndale

Karrikins

First published by Allen & Unwin in 2020
This edition published 2021
Copyright © 2020, 2021 Philippa Tyndale

The names of some of the young women in the book have been changed.

Karrikins
www.philippatyndale.com

 A catalogue record for this book is available from the National Library of Australia

ISBN 978 0 646 84872 3

Maps by MAPgraphics
Index by Puddingburn
Set in 12.5/17 pt Adobe Garamond Pro by Midland Typesetters, Australia

To my father, Otto Zedekiah, and mother, Lucie, who gave me the courage to fight to improve the lives of war-affected girls—Alice

To young women and girls everywhere who daily suffer sexual and gender-based violence; particularly to the girls of Pader Girls Academy who have so generously shared their lives and stories; and to Alice, who continues to prove that one brave woman, armed with faith and boldness, can change the lives of many other women—Philippa

Contents

Uganda

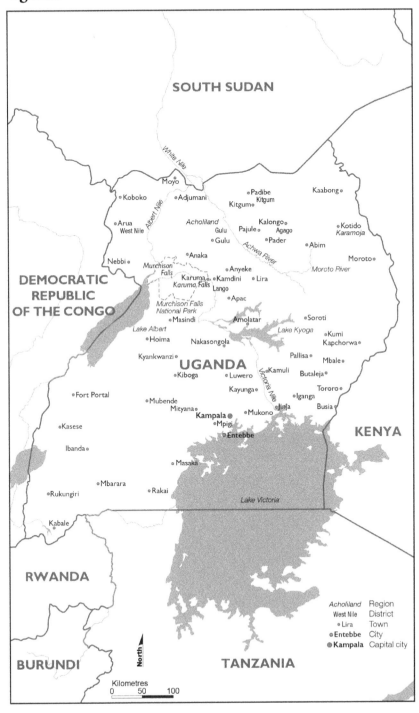

Northern Uganda

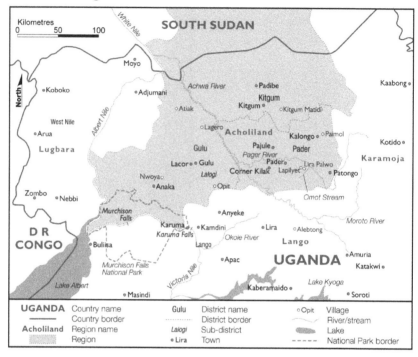

Glossary and List of Acronyms

acoo maber Good morning (reply)

ajwaka Witch doctor

akul A type of enclosure for animals

aleya An informal community system of rotational, cooperative work aimed at sharing the workload

anyeri Edible rat

Apwoyo A greeting (can mean 'thank you')

apoli Little antelope

awal A bottle gourd used for carrying water

bwola The Acholi royal dance

calabash A gourd used as a container

CCF Christian Counseling Fellowship

dada A grandmother

dero Granary used to keep grains dry and safe from rodents

dol Doll

dye-kal A compound, communal courtyard or homestead square

gomesi Traditional women's outfit

HSMF Holy Spirit Mobile Forces

icoo maber Good morning

IDP Internally Displaced Person

jok A class of spirits within the Acholi traditional belief system; when capitalised, it refers to the supreme being

kalang Black garden ant

kasimuru A milk-like drink

kikooyi A sarong-style wrap

kir A cultural taboo

kraal A type of enclosure for animals

kworo A native tree with fig-like fruits

ladit jago Sub-county chief

lak lyec Elephant tusk

lakica Mercy

Lakristo Christian

lakwena Messenger (it can also be used as a proper noun: [Alice] Lakwena, or Alice Lakwena's group)

lanyakidi A grinding stone

Lok ango How are you?

LRA Lord's Resistance Army

malariya Malaria

matatu (Swahili word) A van used as public transport

mego A mother or older woman

Min Mother [of], as in Min Labeja

myel lyel A dance performed at Acholi funerals

mzungu (Bantu word) A white visitor

neko Killing

ngwen White ant, an Acholi delicacy

Nilotics An ethnic group of people indigenous to the Nile Valley

NRA National Resistance Army

nyuka Porridge

nywaro Rape; taking what is not yours

ober Mosquito

obiya Green grass

Obur A masculine surname, which also means the old homestead

OCHA Office for the Coordination of Humanitarian Affairs

ododo Folklore or a story

oro The dry season, from November to March

ottlum A type of grass-thatched hut

pai-pai Pawpaw

panga A machete

posho A porridge made with maize meal

rwot kalam A pen chief appointed by the colonial regime, not by birth

simsim Sesame

togo Green papyrus

tukul A type of grass-thatched hut

two jonyo 'Tired disease' aka HIV/AIDS

UNLA Uganda National Liberation Army

UPDA Uganda People's Democratic Army

UPDF Uganda People's Defence Forces

wang oo A bonfire, made in the evening for family gatherings

waya Aunt

Yesu A form of the name Jesus

Prologue

On any given day, on some part of the planet, people are engaged in war—there has always been war in our world. Right now, in sub-Saharan Africa, half a dozen or more civil wars simmer in places such as Nigeria, Sudan and Somalia, while Sierra Leone, Liberia, Burundi and other countries lick their wounds from their own damaging conflicts. The brutal tactics of choice often involve the rape of girls, and both boys and girls are handed guns and forced to fight. Over two decades in northern Uganda, the Acholi people lost everything in one such war: freedom and life, innocence and limbs, family and property, identity and hope.

The ubiquity of war makes it easier to ignore what is happening 'over there', especially if we live in a safe, peaceful country where our housing and food supplies are secure, and we enjoy good schools, generous welfare and half-decent health services. Sometimes it seems easier to block our ears to horrendous news reports and to cushion our lives to ward off the emotional pain that comes with seeing others suffer.

I've done my fair share of that. But my ability to disconnect from the impact of conflict on individuals—especially girls and women—was challenged the day I walked into the Pader Girls Academy in northern Uganda.

It didn't take long to realise that this was not a usual school, not even for northern Uganda, which in July 2008 was still in disarray after twenty years of civil war. It took just the twenty steps from the Land Cruiser to the school's barren compound to know that here was something extraordinary. Small groups of teenage girls and young women in aloe green dresses were playing games and laughing like school friends anywhere, happy and full of life, with one visible difference to school kids in my own country: their heads were almost bald, hair cropped to half a centimetre in length, as dictated by school rules.

Most tended to babies—*their* babies. Some of the girls chased after toddlers, while others washed infants in plastic tubs, or lounged on wooden benches breastfeeding their little ones.

It was hot, and the smell of beans cooking over an open fire wafted out of the mud-brick kitchen. Nearby, chickens pecked at the dry ground, and a patch of straggly maize plants seemed ready to wither and die. The air around us smelled of dried grass and dust, with a fainter note of sewage.

Before I could be overwhelmed, a strikingly tall woman appeared from the school building, her hand outstretched. 'I'm Alice. You are most welcome,' she said, with the widest of smiles. She led me through a green metal door into the main building, into a large open room with a concrete floor, filled with green double bunks. Here, there were more girls, and more babies on the girls' breasts.

Later, she told me what many of the girls at Pader Girls Academy had overcome to be there. They had been snatched from their village homes by the Lord's Resistance Army (LRA), a rebel group that had been fighting Ugandan government forces since the 1980s, and forced to carry heavy loads on their heads while walking barefoot for day upon day through rugged bush. Beatings and sexual abuse occurred daily, and they were sent out as fodder in battle. Despite bodies that were too young to handle pregnancy, they endured lonely and unsafe births.

'We must give them a chance. Some of these girls are so clever, they could go on to university, to nursing or teaching or business.' Her passion won me over to her cause in an instant.

Alice Achan had faced her own challenges to stay in school as a teenage girl. She shared with me how, as a girl growing up during this conflict, she had lost her idyllic village life, lived in fear of abduction by LRA rebels and hidden for weeks on end. She had lost members of her family to bullets and HIV, spent formative years out of school, and struggled to finish her education. It was beyond humbling to consider the journey that had brought her here. Yet she was using her experience to create opportunities for these young mothers, by offering training in hospitality, sewing, hairdressing and academic studies. Bit by bit, over a few short years, she had reclaimed her own life and built pathways for hundreds of girls to follow. At Pader Girls Academy, she was fighting tooth and nail for the girls' future through education, just as she had fought for her own. But education is just one part of this story.

Through CCF (now known as Te-Kworo Foundation), the grassroots, community-development organisation that Alice founded at the height of the LRA conflict in 2002, she advocates for planned parenting, better maternal and child health, safe births, an end to child marriage, the prevention of domestic abuse, and avenues out of desperate poverty for vulnerable girls. She is an insider fighting for the future of her people and at the forefront of restoring what was lost for thousands of young girls in Acholiland.

This is more than a survival story. It's about redemption and restoration, and how—for girls fighting to survive—forgiveness is the best weapon. Alice's story represents the voices of hundreds of thousands of girls around the world—survivors—whose cries for knowledge, for livelihood, for justice and for the future of their babies in the wake of war go unheard.

Philippa Tyndale

PART ONE

UNDOING

1

Taking Courage

Our elderly father, my Baba, stood his ground the day the
Karimojong came in December 1986, with their spears and
rifles. He was not a man to run, to leave his family, so he
planted himself at the entrance to his hut in the village of
Alebtong, waiting to confront our attackers. 'Make sure the
mothers and children are safe,' he told my brother Charles.
'I will not run and give up everything I've worked for in my
whole life.' That was when Charles came to our huts, hitting
their sides with a stick to wake us.

The Karimojong arrived, whooping their fierce war
cries, but we had all fled—all of us except for Baba who,
at close to 80 years old, stood staring down a Karimojong
so fiercely that his muscles twitched uncontrollably. 'You
can kill me, but you won't take my cattle,' my father said,
pushing away the fear in his voice. They shoved him to the
ground and beat him with their rifle butts, then left him
lying there, not caring if he lived or died.

After this December day during *oro*, the equatorial dry

season, the days and months blurred into one long ordeal of daily attacks and heart-thumping fear.

The first time I fled the attackers, I was thirteen years old. I found myself huddled behind a huge ant hill, shaking at the thought of being caught. I had never before known what it was like to be frightened by man.

That day, I'd woken before dawn, listening for the *mego,* my four mothers who would be up early to set the fire, grind the millet and stir the porridge we call *nyuka.* I so loved the quiet hours of summer mornings before the village awoke, when I could doze in and out of my dreams. I still relied on the mothers to prepare my meals.

From the moment my eyes opened, this day felt different. I felt a crippling heaviness on the village, a weight like a net falling, trapping me. Yesterday, the sky had been bright and blue, and now as I peered through the opening to my hut I saw dull grey clouds hovering low. My heart jumped at the crack of a gunshot from the direction of the *kraal,* where we kept our cows.

'Ugghh,' I heard soon afterwards, and I sat up to listen. There was more gunfire, closer this time.

'Aieee,' came a sharper scream just outside the compound. It was time to move, to gather my nieces and cousins who shared my hut. I shivered at the silence as I stepped out of the small entrance. I looked up to the trees, the shea and acacia, but a hush had come over the birds, and even the roosters did not crow. Then I saw my older brother, Charles, standing in the middle of the compound. 'What's happening?' I called.

'It's the Karimojong, they've taken our cattle,' Charles said, his chest heaving after running from the *kraal.* He was fifteen years old, and already tall and strong, with the build of an athlete. 'They are stealing and burning. Run, or they will kill you.' His eyes looked wild, and he swept his arms up to shoo us away. I stood my ground, wanting to hear more.

'I heard them outside, and I told the other boys, "Wake up, wake up, they are here for our cows",' Charles said, still panting. 'We ran to the *kraal* and tried to free our cows, but they surrounded us.' I had now heard enough and, as the gunshots were moving closer, we had no time to plan an escape. I grabbed the hand of my niece, Jacklyn, and scooped up my crying nephew, Bazillo, who stood naked and rooted to the dirt nearby. I propped him onto my hip, wrapped my spare arm around him, and sprinted into the tall grass at the back of our compound. The dead weight of a two-year-old soon slowed me, and the sharp stubble of cut grass and loose rocks stabbed at the soles of my feet until they bled. I bit on my lip to avoid crying with pain.

I had stopped at the edge of the grass to look back as Charles ran from hut to hut to warn other family members. 'Please run, Charles,' I had whispered. 'Or you will surely die.' I could not stand the thought. I was so proud to see Charles, the closest to me in age, grow into a strong leader like our Baba, Otto Zedekiah, who was a respected county chief, now long retired.

'Run!' my mother screamed, and I saw her herding other children with her arms to hurry them along before she, too, fled in the opposite direction to the shots. Within minutes the entire family—except Baba—had scattered into the surrounding bush.

The Karimojong. The very word made my chest tighten and my palms bead with sweat. They were our neighbours, but they were not our friends. These cattle stealers came from the region to the east of Acholiland, a place more barren and impoverished than our Pader district. Karamoja was drier, more isolated and less populated than our Acholiland. To young girls, the Karimojong were a mystery. Once, in the township of Lira, my cousin Mary had seen a warrior striding along the street with a spear in his hand, with nothing to cover his nakedness but a brightly coloured cloth draped across his shoulder and hanging down by his side. They had not changed in centuries. Whereas we, the Acholi people, had adopted many British customs and had long worn Western clothes: traditional tops, skirts, trousers and dresses.

'Do not stand between the Karimojong and a cow,' Mary had told us, with great authority. 'They think all cattle in the world belongs to them, and they will shoot you with their guns.' She then added, 'And if a boy wants a girl as his wife, he will take her for himself, so no one else will have her.'

'Eww,' was all I could answer, as I shuddered with disgust. In my Lwo language, the act of rape was known as *nywaro*: taking what is not yours.

Once before, when I was much smaller and lived in Lapilyet, Karimojong raiders had come to the village with spears, bows and arrows, to steal our cattle at night while we slept. I had been too young to remember it, but these stories had found their way into our family legend. This time the Karimojong had come armed with guns (which they had stolen from government forces in a border skirmish) and it terrified me to think about what they might do.

Soon the other girls were well ahead of us as I plodded along with the two little ones. I knew this landscape well, from the flat, cleared pasture where cattle and goats grazed, to the brush that dried to gold in the summer season and was then burned off to coax out the *anyeri*, edible rats, and the little antelope, *apoli*. Beyond that was the grassy undergrowth, and then the stream, the Omot, where the grass was tall and thick, and the tops of the papyrus reeds spread out as a canopy. Here I knew we could find shelter. By now the gunfire and shouts had faded, and my breathing had slowed enough to talk.

I found an ant hill that was taller than a warrior; it was so large that anyone approaching the hill could not see us behind it. It was under a thorn tree, surrounded by thick blackberry bushes, and ideal for protection. We made our way under the bushes, carefully folding back the grass so our enemy would not notice footmarks.

'Are you okay, Jacklyn?' I asked. The little girl had not said a word as we ran, though she had deep slashes across her calves and her hair was matted and dishevelled.

'When will I see my Mama?' she asked me, her eyes welling with tears.

'I can't say, but we will make it back,' I reassured her. She looked at me and nodded, retreating into her silence. My instinct for survival told me to run fast and alone, but I could not abandon these little ones.

The sun had still not appeared. The sky was dusty, and it was cool under the tree. I saw holes in the ground, where I imagined snakes coiled up in their own dark hiding place, maybe even as scared as we were. I thought of other dangers—those that occupied me when I played in the grass around the village—such as pythons or scorpions or stinging red ants, which could fight back against small grass snakes. We curled up in a ball of naked legs and arms, unaware of time. I could barely imagine what would happen if the attackers found us. Would they torch the grass, and force us out like fugitive animals? I gathered Bazillo and Jacklyn closer.

God, please protect us from these men, I prayed. Bazillo's little hand clung to mine so tightly it trembled. Some of our family's cows now grazed near the water not far from the ant hill. I could see their slow, deliberate movement and envied the simplicity of their existence.

Go away. Leave us alone, I willed them, leaning forward and fidgeting, knowing that the Karimojong would be nearby, herding them. We had run in the opposite direction to the sound of gunshots, not considering that the thieves might bring the cattle close to our family's garden to the east of the village, to be trapped by the river. I heard faint voices drifting in our direction and saw startled birds rising up from the bush. I felt a rush of panic that transferred itself to the younger children.

'Quiet, now,' I urged, keeping my voice as steady as I could and my face stern so they knew that I meant it. But this set Bazillo off, howling so loudly it could no doubt be heard all around. 'I want Mama. I want my mama,' he cried, growing louder and louder.

'Bazillo, we will return to your mother, but please stop crying,' I pleaded in a quiet voice, to no effect as he fought to stand up. How could I explain to a two-year-old that our lives hung on a thread, and that his crying might kill us?

'Stop,' I hissed, and he did.

I squatted under the thorn bush with my arms around Bazillo and Jacklyn, waiting for gunshots, expecting to be hit in the head or chest. We hid entwined in our burrow for several hours, our legs facing outwards in case we had to make a fast exit. I had no plan. Beyond surviving this moment, I had no idea what the future held. I was still a child myself.

*

We were dozing, worn out from the running and hiding, when I woke to the crack of a twig. That's when I saw the Karimojong man standing over me; it's a memory that continues to haunt me. He was just as Mary had described: tall and slender, the skin on his chest marked with the long horizontal scars of his tribe, and naked but for the bright cloth swathed across his shoulder. His eyes were cold and uncaring, so unlike my father's loving eyes.

The man lifted his arm and motioned for us to come out, speaking loudly and in a sharp tone, in a language that I could not understand. The ant hill formed a solid wall behind us, and the thorn bush was a spiky curtain in front of us. We had nowhere to go. I sucked in the stuffy air of our dirt hole. My stomach rolled and clenched, then tightened all the way to my chest.

My fear turned to anger. 'Get out of our garden,' I growled, knowing that my words would be swept away by the wind before he heard them. The garden was my treasured place, where I had spent whole days playing with the other children while our mothers laboured all day—their backs and legs in a perfect L-shape—digging and weeding, talking and laughing, before returning home, arms laden with fresh maize or tomatoes to prepare the evening meal.

We held each other tightly as he waved his gun, knowing we could never outrun him. 'Dear God, please get us out of here,' I prayed aloud. Beside me, I could feel Jacklyn's quivering body and heard her whisper, 'Amen.'

Then a cow bellowed nearby. The man turned his head to see it sauntering out of the garden, and he bounded away after it. I pulled the others up and we scampered down to the swamp, where we could hide in the *togo*, the forest of green papyrus rising up from the still water. This was where we spent the rest of the day, at least six hours, crouched in the cool water until our legs were numb, and an exhausted Bazillo could only whimper. In the distance, towards the village, we heard gunshots again. I pulled the children tighter around me. I could not bear to imagine what targets those bullets had found.

Late in the day, as the light faded and the cold water became unbearable, the gunshots and voices of the cattle rustlers moved away to the south. 'Come, they have left this area,' I said, and we crept in single file through the towering green grass, *obiya*, in the direction of Alebtong.

We had walked for almost two kilometres when we reached a small clearing, thirty metres long and wide enough in which to walk side by side. I reached behind me for Jacklyn's and Bazillo's little hands, leading them across the treeless corridor to the path on the other side, where we would again be concealed. The sun had set, with just an afterglow to light our path, and a moist freshness rose from the grass around us.

As I turned to reassure them, I caught sight of the silhouette of a tall figure behind us. 'Quick—run,' I urged, as the man lifted his gun and aimed it towards us. A shot whistled past and well beyond us, and then there was silence. We scuttled back into the grass, running out into the open just once more to cross a narrow road before tumbling back behind a screen of *togo* papyrus near the river. We did not see the man again.

It was late now, and I dared not venture beyond the river-bank again for fear of being caught. In the moonlight I could see the rising smoke of a fire not far away, smell the aroma of roasting goat meat that made my mouth water, and hear the sounds of fireside banter. I imagined a scene of victors boasting of their cattle conquest. My empty stomach ached for some of their food, and my shivering body yearned for the warmth of their fire. Most of all, I longed for the security of my own family. I gathered some branches for shelter and settled into a hiding place for the night, with Jacklyn under one arm and Bazillo beneath the other.

For three days we stayed this way, in and out of the cold river's edge, too timid to move in the direction of our village for fear of coming across the men who had stolen our family's cows. Eventually we found our way home through the small passages leading into the village. I was so cold and hungry that death from a gun or a spear did not seem so bad now. Not far from the village, we met three young girls who had run with us on the first day.

'Where did you hide?' I asked them, smiling with relief to see them alive, though looking ragged.

'We stayed in the *togo* with the snakes and rats,' one of the girls replied. She laughed. We were all happy to be going back to our home. We marched together towards the compound, chattering about our experiences. I thought about throwing myself into my mother's open arms.

'The mothers must be worried about us,' I said, thinking of the moment we had fled. But there were no smiles to greet us. The mothers stood under a tree, huddled together, looking confused. My mother shrieked when she saw me, but our happy reunion was short-lived. As the boys moved from hut to hut, collecting food, pots and mats—anything that had been left behind—I realised that all of our huts had been looted, our granaries emptied of maize. I couldn't bear to think about the human toll.

'I found Baba sprawled out on the ground,' Charles said, looking apologetic, as if it had been his job to protect our father, and he had failed. He had been the first back in the village, returning at five o'clock in the evening on the day of the attack.

I ran to my father's hut to find him propped up against the wall, a vacant look on his face. 'Baba!' I cried, moving to comfort him. I fell to my knees at his feet and reached for his hand, afraid to touch his bruised body.

'They've taken all our food, all our clothes, and even my coat,' he replied, without life in his voice. I could never have imagined him in such a defeated state. Charles, crouching beside him, looked at me with tears in his eyes. I felt sick. We all knew what this meant. The pocket of his coat had contained Baba's entire life savings of three million Ugandan shillings, more than one thousand American dollars. Other than a large landholding that we could no longer use, our family had nothing left.

I wondered then if Baba had been the worst casualty of the attack, as he was such a changed man. Even today, I cannot think of this moment without tears. How I wished that he had run—let the raiders have his cattle and his money—and not stayed to defend his honour, to be beaten with the butt of a gun, bruised and swollen and left half dead. As a young man, our fearless father had chased lions and killed elephants and antelope. He was a man who bowed to no one, a chief and leader in the district, a man with three hundred cows, who might have expected to live out his remaining years in peace with his wives and children. Now he sat motionless, his eyes fixed on a distant point, like a man whose spirit had left him, his body a shell.

I had learned so much in my short time in hiding, things I could never have learned from a book or around the fire. I had learned about fear, and how it crushed me and turned my insides to mush. How even when I could walk freely, I was no longer free in my spirit. I had learned how to survive outside the protection of my family. All the adults in my life—even my brave father—were now powerless and afraid, in a state of disbelief. How could they guard me against this new hatred—the men with their guns?

That night I slept clutching my warm wrap, ready to run for my life once again. And yet, in my heart, I now knew it was possible to escape men with guns without being hurt. And this gave me courage.

2

School of *Ododo*

My education started long before I ever saw a book at school. I began to learn how to be Acholi from my first memory, around the flames of the *wang oo,* our family's beating heart. Here, with my legs outstretched and ears picking up every passing word, I learned my lineage from the household to the clan to the chiefdom. I learned life's important lessons: how to take care of each other. How to avoid marrying someone who is our close relation, thereby breaking *kir*, a taboo. By the fire, I discovered how brave Baba had been as a young man. He was old now, no longer the athletic young man who met my mother while hunting elephants in the park at Murchison Falls.

'I killed more than fifty elephants as a young man,' he once told us, our eyes as wide as the full moon. He told us of great feasts after the hunt, where villagers came from far and wide, and how he could trade the tusks for clothes and other goods. The elephant gun still rested on the beam of his hut, ready to defend us.

Every Acholi child learned the same fable in our informal school of village elders: the story of the rooster and the hare. When my father told this story by the fire, I sat with my back straight and eyes fixed on his solemn face, not missing a word.

'This is the tale of the rooster and the hare who, though so different, were the closest of friends. They were so close they even shared the most succulent part of our favourite delicacy, the lower sac of the white ant,' Baba started in his deep voice, speaking slowly to give gravity to his words. 'One day the cock invited the hare to visit, and when the hare arrived, he found his friend standing on one leg. "My friend, what has happened to your other leg?" the hare asked.

'"Oh, my friend, I love you so much I've cut a leg off," the cock replied, and his friend was so excited about his friend's love for him he did not ask further questions over their dinner.' I smiled briefly to think of the hare being tricked by the rooster, but my father's face was serious: these life lessons were not to be taken lightly. He continued, with a slight frown.

'"Come to my house tomorrow," the hare said to the cock as he left that evening. Early in the morning the hare woke up his wife. "Mother of Ebuji, my friend is coming to visit me this morning, so I want you to cut off one of my legs." The wife was very surprised, but she had to obey, so she started cutting, though her husband the hare was in agony.'

We children now sat motionless. 'Soon afterwards, his friend the cock arrived at the gate, walking on two legs. He tucked one leg up under his body and went hop, hop, hop into the compound, where he found his friend in pain and close to death.

"'My friend, from this day onwards our friendship has come to an end because I've found that you are imitating things," the cock said to the hare, as he placed his folded leg on the ground. "Now you've cut off your leg thinking that I've cut off my leg. Can you see that I have two legs?'"

My mouth fell open. I had questions, but could not ask them. *Why would he let his friend die?* 'You see, the hare was friends with many people, but imitation killed him. You must always be you, and not try to copy other people.' It was a lesson none of us ever forgot.

We learned many other things around the *wang oo* in the evening. We learned what made us a cohesive clan: conformity, honesty, hard work and communal unity. We learned our folklore, *ododo*, soaking in the wisdom from centuries of our culture.

During the daylight hours, young girls learned lessons about life and womanhood as we gathered water with the older women, helped weed the vegetables in the garden or sat under the shea tree with the mothers. We learned the most in *oro*, the dry season, when our clan rested and held harvest rituals and marriages, and paid respect to our ancestors. During *oro*, we ate goat and chicken roasted over an open flame and drank *kasimuru*, a milk-like drink made from *simsim* fermented overnight.

Once, my maternal grandmother, Maa, came to visit from Anaka, in Gulu district, a few hours to the west. I didn't know her well, as once Mama married my father, she became part of the Gule clan, and left her own behind. Maa arrived one day in our village of Lapilyet, wandering up the dirt track from the main road, a small bag over her shoulder. I warmed to her straight away, staying close to her as she moved between family members.

Maa revealed many things about her side of the family that my mother did not know. I sat at her feet, entranced, as she told her stories with the authority of a clan elder.

'My mother was captured during the Bunyoro war, and she was given as a wife to a Bunyoro man,' Maa told us in a session that stretched through most of the day. 'But she missed her clan, and she made her way back to Acholiland,' she said with a wide smile. The Bunyoro people were a southern tribe that had long been an enemy.

My eyes slid down to the creased skin on Maa's arms, and then up to her face, which glowed as she remembered her past. I cleared my throat and summoned the courage to speak. 'Is that why Rose Ayo and I are paler than some of the others, Maa?' I ventured. One time I had held my arm against that of my brother Gabriel, and my skin was certainly a shade or two lighter. Until now I had never understood why.

Maa smiled and clucked. 'That could be so, Alice,' she said.

There was no end to the stories that Maa shared with us for hour upon hour under the mango tree. This was the way of *ododo*. Maa was a young woman under British rule when the colonists stirred up rivalries between the powerful Bantu tribal groups of the south—the Buganda, Banyankole and Bunyoro—and the warrior Acholi and Karimojong, the Nilotic peoples of the north. The British had favoured the lighter-skinned tribes from the south, giving them prestigious roles in their colonial administration, and had assigned army and police jobs to those from the north.

My niece Lily and I sat close to Maa, as though through proximity we would capture her wisdom. 'Tell us about the foreigners coming to Acholiland, Maa,' I begged, and Maa started on her intricate narrative of a time long past, when the British arrived with strange customs, and the Arab slave-traders swept over the border from Sudan to steal and then sell young Acholi.

'Tell us about the days of the Acholi kingdoms, Maa,' Lily cried, though we'd heard the historical story before.

Maa closed her eyes, her wrinkled lips curling into the faintest of smiles. 'I can well remember the days of the great chiefs, and how the men welcomed visiting kings with the *bwola*.' She paused and opened her eyes to meet our expectant faces. 'People came from all around Acholiland to see it—it was so majestic,' she told us.

I had once seen a simpler version of these gatherings in our district. I closed my eyes to recall the spectacle of coloured feathers, the shining bodies of the dancers pounding the ground, their powerful male voices and the scores of deep, beating drums that I could feel right to my bones.

'Did the Bunyoro treat your mother well, Maa?' I asked her, but I did not get an answer. There were parts of Maa's past that we would never know.

*

I lived with my four mothers, father and twenty of my twenty-seven siblings and half siblings in the village of Lapilyet, not far from Lira Palwo in Pader district in the north of Uganda. I was the eighth of nine children to Otto Zedekiah's second-last wife, Lucie, and the fifth daughter.

His wives, my mothers, were more fortunate than most. Baba was wealthy in Acholiland, where a man's status was measured in wives and children and cows. Our family had a plough and a grinder to make maize flour. Baba had worked his way up to sub-county chief in the colonial system by being clever and trustworthy, rather than inheriting a title in the traditional Acholi tribal system, and had some three hundred shorthorn cows in the *kraal*. He kept a dark blue suit in his hut, which he wore when he travelled to meetings with government officials and community leaders in the district.

The co-wives knew little of the outside world and did not have any aspirations beyond village life. They lived mostly in harmony, because Baba had been wise. He had divided his land evenly so that each of the four co-wives had her own *dye-kal*, a small compound, with huts for eating and sleeping, and her own granary, a *dero*, for storing the harvests of millet, sorghum and maize so they were safe from weevils and rodents. Each woman had her own cows and goats, so she always had enough milk for her children. But even as a small child, I could see in the little things—such as chicken and eggs being reserved for men and guests—how different it was to be a woman in our culture.

As a young girl, I was free to roam the thick bush around the village with the other girls. There were eight of us of similar age, all half-sisters and nieces, who concocted games with stones and hollowed out branches, and played hide-and-seek around the huts. Lily, Esther and Mary were my best friends, even though we were all related.

There was no question of whether or not I would go to school when I was old enough. My father was progressive, a *rwot kalam* or pen chief, who in his younger years had worked with the British colonial administration. He could read and write in Lwo, and though he had had little education himself, he knew its value, even for girls, by the time I came along.

Baba had made sure that his eldest son, Gabriel, attended primary school in Lira Palwo. He later sent Gabriel to a technical school in Moyo, near the Sudan border.

'Alici, you must go to school, too,' Baba had told me one evening as we sat outside his hut, and I had clapped my hands with happiness. None of my older sisters had made it through school. One by one they had dropped out before finishing secondary school, when they reached fifteen, the age of marriage. My eldest sister, Doreen, had not made it past primary school.

I always believed that I was the favourite child of my father, as he rarely disciplined me. In truth, by the time I reached adolescence, he was old and retired from his role as sub-county chief. As a young man, he had travelled from village to village, on the road and away from his family for weeks at a time. Now he no longer strayed far from his own large thatched hut, very near the huts of his wives and children. He loved to be surrounded by his children and grandchildren. It was simply my good fortune that he had more time to spare, and so he could take an active interest in my wellbeing.

'Baba, I promise you will be proud of me. I will work hard at school,' I replied. I locked that promise into my heart and carried it with me on my first day, when I nervously lined up with the other children outside the hut that would be my classroom for the years to come, met the young teacher and was shepherded into the dark room. The class shared a handful of battered books, the pages often sliding out and fluttering to the ground thanks to the hundreds of tiny hands that had held them over their lifetime. In what seemed like no time, I could make sense of the black symbols on the page, and could read the stories for myself. I was already open to every possibility that school would bring.

*

I had a namesake, Baba's second wife, Achan, the eldest of the mothers, who had become ill and died just as I was born in November 1973. One night around the fire, Baba talked fondly of her. 'She was a very fine wife, so friendly and so good,' he said, looking at the faces of the other wives without judgement. They nodded their heads in reverence at the mention of her name. We were fortunate that in our family the mothers were kind to each other, while in many clans the co-wives fought constantly.

'You children, she loved you so much,' Baba turned to us and smiled. Our admiring eyes were fixed on his. 'When you came to her hut, she made sure you felt at home.' His gaze fell on me, and I felt a pang of longing to know this woman Achan, whose name in Lwo means 'born in a difficult time'. I felt proud to be associated with this strong woman, even if I had never known her, as the older children had.

'I want to be like *mego* Achan when I grow up,' I declared to Baba. The other mothers laughed.

'Yes, Alici, you will be just like your *mego* Achan,' my father beamed.

There was a sisterhood among my mothers that made us all stronger. I never thought to question the idea of one man having many wives, and as a young girl I felt no need to single out one mother. Any of the mothers could feed me, sing to me or scold me on any day. The reassuring female voices I awoke to each morning, murmurs and laughter that made my heart burst with happiness, could have been any of the four women, or even my older sisters and half-sisters. I treasured waking to these voices, and the other sounds that were so familiar to me: the chickens scratching the soil outside, the goats noisily butting each other, the sharp calls to shoo them away, the soothing coo of the native doves, the talk of the young boys back from the *kraal*. I had never wondered if this was how I would choose to live in the future. Our family seemed natural, and for now I knew of no other way to live.

Outside school, my job from the age of eight was to babysit the younger children while our mothers prepared our evening meal. However, one steamy Saturday afternoon, I found my way into the group of older girls, all related, who sat cross-legged under the big mango tree in the centre of the compound. This was our meeting place, where we whiled away the heat of the day. The young women were in deep discussion when I slipped into a gap in the circle and sat quietly, picking up the thread of their conversation. I heard one of them, Agnes Lamwaka, explaining, 'We cannot walk to see our grandmother as you can. It is a long way.' My ears pricked up at this conversation about our grandmothers and the clans they came from before joining the Gule clan of our father's family. This was much more interesting than the usual talk of babies and cooking.

'To see our grandmother, we must catch a bus all the way to Gulu, and we will need several shillings to buy the fare,' Agnes said, turning her gaze to me. Gulu was the largest town in the north of Uganda, a bus ride of more than three hours on a rough road. I had never been there, but I had heard about the vast array of food, cloth and household goods you could buy in the central market. I could barely imagine how thousands of people could live so closely together.

Agnes pointed to me, indicating that we had the same grandmother, the woman named Min Lucie, who we all knew as Maa. I could not move. I turned for a closer look into Agnes's face, and for the first time I recognised the similarity in our high cheekbones. As Agnes continued to boast of her Maa in the big city, it occurred to me that I was closer to her than to the other girls. I felt a rush of excitement. I sat back and let the thought take root. *I need to travel all that way to see our grandmother, to board a bus or a truck when the other girls can walk to the next village.*

In one conversation, my world had grown larger than the village. I pondered the Min Lucie connection, and what this meant. Maa was the mother of Lucie, who was known as Min Ayo. 'Does this mean Min Ayo is also my mother?' I asked Agnes, who looked at me in surprise, then laughed, placing her hand on my shoulder. The other young women laughed, too, and my face warmed. I sat back, hiding my embarrassment.

'Yes, Alice, she is our mother,' Agnes said. 'And you are my full sister.'

I sat up tall, straightened my back and smoothed my skirt until it covered my ankles. Min Ayo was the most industrious and organised of all the mothers. She kept her home swept with her twig broom, her goats were well tended, and she often helped the other women. I had always felt cared for in this community of mothers, but I was proud to have Min Ayo as my own mother.

After this, I quietly set out to piece together the puzzle of which children came from which mother. Soon, I cornered

Agnes with my questions. 'Agnes, who is the first born by our mother?' I asked her as she leaned over a pot of *posho*.

She stood up to reply, wiping her hands on her *kikooyi*. 'That would be our brother, Gabriel Lajul, who was born in 1950, in Pajule.' I learned that after Gabriel came a sister, Rose Ayo, then Edward Nyeko, followed by Susan Akello, Doreen Lapogo, Agnes, Charles and then me. Of the young men, only Charles, born three years ahead of me, remained in the village. David Labeja, who came after me, was still a boy.

I put my hands on my hips and looked her in the eye. 'Agnes, how do you know so much about my brothers and sisters, and I know so little?' I probed, feeling so ill-informed about my own family.

'You are so young, and your sisters have all married into other clans and have their own children. Soon I will be married and leave, too,' she replied, reaching out for my hand. Her words sent a wave of panic through me that landed in my stomach and made me feel sick. I had not thought about this. *Would I have to marry and live in another village, too?*

The next time we went with the mothers to work in the garden, I stayed close to my own mother as she weeded the soil around her tomatoes and eggplants. She had more than one small garden plot: she had one to grow her grains, such as sorghum, millet and maize, and another for vegetables and cassava, and the bees for her honey were on yet another plot. When her friends came from other villages, she offered local beer and tea as well as black millet bread.

One day, as I watched her singing as she laboured with the other women, she stopped working to wipe her cheek. I saw a streak of tears on her face and wanted to ask her, *Mama, what is making you unhappy?* I wanted to cry, too.

But I was young and did not have the courage to ask. I stayed under the tree, playing a game with Lily and puzzling over the cause of my mother's sadness. Our father was never violent, so I knew he was not to blame. *Could it be the visit of my cousin not so long ago?* She had come from Gulu all clean and shiny, with a new suit and shoes, and made us aware of the dirt under our nails from digging, and the rips in our second-hand skirts. Maybe my mother was worried about me?

I dropped the small seeds from our game onto the ground, and looked towards the track that led away from the compound. *My life could be different. If I study hard, I could work as a teacher and not in the fields. I could help my mother have a better life.* I was young and without power in my clan, but I had the kernel of an idea.

3

Seeds of Learning

Most nights, Lily and I shared a reed mat in one of the huts. It could be with any of the mothers—but the most prized were the nights spent with *mego* Esita Akidi, the first of Baba's wives and the one I regarded as a *dada*, a grandmother.

'Please—come to my home, girls. I miss the young ones now my four are all gone from the village,' she would tell us. We needed no incentive beyond the warmth of Akidi herself and the abundance of fruit trees—banana, mango and our favourite, jackfruit—surrounding her hut. Akidi treated me as her own, taking time to walk with me through the garden, explaining how she prepared the fruits.

I knew her as Min Obur, mother of Obur. Akidi was so proud of her youngest son, Simon Obur, and how far he had gone in his studies. He had left Uganda many years before to study in Hungary, and had returned with a European wife named Eva. They called her *mzungu*, the Bantu word for white visitors, which had been used since the arrival of the first Europeans in the 1800s.

Of all Baba's children and grandchildren, I was most like my niece, Lily—we were both tall and slender, and full of curiosity about our world. I had been drawn to Lily from when I was first old enough to totter around after her in the compound. Lily was one year older than me, and the grand-daughter of Baba's third wife, Julie Lapogo, who was known as Min Aduk—mother of Aduk.

We often slept in the hut of Lily's mother, Aduk, who was my half-sister and stricter than the older women. We slept naked, except for a light cloth that was used to ward off the coolness just before the sun broke over the horizon. One morning, we woke in Aduk's hut with wetness leaking out from under our sleeping mat. Aduk's frowning face loomed over us, and her hands were planted on her hips like a two-armed cup. The wetness had trickled beyond the mat, formed a black streak across the ochre-dust floor and was now headed downhill towards the sunlight at the opening of the hut.

'Which of you girls did this?' she demanded. We glanced sideways at each other, and then up at Aduk, with blank faces.

'We don't know, Mama,' Lily replied. Without wet under-wear as proof, Aduk would never know who was guilty. Aduk shook her hand at us and stomped off. She returned with the twig broom from beside the fireplace and beat both of our bare bottoms, but we did not give in.

Lily and I had an unspoken pact to look out for each other, always. We set out from the compound each morning with Esther and Mary, straggling barefoot through the spear grass and onto the familiar path to the school at Lira Palwo, a twenty-minute walk away.

One morning, I breathed deeply and soaked up the musty smell of the bush around me, the rising steam giving it a soft glow. I was consumed by the beauty around me, and wallowed in my contentment. 'I never want to leave the village,' I declared with a long sigh. For now, thoughts of teaching and helping my mother escape her hard labour were far away.

At this moment my life seemed so safe. I had not known of any girl who had left the village for further education, so why was I different from them? Maybe I could live with this as my future: a brave husband just like my father, babies I would suckle until they could feed themselves, a garden I would tend, and millet I would grind on the weathered stone we called *lanyakidi*. I looked forward to graduating to this job, instead of sitting by and watching the mothers work, as I did now. I, too, would crush the grain under the stone with my strong arms, and my children would know my mood by the songs I sang as I worked.

I imagined my songs would be those of thankfulness, and not the complaining songs I sometimes heard from the older women. I, too, would live in bounty in Lapilyet, eating the best honey in the land, and enjoying granaries filled with peas, millet, maize, sorghum and groundnuts (peanuts). I would pick the heavy golden fruits of the compound's mango trees in season, and the nuts from the nearby shea trees, which I would beat into butter and mix with sweet potato.

Ours was a community of people who did everything collectively: the boys hunted as a pack, while the women and girls gathered seeds and grains together and tended the garden in a group. We always ate as an extended family. 'Only those with bad hearts want to be by themselves,' my mother had told us.

The young girls were also relegated to rotational jobs in a system we called *aleya*. One such job was collecting water. We set out as a group with our *calabashes* riding on our heads to the water point, a fifteen-minute walk away. We made the trip four times a day so that each household had a good supply of water. Some days we scoured the bush as a large group, returning with bundles of firewood under our arms, and then went from one household to the next depositing it in dry places near the huts. Though some of the girls complained, the displeasure never lingered. My older brother Charles and the other young boys had different jobs from us. They tended to and milked the cows, or hunted for bush rats. From two years of age, young Acholi boys could wander far from home, as far as the next village, without worrying their mothers. We instinctively learned how to live in a community, and how to be Acholi. Many days, I knew nothing but contentment with my life.

I especially loved Fridays at school. At the end of the school day on Thursday, the teacher always asked us, 'Girls, what do we do on Friday?'

'Smearing,' we'd reply in unison, clapping our hands. The next morning, I would rise half an hour earlier than usual and head down to the *kraal*, where the boys would help shovel fresh cow dung—still steaming—into my pail. It was heavy, so I would share the load with one of the other girls, setting out through the grass and making our way to the school. We'd set our pails down outside the classroom and eagerly work our way through lessons until later in the day, when we would finally be allowed to put our pens down and start the job we enjoyed so much.

'Girls, you may get your pails now,' the teacher would finally announce, and we'd dart out the door and back, plunge our bare hands into the buckets of firm cow dung to mix it with water before lifting it out in big handfuls and smearing it as finely as we could across the floor of the school hut, starting from the furthest side and working our way to the door, finally backing out of the dark space as we coated the entrance with the last lumps. On Mondays, we girls would arrive at school before the boys to admire our handiwork: the dried dung now faded to a pale greenish grey, and the schoolroom looked fresh and smooth again. Not only did the smearing protect the classroom floor from the rain, it also kept the termites away from the hut.

I never thought to question why the girls, and not the boys, had this job or other menial tasks—such as bringing water to the school and sweeping the floors—that kept us from our books while the boys studied. In our early years, we were already falling behind.

*

The first educated woman I met was Eva Mezo Obur, the Hungarian wife of my older half-brother, Simon Obur. I was eight years old when he first brought Eva to Lira Palwo. They had met at medical school in Budapest, where they both qualified as doctors. I didn't know this piece of information at the time: I had never met a doctor and never considered that this could be a job for a woman.

Simon Obur and Eva had fled to Kenya when Idi Amin became president of Uganda in 1971. Simon had feared that he would be among the thousands of educated Ugandans who were being targeted by the illiterate Amin. Amin had slaughtered many of those in authority—clergymen, university lecturers, political opponents—whom he perceived to be a threat to his despotic leadership.

When Eva arrived, I was enthralled, as if I was seeing a rare and exotic animal for the first time. Clad in my dirty weekday dress, I watched from behind a shea tree as she daintily stepped down from the high seat of the Land Rover, her fine shoes and light blouse too delicate for this land, the dust enveloping them. I had once seen a priest with white skin at the Kalongo Hospital, but never before a white woman. I did not want to be near this foreigner with luminous skin, but observed as each of my family members lined up outside Akidi's hut, waiting to be introduced.

'Welcome to our village, sister,' and 'You are most welcome,' they said, shaking hands or bobbing into a reverent curtsy.

From my vantage point, I saw her fear as she re-emerged from the hut, the expression on her face like a deer cornered by a hunter's bow. I could see her loneliness, even as she was surrounded by a crowd of people who wanted nothing more than to draw her into their community, and that made me soften towards her. With an air of ceremony, Eva and Simon Obur presented our father with a pale pink teacup and matching saucer, made from the finest European china. In return, Baba gave them a *lak lyec*, an elephant's tooth, as we called the tusks. To my shame, I later broke the cup as I lifted it down from the ledge in Baba's hut. For this, I received the only spanking I can remember as a child from my father.

The next time Eva came, it was with bags of sweets. I was among the riot of jumping children corralling her. 'Go away, go away, go away,' she called, waving her hand at us, but of course as excited children we did not respond to her English spoken with a heavy Hungarian accent. We were only just learning the language at school. For many years afterwards, I believed that 'go away' was a name she used for us.

The last visit was in 1984, when Simon and Eva again came to stay in Akidi's hut, this time with their three young children, each with a different shade of coffee-coloured skin and pale eyes. I had never seen children who looked like this. When they pulled into the trading centre in Lira Palwo in their four-wheel drive, a crowd gathered to stare and point. They called the children *dol*—dolls—because they looked too delicate to be real, as if they might break if they lived in the village.

We never saw Simon Obur and his family again. The winds of political change had made it impossible for them to visit safely. They remained in Kenya, in exile.

4

The End of School

As I reached the age of twelve, tension began to seep into our village like a fog. The mothers began whispering so we could not hear what they said; they stopped singing their contented songs, and often stayed at home rather than walking the twenty minutes to tend to their gardens. When they went, they walked together, and stayed for less of the day, sure to be home well before dusk. These days we rarely walked to the trading centre in Lira Palwo to buy the few things we could not grow or make, such as sugar, salt or oil, or to trade shea nuts or eggplants for flour or clothing. We went without.

'Obote has been overturned,' I overheard one day in July 1985. Milton Obote was the president, whose Uganda National Liberation Army (UNLA) soldiers we had seen nearby, and now he had been overthrown in a military coup by General Tito Okello, an Acholi from Kitgum district. Within six months, Okello's military junta had also been replaced, and Yoweri Museveni—a guerrilla leader who had trained in Tanzania and headed the National Resistance Army

(NRA)—had taken charge. In our quiet village, we did not endure the turmoil of the capital city, Kampala, where food supplies were cut off, and banks and trucks and fuel stations all over the city were robbed or hijacked by both soldiers and civilians. But we felt the uncertainty.

Before long, my world had shrunk to the size of our compound, with only occasional forays into the long grass to play games, and visits to the water point to pump as much water as we could carry. 'Stay where I can see you,' my mother demanded, her face solemn, without telling me why. I groaned and felt the invisible cord around me tighten. I was almost twelve years old, but less free than I had been when I was eight.

There was so much happening around us to keep up with. I learned, through the mothers gathering at the water point, about a spirit medium named Alice Auma. 'She is a miracle woman. She can protect herself from bullets with just shea butter and honey,' a woman from a nearby village gossiped to my mother as I stood sullenly watching. 'She has named herself Lakwena.' The woman spoke in a reverent tone, as if this Alice Auma—now Lakwena, meaning 'messenger' in Lwo—who came from the simple village of Opit, near Gulu, was a saviour of the Acholi people.

'Ahh, yes, I've heard of her,' Mama replied as she picked up her *calabash*. I followed as we marched back along the path to Lapilyet.

After a few moments, Mama turned to me. 'I'm not convinced about this woman,' she said and then kept walking. I took her lead and slipped into thinking about what I knew of Alice Lakwena. She was a growing force in the north of Uganda, gathering followers to her Holy Spirit Movement like flying ants to a flame. In the beginning it had all been done without violence, with a spiritual approach that gave her authority among some Acholi. Lakwena claimed to have prophetic powers, and to channel spirits who told her what to do, and already her legend had grown: we had heard how she had led her followers, many of them children, into battle singing hymns and holding rocks as their defence against guns, and in this way her Holy Spirit Mobile Forces (HSMF) had won several battles. Then, she had taken firearms as the spoils of victory, making her marches more deadly.

Lakwena's followers came to villages and spoke in our Lwo language, presenting themselves as a local alternative to the former and present government forces battling it out. Lakwena was an enemy to every other armed group, so anyone who crossed to Lakwena's camp became an enemy of all others.

Later, in October 1987, Lakwena's HSMF would make it to within 100 kilometres of the capital, Kampala, before government forces stopped her and she fled across the border to Kenya. It was Joseph Kony, the second leader of this movement to rise up after Lakwena, who would become the most destructive force of all, under the banner of the Lord's Resistance Army (LRA).

Even before Joseph Kony came onto the scene, Alice Lakwena's tactics had become increasingly evil. She had instructed her troops to use our most precious commodities, shea butter and honey, in a ritual to protect themselves from bullets, and at the same time sent orders for the rebels to kill any villager who ate them. At the height of Lakwena's reign, my sister-in-law Pauline's mother in Lira Palwo was caught eating shea butter and murdered in front of her family.

*

One day in March 1986 a man arrived breathless at the door of our father's hut. '*Ladit jago*, I need to talk with you right now,' he said, stumbling straight into the dark space, wheezing for breath. He was one of the neighbouring farmers, a man we all knew.

'They're all gone, the family across the road. There are only two children left from the family of eight,' he cried. 'It was that man Samuel. He joined an armed group and came back to kill them with a *panga*.' His hands shook as he spoke.

'That is terrible,' Baba gasped. He knew both Samuel and the family of eight and was at first confused. 'I have never heard of such hatred.' He sat back to ponder what could cause a man to ignore the pleas of a child, to slash and slice with a machete as if harvesting cane and maize. Baba sat alone for some time after that, long after the panting man had returned down the road.

'Gather the men,' he barked when he came out again, and soon his sons and the clan elders—some in their best shirts and trousers—had assembled. He shooed the younger children away, out of earshot. We gathered around the mothers, who waited anxiously. In our clan, the men made the big decisions—it had always been this way.

'We could be next,' I heard one of the mothers say. My legs twitched, ready to take flight.

The men talked for many hours, at times sounding agitated. I heard my father's voice consistently: deep and firm, even in his old age. That night, after the elders had left, Baba stayed by the fire with his sons, his head bowed for a long time. The men sat in silence, only occasionally speaking quietly to each other or rising to feed the fire. At daybreak when I crawled from my mat to peer out into daylight, some were still there.

After our breakfast of black tea and porridge, Baba called us together. 'It is time for us to move,' he said, his voice weary. A murmur of displeasure rippled through the group. Baba ignored the grumbling. 'We are not safe here. Who knows which army will come along this busy road?'

'What can we bring with us?' Mama asked in a matter-of-fact way. She was well aware of how insecure we now were, through rumours in the community. One of the other mothers cried, while others started to gather their pots and pans and the firewood sitting nearby.

'Bring only what we can carry. We will move to our farmland in Alebtong, far from the main road, where there is nothing to draw the attention of the soldiers,' he said, his face sterner than I had ever seen.

It was a warm day, yet a stony coldness—fear—descended on the mothers. None of us wanted to leave our home, but we had to trust the judgement of the patriarch, whose role as the head of the clan was to keep us safe.

I stood on the sidelines, my heart breaking to think what this hasty move might mean for my education—we would be far from any school. As the mothers gathered our possessions, I escaped to a small clearing where I could sit and cry without being seen.

School had been my hope, even our tiny village school with two huts as classrooms and barely a pencil between us. It was now six or more months since the day the teachers had sent us all home, unable to protect us anymore, and I missed it every day.

The sounds of my family's activity—clanks of pans, sharp directions to children, goats bleating—drifted through the grass, but I stayed hidden, lost in memories of my school days. We had learned the symbols of my Lwo language and I could read and write and do some mathematics. I had learned about life in stories—important stories about respect for other people. We had started to learn English, with our teacher reading us stories that made us laugh. Every day in school was an adventure. We had played sports and games, and danced, and sometimes the girls had gone to the garden to dig. I had loved to go to school every day, not only for our lessons, but also because my mother packed my favourite food—sweet potatoes with *simsim* paste—for lunch.

I thought about my last day of school, close to the end of second term, when I had reached the level of Primary 5 (equivalent to the last year of primary school in Australia). I had set out with Lily, Esther and Mary, along the same road I travelled every school day, wearing a clean shirt and skirt that fell below my knees. We had made a detour onto the grassy verge to pluck sweet *pai-pai* (pawpaw), which we planned to eat later in the day. I was already thinking about my lessons for that day.

Soon after we left our homes, we heard the deep thuds of heavy shelling in the distance, only kilometres from Lapilyet, from the direction of Lira. I stopped in my tracks. 'Should we go back home?' I asked the other girls, looking ahead towards the school, just behind the row of shops in the trading centre. 'No, let us see what is happening in the trading centre,' Mary replied, striding ahead without slowing. 'They will not let us come to harm,' she said, with a confidence that drove us all forwards. I was still not sure we should be moving further from the protection of our family, but followed the other girls.

At the school, the atmosphere had changed, even from

the day before. Teachers stood in groups speaking in hushed tones to each other, occasionally glancing at the students with worried faces. None of the children standing around were ushered into the classrooms. Even the most exuberant of the children could not raise their spirits enough to play.

At ten o'clock in the morning, a truck laden with military men from the local barracks rattled past, speeding towards Lira district to the east, the direction from which I could still hear the pounding of bombs from time to time. The soldiers were crowded in the tray of the truck, shaking their rifles, which were all pointed towards a featureless sky. They whooped and chanted battle cries, they lifted their heads and ululated in shrill tones—the same effortless sound that in other circumstances might herald joy, but today was whipping them into a mood to fight. We stood planted by the side of the road, our eyes wide and fixed on the truck, even after it had spewed powdery dust onto our clean uniforms.

'Aahh, this is not like a usual day,' I said to Lily, looking up at the hazy sky, which promised neither sunshine nor rain. We stood around the school grounds for most of the day, none of us in a mood to play or chatter.

'How can I defend these children? We cannot,' I heard Miss Helen, our young teacher, tell the senior teacher. By the afternoon, the shutters had come down on the rickety row of shops, and the shopkeepers had packed up their measly supplies of rice, flour and soap to take home with them, perhaps unsure if they would open their shops again in the morning. Like the teachers, they gathered in small groups, leaning towards each other in earnest conversation. There were no bombs and the air was quiet, but the mood of foreboding had grown heavier.

'Please go home to your mothers, and may God protect you,' Miss Helen said, pressing the palms of her hands together, as if in prayer. I felt a knot of anxiety and grabbed Lily's hand.

'C'mon, let's get out of here,' I called, and hastened the other girls to come with us. Together we ran home, without a backwards glance, without even pausing to run our hands across the soft heads of the *obiya* grass. I had no idea that I would be without school for many months—in fact, that I would struggle to finish my education.

The mothers waited for us in the village, looking miserable. Mama rushed to me as we arrived at the compound, gathering me up into her arms like a chick under a wing. That evening, she hurried me through the evening meal and sent me off to bed at sunset. I slept lightly, waking to urgent whispers outside, snatches of conversation, whimpers of young voices. I was too tired to go out in the dark, but in the morning when I looked through the doorway, I saw strangers: women and children and a few men, some resting on reed mats, their pots nearby.

'What is happening, Mama?' I called, not wanting to leave the safety of the dim room.

'The soldiers have forced them from their homes, and they cannot return,' she replied. Her voice was flat, her manner stricken.

It was after school had been shut down for several months that Baba called us together to announce our first move, when we gathered our pots and mats, our few clothes, the implements to grind maize and till the new soil, *calabashes* for water, and the maize and seed we needed to survive. The women and girls who weren't carrying babies loaded goods onto their backs and heads, then set out on the five-kilometre march to our new home in Alebtong in the interior of the sub-district. Our numbers had swelled, as the older sisters brought their children to stay where they thought they could be safe from the brewing storm. Some of those who had been displaced by the soldiers joined the procession through dense bush, on narrow paths well worn by cattle and goats and their herders.

I had been to the hamlet of Alebtong before. The boys sometimes drove their cows along this route so they could graze on fresh grass, while the girls trailed along beside them, gathering wild fruits and mushrooms to bring home. We soon set about rebuilding our community, starting with bricks formed with our own hands from the chocolate-brown mud, which lightened as it dried in the sunlight. The men crafted the rounded sides of the *ottlum* in the same way Acholi had for centuries. They cut spear grass, tying it into sheaves to dry before packaging it into long bundles to lie on the roof frame. They strengthened the *kraal* with twigs and vines from the bush, and set up a new granary not far away. We soon settled into our new home, but we were anxious, as if the elders sensed our days of freedom were at an end.

We had moved to a backwater, a quiet place in the bush further from danger, but I soon grew bored and restless. I had Esther and Lily nearby, and the mothers around me, but without school—or even the prospect of school—what were we to do? The mothers did not even have a proper garden to work in—the seeds they planted and nurtured near their new huts would take weeks to yield, while the granaries grew perilously empty.

I missed the carefree giggles of my siblings, the steadying voice of my father, the warmth of nights by the *wang oo*. More than anything, I lamented the loss of my other source of learning: the school of *ododo*. Now, we were too busy surviving to tell stories by the fire.

5

Falling to Pieces

Without seeing them, I knew when the enemy was near: the smell of gun smoke would waft through our tiny village, making my stomach churn. It overwhelmed the sweet aromas of musty grass and maize cooking on charcoal that I so loved. It reminded me how much my life had changed.

We started to hide at night, worried about abduction. Late one morning, we'd crept back home, eyes peeled for solitary rebels who had stayed after dark. My rolled-up mat was under one arm, and I had linked the other with Lily's as we got closer to our home.

'Mama?' I looked around for her, and I heard a hum of voices in the direction of Min Obur's hut. I could see a small crowd outside, coming in and out of the low entrance. Mama saw me and hurried over, the distress on her face and the muted mood telling me the story. She gently led me away to our hut, where my cousin was waiting.

'It's Min Obur. She passed away last night,' she whispered. 'Natural causes,' she added before I could ask. I hung my head. Min Obur was Baba's first wife, and much loved by all the family. The mothers had already laid out Min Obur on the bare floor to prepare her body for burial, and family members were filing through her sparse hut to farewell her. I felt sick at the haste of this goodbye of a loving mother. I collapsed to my knees and rested my head beside our hut.

We buried Min Obur quietly, in a silent, soulless way, wrapping her small body in a white sheet and lowering her into a shallow grave behind our compound. Acholi wrapped their dead in cowhides, and later, in white sheets or blankets. In a time of peace, the burial of a woman of Min Obur's stature would be graced by ceremony—the women wailing around her grave, the men dancing the *myel lyel* and beating the air with sticks. We'd have mourned for day after day to usher Min Obur's spirit into the next world. But now, with hostilities escalating between the warring groups—government, former government and LRA rebels—we could not afford to attract attention.

'Until we meet again in Heaven, farewell Min Obur,' I whispered, as Lily and I stood at a distance, watching the bundle being lowered into the ground and covered with soil. I became distracted by a thought. 'Maybe Min Obur is the fortunate one, to be leaving this life for a better place,' I said.

'Yes, and she is fortunate that most of her life was happy, even through the time of Idi Amin,' Lily replied. She could find something good in any situation.

Min Obur was the first person I had seen buried in this way, but after her simple funeral it became commonplace to farewell lost ones in a way that defied everything in our culture. Forebears might have slaughtered a bull or a goat and sprinkled its blood on Min Obur's body to appease Jok, the supreme being, and to calm the anger of the deceased. Children could not see or bury the deceased, for fear that the angry spirit might harm them. In Acholi belief, the spirit of a family member lived on after the body died, near the water or the forest, or sometimes at the top of a hill, and it would disturb the home unless the living performed certain rituals. Many people would not move at night for fear that the evil spirits would catch them. (Our family was *Lakristo,* Christian, and we had given up the ways of the witch doctors, the *ajwaka*, to follow the ways of *Yesu,* so I had never been scared of Jok or joined in these rituals.)

After one year, the family would have gathered again to remember the loved one and to give their personal belongings, such as walking sticks, chairs and clothes, to others in the household. But Min Obur had had nothing left when she died. Rebels had stolen her chickens, cows and goats, as well as her stored supplies of rice and seeds, and her hut was bare. Our future was too uncertain to plan a gathering in one year's time, or even one day's time. When Min Obur died, we could not wail—but we could still cry, and we did. Later in the war, as the list of atrocities grew, I saw how people became immune to the violence, too sick with pain or too hardened even to cry.

I was only six when Idi Amin was deposed in 1979, after he had created havoc in Uganda during his rule through the 1970s. By every account, Amin's rule was barbaric. He forced 60,000 Asians—many of them business owners of Indian heritage—out of the country, and slaughtered as many as 300,000 Ugandans. He reserved a particular hatred for the Acholi and Langi people, even though he was born in West Nile, to the north-west of us. Baba had protected his family from the worst of Amin's poison by isolating us in the village, and we had come out unscathed.

But now danger came from many directions, and we were exposed to it all. After the first raid on our village by the Karimojong in December 1986, the warriors came through the district almost daily, herding stolen cattle from around Pader and Lira Palwo over the border to their homeland in the east. Though they did not steal women or girls, we did not feel safe.

I could not have imagined that there were worse raiders, or that the carnage around me could escalate. But there were, it did—and it happened quickly. Where the Karimojong intimidated us by beating the men, stealing our livestock and, at times, raping the women, they did not abduct children. Alice Auma, now Alice Lakwena, had passed her Holy Spirit Movement on to a young man named Joseph Kony, rumoured to be her cousin, who renamed the rebel force the Lord's Resistance Army (LRA). Like Lakwena, Kony claimed to channel spirits for guidance. He employed a new tactic that scared us more than any of the rest: he enlisted boys by force—boys like those in my school, boys like my nephews—who became young killers in army fatigues with guns they could hardly lift.

Soon, the Karimojong were the least of our worries. Along with President Yoweri Museveni's forces pursuing both the LRA and Milton Obote's former government soldiers, there were three other warring groups around our village. We were never sure which armed group was the enemy and which was the ally, who was good or bad, who was there to defend us or kill us, or what any of the groups hoped to achieve. An armed group could be government forces looking for rebels, or rebels asking where the government forces were. The government forces, knowing that the rebels also spoke Lwo, were at times as brutal towards us as the rebels. Sometimes the rebels dressed as government soldiers to test the villagers: if someone tipped them off about the rebels, they'd punish the whole village by razing it to the ground. Government soldiers would be just as vindictive if they suspected rebel collaborators.

Several thousand of Obote's soldiers had escaped to southern Sudan with their AK-47s and hand grenades, then regrouped and come back across the border into Acholiland as the Uganda People's Democratic Army (UPDA). Museveni sent his forces to Acholiland to flush out the remnants of the UPDA, enlisting men from Bantu-speaking tribes into his National Resistance Army (NRA).

We had run once, from Lapilyet to Alebtong, before the first raid. In the midst of this, my family ran again, to a tiny hamlet called Lalogi, collecting what was now left of our belongings and moving deeper into the bush to escape the threat of attack. The mothers were weary, walking slowly, bent over with what remained of their belongings: spare sets of clothes, their reed mats and rough-woven rugs for sleeping, their few aluminium pots, woven baskets of maize, and wooden cooking utensils. It took us two full days.

My father refused to move with us this time, even though he urged us to go. Charles chose to stay with him, knowing Baba was too old and too broken to survive by himself in Alebtong. A dozen of the stolen three hundred cows had found their way back to the village, and Baba guarded them as he would prodigal sons. His cattle were his most valuable possession, a measure of his wealth and status. Cattle allowed a man to support several wives and pay the bride price to his daughters' suitors.

In all these years we had never been without Baba, even in his weakened state. We now moved without hope or joy to a place even further from the main road, in the sub-district of Lalogi, which was closer to Gulu. We were more than a two-hour walk from the trading centre, but it wasn't all bad. In Lalogi, we could safely gather wild fruits—black plums, tamarinds, custard apples—as well as nuts from the shea trees and borassus palms. Firewood was plentiful, and for a while we felt safer, never imagining outsiders would venture to where the water point was well over a kilometre away, and the landholdings far apart. Here, we crowded into the huts of distant clan relatives, who had no choice but to take us in.

For a time, the pleasure of roaming freely again in the bush enlivened me, distracting me from the pain of missing out on school, but the security of our new home was short-lived.

6

A Girl Survives

'First you must kill your mother,' the LRA ordered the boys they had just captured. The pact was simple: kill or be killed. I had heard these words from an eyewitness and could not get them out of my head. *How does a boy go from herding goats to killing family and neighbours?* I asked myself. I thought of my brothers and nephews, and felt a chill run down my back.

The rebels taught our boys how to kill. But they taught the girls they captured to die again and again. Every day in captivity, a young female was subjected to beatings, rape and hours of trekking—with heavy bags and firewood on her head—through rocky terrain in bare feet.

By late 1987, as I approached the age of fourteen, I was on my knees every morning, praying that I would escape abduction. I feared it more than death. The LRA rebels had descended on our district like a pack of wild dogs and now prowled around our villages after sunset looking for girls like me. They wanted females in their early teens, those strong enough to carry supplies for day upon day, and old enough to service the sexual needs of the commanders at night. They needed young males who were pliable enough to be trained as merciless killers, often by killing their own families first.

A year after the first raid on our village—my awakening to fear—I met each morning with tightness in my chest. *Will they come for me today?*

It was not safe to venture from the village for firewood or to gather bush foods, yet we could not survive without water, so we went as a group to the water point. *Surely they could not catch six girls at once?* I reasoned. At least one would make it home to raise the alarm. One day, I bravely set out in broad daylight to the water point with just Esther and Mary. It was a place with towering shea trees and creamy yellow ant hills that rose two metres above the ground into a rounded point. The water was filthy as animals had been there—but with rebels and soldiers nearby, no one maintained the water sites. We had no choice but to risk sickness and drink the water.

I walked in front as we cautiously approached the water-hole, my eyes scanning the grass for signs of movement or gun smoke. I lifted my head high to tune my ears for the telltale murmuring of voices. When nothing alarmed me, I turned to the girls behind me and said, 'It's all clear.' We kept walking along the dirt path in our bare feet, the empty *calabashes* riding on our heads.

We were still some way from the water point when Mary caught a glimpse of a man's head above an ant hill. 'LRA!' she screamed, as the man quickly squatted down out of sight.

We threw down our *calabashes* and scrambled as fast as we could towards the river. We could not allow ourselves to be caught. We knew our fate if we were: we'd become sexual slaves for the LRA commanders.

Three khaki-clad rebels jumped out from behind the ant hill, running after us with their guns rattling by their sides. I dived into the river first, with the other girls close behind me, drawing my arms through the cool water in long strokes, my head held up, for as far as I could. We swam towards a thick clump of *togo* growing like a bushy island in the river, pulling ourselves through the slimy stalks. My skin bristled, and my heart pounded. I raised myself high enough to slowly pull the *togo* apart, careful not to make a sudden movement that might draw the enemy's eyes to our hiding place.

'It's all clear now,' I said, after the third time I peeked through the grass. 'We can go home.' I had declared the path to be clear, and prayed that I was right. We retraced our way back to the shore and walked in the opposite direction, well away from the ant hill.

After that, the mothers sent all six girls to hide each night. 'You must go, Alice,' Mama told me the first time, her eyes shiny with tears. 'I will help you find a safe place to hide so the rebels will not take you.' She went into the scrub around our huts to find hollowed-out trees, bushes we could crawl beneath, and mounds with protective trees behind them.

'If you come back and I'm not here, I've left groundnuts and drinking water just here,' she told me, pointing to a thick bush a short distance from the hut.

'Yes, Mama,' I replied, not wanting to miss a word of her instructions.

'When you find a safe place to sleep, do not move,' she said. Her face was grave, and she held back tears. 'If you move to another tree, the rebels may be there. And stay quiet, so they will not hear you and come for you.' I trusted her to keep us safe.

We had rested that day, until five o'clock, when my mother started to look anxiously over my shoulder to the perimeter of the compound. 'Here, this will help you run,' she said, thrusting a small package of food into my hands. 'May God protect you,' she cried. I glanced back as we melted into the bush with our small bundles of supplies under our arms. My mother had turned from us, and I saw her thin body bent over and shaking.

I cried, too, that first time, though not until we had started our march into the elephant grass and I could no longer fight the lump rising in my throat and the pity I felt for us all. I let the tears roll silently down my cheeks until the task at hand—stepping over sharp twigs and ducking under overhanging branches—made me focus on where I placed each step.

In the last light of the day, we moved as a group to one location and then fanned out. We rolled out our bedding in the places our mothers had staked out for us. 'Separate into pairs,' they had told us. 'Having six of you in one place is too risky.'

We soon learned that we could sleep well if we planned ahead and hid away as securely as birds in their nests. As long as we remained silent, the heads attached to the legs striding past us would never know we were there.

One night, the moon bright above us, I lay curled up and sleeping on the inner side of our hiding hole. I woke to a rustling sound and, without thinking clearly, nudged Lily, who was sleeping on the outside and closer to the noise. She awoke with a start.

Within the small ring of moonlight reaching into our hiding place we saw a slim, sinister-looking snake gliding within arm's reach of our mats. I opened my mouth to scream, prepared to run, but heard in my head my mother's firm voice telling me, 'Do not move, and stay quiet.' I took three long breaths to calm my racing heart. In the still moment, the snake glided into the darkness.

I lived this way for two years: spending nights in the bush, and then arriving home in the morning to my mother—all the mothers—crying out with relief. My mama was so solemn now, though she never expressed her deep fear, as if sharing it might endanger me. She stopped smiling and chatting with her co-wives. She waited each morning, threading her hands in front of her, like the other mothers.

At times the rebels stayed near our village for days, blocking our way home. They would not have hesitated to take us into captivity, even in daylight. During these times, our mothers feared the worst: that we'd been found and taken away. Sometimes our mothers were so frightened by crossfire around the village that they ran from the rebels themselves. On those days, we returned to our deserted huts and waited.

We hid in all seasons: during the dry season, when the grass was long and gave us protection, and during the long rainy season in the middle of the year, when the downpours became our blanket. Though it rained and rained, there were times I could not even feel the droplets, or the coldness that seeped into my bones and made me shiver. The fear of being abducted or killed had numbed my senses. Some nights, thunder and lightning exploded around me, lighting up the sky as bright as day, and for a few seconds I was completely exposed. Other nights, when low clouds obscured the stars, I slept in complete darkness, as if in the void of a cave. In this way I grew African eyes—inner eyes that sensed the movement of other living things, and perceived danger without seeing it with my physical eyes.

I felt the closeness to my mother slipping away as our interactions narrowed to matters of survival. 'Where should we go tonight, Mama?' I might ask in the afternoon.

'You should stay close to the river.' Or, 'You must go in the direction of Lira, as the rebels are on the road from Patonga.' She had always done her research, by questioning anyone who came past, or older people who always seemed to know the movements of the armed groups.

Then, in the morning: 'How did you survive last night?' she would ask, still busying her hands with the beans she was preparing for the evening meal.

'We found a small patch of berries and that helped us,' I'd say, too tired to engage beyond the simplest of replies. And there would be no time for further conversation.

One morning, I woke after a night on cold soil and saw fresh blood trickling down my leg. I jumped to my feet, backing away from the hiding hole as if it contained a predator. *Am I dying?*

'What is this?' I cried, looking for a wound or a dead animal nearby. Lily put her arm around me. 'It is okay, Alice. It is your body preparing you to be a woman who will have babies,' she reassured me, ripping the sleeve of her shirt and handing it to me to stem the flow.

Before a second month had passed, I was able to get some more reassurance from my sister Doreen, who was much older than me. 'I was so confused,' I explained, as we stared at the flickering fire near Mama's hut. 'I was not expecting this.'

'Why didn't you ask me before this? What about our mother, or the other sisters? You could have talked to them,' she said, in a kind voice that invited me to keep talking. She placed her hands in her lap and turned to face me, offering her full attention.

'I did not want to add to our mother's burden, and you all have young ones to care for,' I replied. I ached for my loss: the lessons about womanhood that I had missed while hiding from the LRA.

'You must wash when you can,' Doreen said, rubbing her hands together in a washing motion.

'Ha. That is hard to do,' I said. I shook my head, annoyed, before softening. In truth, I was just covering my shame at being unclean. 'There is no soap or water when I am in the bush, so I cannot wash myself.' There had been stretches when I could not so much as rinse my body for many days at a time. I was so ashamed of my dirty state that I would pick handfuls of long grass to dampen and scrape across my blood- and mud-stained shirts and skirts. I quickly pushed down my frustration with my sister. Doreen was not to blame for my predicament, and I was relieved after speaking with her—at least I wasn't dying.

I fixed my gaze on the fire, wishing it could sweep across the north and consume this whole war. How else could we escape it?

*

The battle between government soldiers and rebels around the district had become so ferocious that by late January my forays into the bush were lasting longer and longer. One time, I lived like a wild person in the bush for two weeks, foraging for leaves and seeds to relieve the ache in my stomach. I gulped down brown water that could have given me diarrhoea, or carried diseases such as cholera or typhoid, or any number of parasites. Adrenaline pulsed through me as I heard the deafening cracks of guns that seemed to be coming from every side.

Then one morning I awoke to a sky so wide and open that I wondered how it could contain the misery of war. It was silent, for the first time in recent memory. The dew dazzled on the grass around me. I wanted to run my hands through it, to feel its cool wetness. I heard a thrush sing, so rare these days when even the birds did not feel safe. With the song came a flash of carefree summers from my childhood. I had lost count of the days I'd been in the bush this time.

I left my companions and ventured into a small pocket of low grass nearby. Here I lay down, feeling my body relax for the first time since I'd fled. I stared up at a block of turquoise sky draped with pockets of white clouds, letting my thoughts roam. I allowed my senses to reawaken, capturing the heady bush smells of my childhood. I laughed out loud—just because it felt good—and I wondered how I had survived as a fugitive, away from my home and family, for so long. It was a blur of running and hiding, my heart thumping with terror, my belly hungry and thirsty. But I had survived.

I smiled without trying, feeling the breeze on my teeth. Warmth flooded my chest as I dared to let happiness in. I realised that during this time of hiding from the rebels, sometimes in the rain, drinking unhealthy water, being bitten by mosquitoes over and over, I had not fallen sick for one day. When I thought about it, nobody in the village had suffered from malaria or died of illness. Anyone I knew who lost their life at this time died from gunshots. At least a dozen times I had narrowly slipped from the clutches of the LRA, and I knew it was not because I was smarter than others, like some boys I knew who had been taken. I rolled in the spiky grass, my spirit lifting, feeling fully alive. I thought about the village where we now lived: there were two-metre-long pythons that moved at night, large enough to swallow one of the small children. How many times had I awoken to hear that a python had taken a goat, yet none of my family had died in this way. The longer I lay in the grass that day, gazing up at the blue sky, thinking of the goodness in my life, the more peaceful and less alone I felt. I grew more and more confident that my life would not end on this day, or in this war. In that blue sky, in my own frailty, I saw a protective hand stretching over me, and my heart was relieved. 'Thank you, God,' I called out, my arms outstretched. Peace flooded my veins.

My blue-sky day was a watershed. The next day, the guns blazed again, and I again cowered under a prickly bush, focused on staying alive. The euphoria had quickly worn off, and I was soon aware of stabs of hunger, and the cold I could not keep out of my bones when the temperature dropped at night. My simple dress—one of the few I had—was worn, with holes and rips, and was too light for the cool nights. Yet when I lay down that night I slept soundly, as if my body was telling me to hold on to every tiny bit of strength I had in reserve. The next morning I awoke so hungry that I was willing to risk my life to eat.

'Let's see if we can find some groundnuts in the village,' I urged the other girls. We left the protection of our hiding hole to creep through the long grass to our home, knowing it was unsafe to do so. We came close to the clearing, where the shield of grass abruptly finished and the open space of the village started, expecting to hear the sounds of family members. But it was silent.

'Help me.' I heard a weak voice and looked across towards the huts to see a man with his head raised from the ground, calling. All around him lay dead bodies, some soldiers in uniforms, others familiar to me. They were all bodies of men. I knew LRA tactics, how they rounded up many soldiers and civilians together, crowded them into one hut wearing blindfolds, then brought them out one by one to be executed. Most had been cut or hit, the red streaks of their blood a deeper shade than the dusty soil, and running in every direction. I was too scared to look, fearing I would find my brothers and cousins among them. I could not bring myself to respond to the call of the wounded man from among the dead bodies, and pulled Mary back when she moved in his direction.

'Don't touch him,' I yelled. 'This could be a trick—he could be LRA, and he will take you.' I was ashamed of my own words as they came out of my mouth. I turned and ran away from the destruction, back into the security of the bush, tormented by the image of a river of blood flowing through my home.

When I ventured back soon after, my mother and sisters had returned. 'The rebels brought a group of men to our village. We ran for our lives,' my mother told me. 'That man you saw, he was beaten very badly but he survived.' I dropped my head in shame. I re-enacted the scene in my head, reasoning with myself, and still arrived at the conclusion that my mistrust was well founded. Already this conflict had stolen so much from me. The trust in adults I had once felt as a child was just one more thing that was irretrievably gone.

7

Learning to Run

'Neko! Kill them!' I heard a man shout in a fierce voice, close by in the grass. Mama and I dropped the knives we had in our hands and ran for the shelter of the hut. I had long feared this: being trapped in the hut when the rebels came. It was midday on a clear day during summer. I had been sitting with my mother outside the hut, peeling wild yams, our hands moving quickly as we worked in silence, listening for unfamiliar sounds. In the distance I had heard the rapid firing of an AK-47, a sound I knew well.

Some minutes later, I poked my head out the door to find the compound empty. No one had burst through the grass to steal me, and the voices were more distant. 'Mama, do you think we are invisible?' I asked my mother, lightening the mood.

'They just want to kill each other, and we are in the way,' she replied. 'We are not even real people to them, we are not people with beating hearts.'

Just as I emerged from the hut, the bush erupted around us. Suddenly the shouts were close by, and bullets whizzed past me from one direction and then the other, so I did not know which way to run. I could feel my stomach turning from the fear and knew that soon my body would empty itself. This is how I reacted to gunshots these days.

Both sides had laid ambushes. The rebels knew that they were being pursued, so they had made plans to hide in the bush to catch the government soldiers. It was an invasion of the village on a grand scale, a difficult battle where every bit of ground was won and then lost by each side, like a deadly tug of war, with the rebels throwing all their efforts into resistance, while the UPDF—the government forces—called for reinforcements. Everybody in the village ran that day.

For four days, the rebels and government forces battled it out around us, the sounds of whistling bullets and explosions reverberating into our hiding holes. For those four long days I hid with three others, my stomach crying out for food and water, but we were unable to move. With me were Lily, Mary and Esther. When the battle had started, we had run separately, in different directions, but soon found ourselves close together in the tall, dry grass, cowering from the shooting.

From my months of hiding, I had become attuned to every sound and smell, every faint movement around me. 'Kalang,' I whispered to Lily. 'Watch out.' I pointed to a black ant creeping across Lily's bare ankle, but even when it bit her, leaving behind a red welt, she winced in pain but did not cry out. The crawling insects were a momentary distraction from questions that occupied my mind. Where are the guns now? Will they find us here, or should we find another place to hide? Will they set the grass on fire? Where will we run if there's a fire?

In the middle of the fourth morning, before lunchtime

when the sun was still rising, I heard a piercing buzz like the *ober*, which came at dawn and dusk with the threat of the deadly sweating disease, *malariya*. Before my mind could process why a mosquito would be flying at this odd hour, the ground beside the hiding place exploded, ripping up the grass that hid us.

The flames took hold of the grass, and I jumped to my feet. I tumbled through the undergrowth, sharp stabs of pain running up and down my legs, feeling like my whole body would soon be consumed by fire.

'Take my hand,' Lily called, grasping my shaking hand and leading me away as a wall of flames danced through the bush around us. Within minutes we lost sight of the other girls and could not hear a sound other than the crackling grass. Then a wall of thick smoke separated Lily and me.

The pain prickled—it seemed to be all over my body— and I swiped at my legs as though shooing the pain away. I could no longer stand. I had crawled as far as I could, over-whelmed by the pain shooting up my legs like flames on burning logs, until I hid under a sapling tree in an untended garden. Hours later, as the sun slid beyond the horizon, I took stock of my injuries. I looked at the skin on my lower legs, now melted into red and black swirls, and saw splinters of the bomb speckling my body. *I will die here, in this garden,* I thought, as I slipped in and out of consciousness.

I let my mind escape to images of our own garden, the scenes of laughter, where I had grown up around the ankles of the mothers as they worked, before coming back to reality: I was now in the place of my deepest fear. This garden was where adults I knew had recently lost their lives. The rebels were not interested in adult labour—adults could fight back.

They hacked men and women to death with garden hoes because they did not want to waste their bullets.

It was only later, when I came around in the cool darkness of the garden, that I remembered the other girls. In my mind I saw the two who were left behind, burned or suffocated in the fire because they'd been unable to escape in time. I felt a rush of guilt. I had survived when I should have perished as well. *Could I have warned them?*

'Lily?' I cried out, lifting my head. *Where is Lily?* I could barely summon the energy to say her name before I collapsed back onto the ground.

The local hospital had closed down. For many months, no one in our district had received medical care. There was no one to treat the malaria that killed so many, to tend wounds from the daily attacks across the north, or to help women and girls through difficult labours. Twice in the past two years when the clan was under siege, I had seen women struggling in childbirth who later died of treatable complications, such as high blood pressure and heavy bleeding. I knew not to expect formal medical treatment.

The garden was less than a mile from our home, but it took me more than an hour to get back to the village. I found a long stick that helped me as I dragged my leg; when I became tired, I reached out for a tree to hold me up. *Not far to go now,* I reminded myself with each laborious step. The stabs of pain became so strong that I had to start crawling, and this is how my mother saw me from across the compound when I arrived. She dropped the pot that she held with both hands and rushed to my side. I saw the surprised faces of other family members and heard my name called out, but could not take it in.

'Alice, what has happened to you?' Mama cried, looking down at my legs. She pushed her right shoulder under my arm to support me, and together we limped to a bench near the hut. I struggled to find the words to explain what had happened.

'It was a bomb . . . in our hiding place,' I said through tears. Mama stepped into our hut and emerged with a bowl of grey water. She cupped the water in her palm and splashed it over my wounds. I bit my lip to allay the pain.

One of the mothers, Julie Lapogo—Lily's grandmother—now saw me and rushed over to ask, 'Have you seen the other girls? Where is Lily?' I had seen with my own eyes the ferocity of the flames, and guessed they had enveloped Mary and Esther, but I could not bring myself to tell her. 'Lily ran in another direction,' I replied, before I lay my head on the bench, too exhausted to talk, and slept. I awoke to Mama's gentle hands on my legs.

'We will save your legs, Alice,' she said, as she deftly cleaned out dirt and specks of twigs that had been driven into the skin with the shrapnel. I almost fainted with the pain. Only the older women knew the traditional remedies that Acholi had used for centuries: the bitter leaves from wild bushes, the ground stem bark of the knobwood that kept infection at bay, along with many other ailments, and the catechu tree that brought healing.

Each morning and night, Mama prepared her soothing balms and rubbed them over my lacerations with hands like feathers until the heart-stabbing pain subsided and the skin paled from a charred red. The melted skin had twisted into knots down my calves, and every movement hurt.

Outside the village, there was still trouble. But thankfully for now, when I could not move far, the rebels and government soldiers had taken their skirmishes elsewhere.

When Lily returned home a day after me, in a terrible state, I was too disorientated to celebrate with the mothers. Yet despite the pain, as I spent hours alone on my mat, my resolve to fight back grew stronger. I would fight by making something of my life and not yielding to the calamity around me.

As soon as I was strong enough to be moved, my brother, Charles, carefully lifted me onto his bicycle, while my family gathered mats and pots and moved to a tiny settlement across the river where we hoped to feel safe again. The rebels had cleared our granary and stolen everything of value, so our load was light. I did not feel safe, even while clutching the shoulders of my strong brother. Not while I still smelled the smoke of gunfire or heard its thunder, and wondered if I could hold my stomach together.

8

Escape

I was preparing to escape with my brother, Gabriel, and his children any day now. Before the war erupted around us, Gabriel had left the village to find work as a truck driver in Gulu, the largest town in Acholiland, some 110 kilometres to the west of Pader. As news of rebel attacks became too distressing, Gabriel had borrowed a bicycle from his neighbour in Gulu and pedalled for a whole day to reach the hamlet of Lalogi, where the conflict was closing in on our quiet community. The bush around Lalogi had become the centre of some of the worst fighting in Uganda—more dangerous than anywhere we had lived. LRA rebels had raided the military barracks at Kilak, a village on the junction of the road between Lira and Kitgum, and we knew that we would soon be trapped. There was certainly no returning to the family home in Lapilyet, but we could make it to Alebtong, where we'd left our father with Charles and the last of his herd.

Gabriel moved quickly to get us out of Lalogi. 'It is not safe to stay here. It is now quieter in Alebtong, and it is good for us to be with our father,' he announced to the relieved clan.

However, within days of the move back to Alebtong, he came to me and Rose, my cousin from West Nile, and told us, 'Tomorrow we will set out for Gulu. This fighting could go on for a long time around here, and you need to get back to school.'

The government military, the NRA, had their main barracks in Gulu, and the presence of soldiers had kept the LRA at bay. There was still food in the markets, and the schools in Gulu district still operated. Gabriel's two daughters, Faith and Grace, who were a few years younger than me, and his son, Emmanuel, who was still a toddler, were to come too.

'Will Pauline travel with us?' I asked. My sister-in-law was like another mother to me. She was heavily pregnant and already tired from the move between the two villages.

'Pauline will stay in Alebtong until the baby is old enough to join us,' Gabriel replied.

I could barely sleep that night as my mind raced through what might lie ahead. Before we could leave, I had to say one important goodbye. I found Baba sitting listlessly on his wooden armchair, the royal chair with stout arms and a high back, outside his hut. He looked unkempt, like his surroundings, which through neglect had become overgrown with weeds and long grass. He still managed a smile when he saw me approach and held out a bony hand. I paused for a moment to brace myself. Gabriel had seen him already and prepared us for a sad sight. 'Oh, how I cried when I saw the loneliness of our father,' he had told me on his return to Lalogi from seeing Baba.

I was still not accustomed to seeing him so diminished. I held back my tears, sitting down beside him on the ground and taking his hand. None of us knew that prostate cancer was invading his wizened body, and there would be no way back. 'I've come to say goodbye, Baba,' I said, my voice trembling. He nodded, and leaned back against the high-backed chair. Then he looked me in the eyes with a love that only Baba could give me.

'Alici, you know one day soon I will die, but if I die you are not to worry so much,' he said, in his strong, deep voice. 'The most important thing is your education. You have to study.' I could no longer hold back my tears, and let them roll down my cheeks.

'Baba, I will finish my studies,' I promised him, holding both of his hands in mine. I considered how fortunate I was to have this man as my father. How he had encouraged me to keep learning when so many fathers had already arranged marriages for their teenage daughters by the time they were my age, almost fifteen. From eleven years old, some girls wore red bangles on their wrists so that boys knew they were already promised in marriage. I wiped the tears away and stood up to leave. I had to steel myself: I knew that the war would kill my father, and that this farewell would be the last time I saw him. As the eldest brother, Gabriel would be my guardian in the future.

The roads between the main towns of the north had become more and more dangerous. Every day we heard of ambushes on the road between Pader and Gulu, so we would need to choose our route carefully. I had grown so weary of the running and hiding—and the pervasive fear of abduction—that I almost welcomed this risk as a reprieve.

At one point during the night, I awoke and remembered that I was heading for school. I felt a flutter of anticipation in my stomach. I sat up and looked around at the darkness, then settled back into sleep—tomorrow's journey would be long and treacherous.

We set out just before sunrise the next morning, with the two little girls, Faith and Grace, perched on Gabriel's bicycle as he pushed them along. None of the children had shoes, but our soles were toughened from a lifetime without them. My legs had not fully healed, and I wondered how I could wash them as we fled. At fourteen years old, I was the eldest—old enough to carry Emmanuel, who was strapped by a cotton sash to my back, slowing my progress to a plod. Gabriel was no faster. At the age of two he had contracted malaria, and doctors had given him an injection of quinine into his left buttock. For some reason it had made his left leg numb, so it couldn't bear weight, and with lack of exercise the leg had atrophied and his foot had become deformed. Though our family did not have much money, Baba had made sure that Gabriel had a series of operations that would allow him to walk on his foot, though he would forever have a limp.

Rose and I laboured along, carrying clothes, fruits and groundnuts, and balancing water in small plastic containers on our heads. At times we slowed to a plod.

'Come on, girls,' Gabriel urged. 'We will make it, but we need to keep moving. And keep your eyes open.'

'I'm too tired, Gabriel. Can we take a rest?' I complained as darkness fell on the first day, but he would not listen.

'We will go together, and we will make it all the way to Lira tonight, and then we can rest,' Gabriel replied confidently, beckoning me with his hand. I later discovered how nervous he was. He had heard stories in the village of how others from our district had set out in this same way, only to be stopped by rebels or soldiers. He had heard of brutal killings, too, but he had kept this to himself.

We chose a narrow corridor where we knew the rebels were not active, well away from villages or huts. At times we took single-file tracks used by cattle herders, to avoid talking with strangers, in case we were accused of collaborating. When we saw a person or a group in the distance, Gabriel herded us into the bushes until the threat passed. We skirted around stark villages, where from a distance we could see only men, assuming they were rebels.

*

The Ashwa River was full and fast flowing, with a series of channels gushing over and around rocky outcrops, some with hardy bushes perched on them. This river wound its way through the district and then north into Sudan, to the great White Nile River and a world that I could not even imagine. I looked at the swiftness of the current and froze. I backed up the low riverbank, looking behind me for a way out, and then glanced in either direction for an alternative place to cross. How could I possibly cross this divide when I was not a confident swimmer? I knew I could not make it to Lira, the first town on the way to Gulu, without crossing it, and Gabriel would not leave me behind or allow me to turn back on my own.

'Gabriel, this is too deep, it will take me away,' I called, but Gabriel was already ferrying the younger girls and baby Emmanuel from rock to rock across the river, leaving Rose and me to contemplate how we would negotiate the dangerous crossing.

'Let's go,' Rose said as she held my hand tightly, and we stepped out into the current. The water around our ankles was cool, and it got colder as we waded towards the deeper water of the channel, where the swift current swirled around our waists. I lifted my hands above my head, and with each step searched with my bare toes for stones under my feet.

'It's so slippery,' I yelled out, wanting to cry. I was well into the river when I felt my feet slipping on the mossy stones. I pulled on Rose's hand, but she was slipping, too—we were both toppling over.

'Help us, Gabriel!' Rose cried out. He quickly doubled back to reach us and pull us from the water, one on each strong arm.

I sat on the bank of the river for a long time after that, gathering myself. 'I could have drowned. I could feel it,' I said, shaken. Rose nodded. Soon Gabriel called us to follow him. We had passed the only natural obstacle on the way to Lira, and if we could just stay clear of government soldiers and rebels, we would have our freedom.

The closer we walked to Lira—the main centre for the Langi tribe—the safer I felt, the higher my spirits rose, and the less my aching and lacerated bare feet screamed out for attention. We reached the outskirts of Lira after two full days and two nights of walking, but we were just 40 kilometres from home. My legs had swelled from the burns, and the infected wounds were getting worse. I looked forward to treatment in a few days' time in Gulu, if we finally made it.

The Lango district had escaped the worst atrocities of the conflict. Here, we were among friends: Langi and Acholi shared many of the same customs and could understand each other's language. Finally, we could rest, though only for one night. We laid out our mats under the cover of an awning of a public building, and, for the first time in days, slept soundly.

The next morning, Gabriel negotiated our passage on the back of a truck crowded with fifty others, all as weary as we were, each with a story of hardship and loss as bad or even worse than anything I had seen. When we reached Kamdini, a junction on the main highway linking Kampala to Lira, West Nile and Sudan, I could feel freedom in my veins. It was so close now. Kamdini was near the Nile River crossing at Karuma Falls, and 70 kilometres west of Lira. The fighting ended at the Nile River: it was a flowing demarcation line between safety and misery. However, to get to Gulu, the truck had to travel 60 kilometres north into dangerous rebel-filled territory.

At the trading centre of Minakulu on the border of Acholi and Langi lands, we sat for hours in the blazing heat without any cover, waiting in silence for other vehicles to arrive to form a military convoy. There were trees, but we did not want to move far from our transport. When the convoy finally moved, it was at a crawl, and twice it stopped when word came down the road that there were rebel ambushes ahead.

'Get out,' yelled the government soldiers leading the convoy, who were there to bring us to safety. They shepherded us off the back of the truck with their rifle butts, and we stood around like lost sheep beside the road, our mouths dry and stomachs empty.

Is this it? I wondered, looking at the others in the group, who seemed nervous.

The soldiers were angry—perhaps at the war or their own poverty—and at times fired shots in the air in frustration. Many of the NRA military came from the south and were resentful of being poorly paid in this civil war. I saw the hatred in their eyes and the guns in their hands, and I shuddered. 'I'm afraid they will kill us,' Rose whispered to me.

'Don't look at them,' I whispered back, casting my eyes to my dirty feet. We kept our eyes averted as they pushed us back onto the truck, and we were soon back on the gravel road. Ten hours after leaving Lira, the truck rattled down a hill and along the main street of Gulu. The place bristled with a life I had never encountered: groups of people walking by the side of the road, rows and rows of shopfronts and buildings two or three storeys high.

*

Gabriel had a home right in the centre of Gulu, a one-bedroom house with a tin roof, concrete-block walls and a locking door that offered some security. I stepped inside and felt the luxury of a cool concrete floor on my bare, worn-out feet. The walls were solid, but the closeness of the people in the houses around me felt foreign after a life spent in the village.

'Thank you for bringing us here,' I mumbled as I looked around the room. I realised how brave my brother had been to leave these four solid walls and come for us in the heart of the conflict.

He smiled, looking pleased to have us filling his empty home. 'You are most welcome.'

I hardly had a moment to take in my new surroundings when Gabriel announced, 'I must go back to work now, if

I am to provide for all of you. Alice, you will take care of the younger children.'

'Where will I find food? And water?' I replied in a panic. I knew where the water points were around my district, but where would I go in a city?

'We have good neighbours—one of them is our nephew. They will help you with all you need.' And then he was off for days at a time, to remote places such as West Nile, towards Zaire (now the Democratic Republic of the Congo). I was left as provider and protector. As I approached my fifteenth birthday, I had to learn how to be a mother in a hurry. Some days, when the roads were bad, we all waited and waited for Gabriel to return home with food. Many times, he simply could not get back, so we went hungry. Sometimes, I had the courage to ask our neighbours for help, and other times we curled up together to sleep with empty stomachs. Often, I waited until the younger children slept and then quietly wept for my mama.

The fighting in Gulu was mild compared to the Pader district we had fled—most of the conflict in the district was between the former Obote government's UNLA under a Major Kilama, and the Museveni government forces, who lived in the military barracks on the outskirts of town. In Gulu, the LRA targeted barracks and not civilians. Yet I felt less secure than I had in the village, where I could run to my hiding places under bushes or in the long grass.

My dismay at being put in charge of the family was soon tempered by a return to school. I'd learned that in January 1988, I would be starting in Senior 6, with all the other students. I spent days preparing myself for my first day at Holy Rosary, a large Catholic school in the middle of town near the market. I had walked past the school almost every day since we'd arrived and had looked on with envy at the children in uniforms playing in the school grounds as though they had no cares in the world.

That first day, I made sure that the younger children were clean and had eaten a bowl of *posho* I'd prepared over the fire, and that there was water in the house and something to eat when we came home in the evening. My niece Faith, Gabriel's eldest daughter, was also of school age, and my cousin Rose would join us at the new school. She had gone to live with her older sister in another part of Gulu. Faith and I set out together in second-hand school uniforms donated by family friends. We deposited Emmanuel with the neighbours, and Grace at the kindergarten nearby, and continued along the main road to the school, where we paused at the gates. It had been many months since the closure of my tiny village school. With its long, low, mud-brick blocks, Holy Rosary was huge by comparison. I hid my nerves by locking my arm with Faith's and declaring, 'This is a good day for us, Faith. Today we will go to school.' Faith was a smart girl—I knew she would thrive here.

By the end of my first day, I had made three good friends: Atim Harriet, Adong Alice and Lily Rose. Two of these girls would remain my friends for many years.

I'd also found an ally in Sister Margaret, a nun from Pader district, who knew I'd escaped fighting in the village. When she came into our classroom to greet the class, she made a point of welcoming me. Her smile radiated love and kindness, and calmed my fears. From the moment her soft eyes met mine on that first day, I knew I could trust her.

One morning I rose as usual at dawn to fetch water from

the water point, moving quickly through the hushed streets before they came to life. Most days I was at home before the younger ones awoke. But on this morning, as I ventured out with an empty jerry can on my head, I was distracted by thoughts of the day ahead at school. The night before, I had worked on an assignment by candlelight, and I hoped I would earn high marks for it.

Before I knew it, I had covered the ten blocks to the creaking hand pump, where I lined up behind the older women for my turn. Some mornings we enjoyed relaxed conversation, but today we waited in silence. There had been warnings of heightened tension in Gulu, and the women were not in the mood for lighthearted chatter. I filled my yellow plastic container, labouring to lift it onto my head, then stepped away from the water point to trudge home, the water sloshing over the sides as I swung my hips.

I had barely started out on the homeward journey when a crack of gunfire cut through the stillness of the morning. I dropped the jerry can and threw myself onto the dirt road before the return fire split the air. These were the opening salvos of a ferocious rebel attack, one that brought fiery exchanges and would rock the streets all day. The government soldiers rapidly set up roadblocks to stop people moving around the city, so groups of civilians—local people trying to go about their everyday business—sat waiting for hours and hours.

Don't you care that we are trying to live here? I inwardly scowled at the soldiers, but I would never have been brave enough to voice the words. I sat by the roadblock the whole day, my thoughts growing more and more frenzied about my three young charges alone at home without food or water. *What will become of the children if I am shot during the crossfire? They will be hungry. I hope Faith will know to ask the neighbours for help.*

This was not a lone incident. A few times, police blocked me from making my way home. On one occasion I ended up sleeping on the dirt floor of a stall in the market, arriving home early the next day. On these days I skipped school, too tired to walk all that way and too tired to learn. At school, Sister Margaret covered for me on the days I arrived late or not at all. She took the time to ask why I was late and to make sure that I was all right, where other girls might have been punished. My confidence grew under Sister Margaret's care. I did not know then that she would continue to support me for decades to come.

We lived in this disorganised way for almost a year. My sister-in-law Pauline arrived from Pader district with her new baby, Gideon, and took over the care of the children. As my high-school years approached, I was finally able to devote myself to my studies.

One night, later that year, Gabriel gathered us all around him in the living room. 'I have something to announce,' he said with a wide grin. 'We are moving to Jinja.' Jinja was a city in the south, on the shore of the vast Lake Victoria. Uganda was like two countries: the north, now torn apart by warring groups, and the south, still struggling to recover from Idi Amin's past ravages, but safe. And while Winston Churchill had famously called Uganda 'the Pearl of Africa'— for its fertile soil and profusion of birds and wildlife—I had heard that Jinja was considered a pearl on Lake Victoria.

I clapped my hands at the news, and turned to hug the younger girls. We would finally be far away from the war.

Gabriel looked perplexed and turned to me. 'Alice, it is

best if you stay here for Primary 7,' he said. In the past we had talked about secondary school, and how I might go to St Mary's after my last year of primary. 'You can join us when you finish school.'

My lip started to quiver when I realised that I would not be going south, but he did not notice. I bit it to stop myself breaking down, as that would not help. He was my guardian—I could not argue with Gabriel.

Soon afterwards, I stood in the central bus terminal, right beside the market, clutching a soiled handkerchief. Around me were rows of battered buses that had withstood the wartime ravages of ambushes and bullet punctures. The Kampala bus sat idling, smoke streaming from its exhaust pipe, as passengers who were taking their chances on the perilous road south looked around nervously. I tapped on the window to catch Pauline's attention and saw beside her the bright faces of Grace and Faith, who turned and grinned. I choked.

Until Pauline had escaped our village to join us, I'd been like a mother to those girls. I felt a pang of jealousy that my niece, Lucy, who had recently joined us, was with Gabriel's family and I would be left behind. Pauline, always so kind, caught a glimpse of the tears now running down my cheeks, and I saw her eyes become watery. The driver clunked his vehicle into gear, the diesel fumes forcing me to take a step back, and the bus edged away from the stand. I lifted my arm and mouthed, 'Goodbye,' then sagged the minute the bus was out of sight. *What if they don't make it down that road?*

I had never felt so alone. I started walking in the direction of our little home and wondering how I would cope, even though I still had my nephew and other relatives nearby. But before long, all I could think about was my good fortune. I appreciated the sacrifices Gabriel had made to keep me in school, when he struggled on a meagre truck driver's wage to feed his family members and to keep his own children in school.

One day, he had even come to the school to speak with my teacher. I had watched him from behind a shade tree, where I sat with friends. I saw his open hands and earnest expression, and knew that he was pleading on my behalf for the school to allow me to stay without paying fees, as he could no longer afford to pay for me. With help from Gabriel, I had secured a precious place at St Mary's for secondary school. I was indeed fortunate to be getting an education.

Early in 1990, at the age of sixteen, I started high school in Senior 1 at St Mary's Secondary School at Lacor, on the outskirts of Gulu. In all of the north, there were only two boarding schools exclusively for girls: St Mary's Secondary School, and another school in Kitgum.

I had good reason to pick up my pen and open my workbooks: memories of sitting bored in the village, day upon day, of my mother's tears in the garden, and of my pact to do better in life all remained fresh. I arrived at the school on the first day singing, grateful for this good turn in my life. I had made a pledge to Baba, and to myself: I would channel all my attention into my studies.

St Mary's was a good school, with a good reputation in the district. In the middle of the school grounds stood a large chapel, where I spent many hours reciting the rosary, and there were separate houses for the priests and nuns. The school was close to St Mary's Hospital, with thick bush stretching out behind the dormitories. When I joined St Mary's, the LRA

During the 1990s, around one million Acholi people in northern Uganda were forced by the government into Internally Displaced Person (IDP) camps, ostensibly for their own safety.

At the peak of the war, there were more than sixty overcrowded camps with inadequate sanitation and no privacy. Malnutrition was common, along with malaria, dysentery and many other treatable illnesses.

Anxious mothers gather to hear news of their abducted children.

Families wait for vital food supplies from the World Food Programme (WFP) and other programs, including Childcare International (now the Irene Gleeson Foundation [IGF]). They provided the only food available once families moved into camps and could no longer grow their own crops.

People in an IDP camp line up at a borehole to fill their plastic jerry cans with water. It was often unsafe to move outside the camps to traditional sources of water. It could take all day to get water.

Fire was yet another hazard faced by those living in camps; flames could skip easily from hut to hut, causing untold devastation. Some fires were caused by gunfire during rebel attacks, others by women cooking over open fires in their huts.

Without easy access to water, there was no way to contain a fire.

The aftermath of a fire breaking out in the camp.

Cleaning up after a fire. The dry season was the time of greatest risk.

There's nowhere to go after a fire. Families who have already lost their village homes, livelihoods and peaceful lives now face further loss: food items, bedding and clothing.

A mother and baby at Padibe IDP camp, which housed more than 30,000 people and was one of the largest.

A meeting of mothers in the community. Women took leadership roles in the camps and frequently gathered for consultations with humanitarian and government representatives.

The reintegration process—a young girl, newly returned from captivity with a wounded leg, is supported by her parents. Others in her community gathered to welcome her. Not all returning children receive a warm welcome. CCF helped to reintegrate hundreds of children as the war wound down after 2006.

An unattended child in a camp, amusing himself with charcoal.

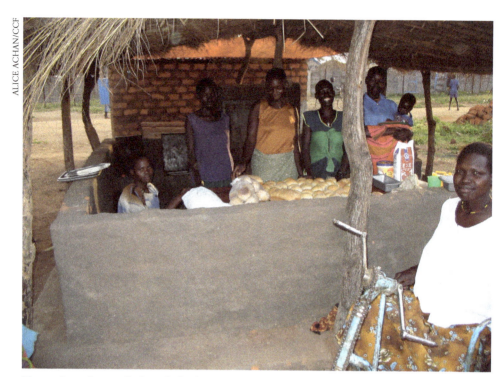

The girl mothers sell their baked goods in Pader. Learning to bake was an early activity in the reception centre, designed to teach the girls how to make a living.

Craft classes at the reception centre were a means of therapy. They also helped with reintegration into the community.

Reclaiming a culture lost in the conflict: the girls learn traditional Acholi dance as a form of trauma therapy.

Practical support arrives at the reception centre. When help came, it arrived in many forms: food, clothes and medicine, along with these bunk beds that went into two UNICEF tents.

Girls and boys returned on Eagle Air flights to Pader, Agago and other districts, where they were reunited with their families. They arrived with clothes and sleeping mats donated by humanitarian agencies. Here, a social worker gets to know one of the girls and documents important information, such as her name, parents' names, home village and district.

A thirteen-year-old girl soon after giving birth. She returned to Pader from captivity while heavily pregnant and was reunited with her mother through CCF.

Faith and her mother, Pauline, in recent times. Despite the dislocation of the war, Gabriel and Pauline's focus on educating their children has prepared each of them for successful careers.

The bustling town of Gulu in 2008, two years after the fighting ended.

The main street of Pader township. During the time of the IDP camps, the town was crowded with NGO four-wheel drives and foreign aid workers.

ANDREW TYNDALE

Philippa and Alice in Lira Palwo in 2008, at the time of the dismantling of the camps, known as 'decongestion'. Small tailoring and vegetable businesses had sprung up along the main street of the trading centre.

LINDA GOLLAN

Philippa with the Pader girls in June 2008, just months after the school's opening.

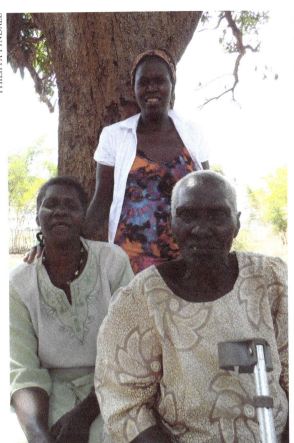

Alice, Doreen and their elderly mother, Mama Lucie, on a return visit in 2016 to the family home in Lapilyet, where Alice spent her early years.

Mama Lucie and Gabriel at his home in Gulu. Approaching ninety years of age at the time of publication, Mama Lucie spends her time helping to prepare daily meals.

Florence Komakech, a community leader throughout the conflict and beyond. Florence was among the first people to support Alice in 2002 as she met with girls under the *kworo* tree. Most of the early group had returned to the camp from captivity.

Alice making her dinner in her small room in Pader. After working in the camp and at the reception centre all day, it was a relief to have her own space.

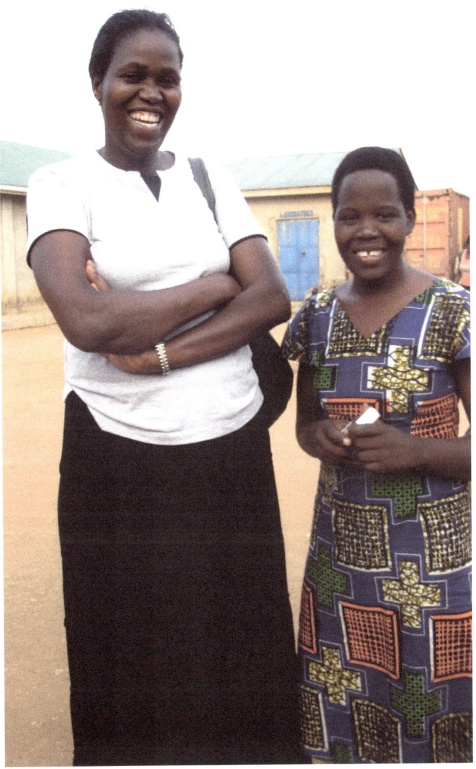

Alice and Polline, who arrived at the school from Nairobi, having survived life in Congo in the camp of the top LRA leadership.

Alice with one of the Pader Girls Academy girls. Many still look to Alice as a mother figure and mentor when she's at the school.

The CCF guesthouse, opened in 2012, before the addition of a lawn and garden as well as a secure perimeter wall. The guesthouse was developed to provide an income stream for the school, and as a place where the girls can learn about hospitality.

was active around Gulu, but while the rebels had descended upon villages and stolen children all across the north, they had spared missionary schools. As a result, institutions like ours were open campuses without fences.

One of the nuns, Sister Miriam, came from West Nile, and knew several of my brothers, including Gabriel. She kept a watchful eye over me at St Mary's after Gabriel and Pauline left. I felt safe at school—safer than outside, where there were skirmishes with the LRA, and girls were targets for lustful boys—and I slept soundly in my dormitory after we locked the door behind us at dusk. The footsteps I heard outside the dormitory during the night were guards paid to protect us and offer advance warning of any danger. There were two girls' dormitories: one for the girls in Senior 3 and 4, and the one where I lived, for the younger girls in Senior 1 and 2, the first two years of secondary school.

The dormitories were wide and long, with concrete floors and mattresses lined up either side of a corridor. My mattress was right at the end, one of the furthest from the entrance to the room. It was a simple arrangement: my metal suitcase acted as a headboard, and I had a single sheet and a blanket for cover. A basin for bathing and jug for water sat near my feet. There was no pillow. A pillow and a change of sheets were luxuries reserved for children from families with more shillings than mine.

Each evening at five o'clock, I lined up with thirty other girls for bowls of rice and beans, which we quickly devoured before preparing to settle down for the night. By seven o'clock, we were locked into the dormitory until sunrise. I enjoyed the nightly routine, knowing that after seven o'clock I would be nestled into my corner, more secure than I could ever remember being. In my safe corner, I could let my mind wander. I thought of the village school and the first time that I picked up a worn-out book and laughed at the sketches of strange creatures from another country—we certainly did not have black bears or mule deer or red-breasted robins in Uganda. Even in my earliest years of schooling, I could read more than my mother. I remembered the pact that I'd made with myself: I would never constrain my life to the village and babies—it would be bigger than that.

Late in September 1990, the St Mary's drama students were well advanced in their rehearsals for the Independence Day inter-school competition, while the dancers and singers in the school met in the school grounds each morning to practise their performances. Independence Day is celebrated on 9 October to mark the day in 1962 when Britain handed Uganda back to Ugandans after almost seventy years of colonial rule. We all marched to a brass-band recording, our backs as straight as poles and our arms swinging in unison. For one day, we united as Ugandans and put our wars behind us. Our youthful confidence was not dampened by the booms of shelling or the knowledge that clashes between soldiers and rebels erupted every day around Gulu. I held my head high and marched proudly shoulder to shoulder with my classmates. At the end of the march, we held hands and laughed without a care.

9

A Knock on the Door

The school of *ododo* could only go so far in preparing me for life in conflict.

In the early hours of the morning of 1 November 1990, All Saints Day, there was a knock on the door of the dormitory next door, the one for older girls. 'Open up,' a high voice called, convincingly enough for the girl closest to the door to climb out of her bunk bed to listen.

'Who is it?' she asked.

'It's matron. Open up, I need to come in,' the voice answered. Through the door it must have sounded just like Sister Karla, the much-admired school matron who was known to check on us at any time. Without another word, the young girl slid the metal bar from its latch and, before she could open the door fully, gun muzzles pushed through the crack, and sweaty men in khaki uniforms swarmed into the dormitory. It was a small band of LRA rebels who, in the darkness, had slipped past the sleeping guards. They strode through the dormitory, grabbing the girls and pulling them outside.

Soon we were awake, too, and could hear the screams next door. I felt the cloud of fear rising around me, and sensed the short breath and beating hearts. We had no way to escape. Some of my schoolmates cowered to appear small, while others found friends and clung to them. I froze in my corner.

Then we heard a voice at our door. 'You must open up. If you open the door, we will not kill you,' the rebel said in a quiet, strong voice. The rebels had ways of keeping frightened children quiet without a single gunshot. 'Do not make one noise or we'll kill all of you,' the rebel threatened, and we all knew they would. We had no way out. If we cried out, we would die. If we raised the alarm and soldiers came to our rescue, many of the children outside—our friends, schoolmates—would perish in the tussle.

A girl closest to the entrance stepped up to slide open the bolt on the door, and six or more rebels with guns on their shoulders stormed through the dormitory. They ripped at everything, pulling the mattresses apart, and then beat the girls while yelling at them. It was two o'clock in the morning and completely dark. Nobody cried.

'You and you. Come with us,' the rebels yelled at a shivering huddle of girls who had been corralled into a corner. The men had clear targets: younger girls, the girls under sixteen years of age, who were less capable of escaping.

I was so frightened that I couldn't think what to do. I was trapped—it wasn't like the village, where I had time to run and places to hide. The rebels were in a hurry now. They'd already collected a large number of girls from the other dormitory and would soon escape back into the bush to meet their commanders and slip out of range of the government soldiers. They rampaged up and down the corridor, pulling young girls out of their beds by their arms and bundling them out. I crouched in my corner, waiting for my turn. My stomach churned, and I fought the urge to be sick. My thoughts ran out of control. *All these years of running, and I had escaped this. All these lessons will amount to nothing if I am taken away to the bush.* I waited, praying a simple prayer, as I had when I was twelve years old. *Please protect me, God. Please let me live. Spare my life.*

In the confusion, a mattress was flung towards my hiding place, covering me. Then another fell on top of that, and a blanket. After a few minutes, the noises around me—the shuffling and muffled whimpers—grew distant. I was in a cocoon under the bedding, where it was now quiet, apart from the sound of my heartbeat. Soon there was complete silence. I was burning up from the layers, but I could not move. I stayed there a long, long time in a daze, wondering if they might come back for me. When I finally lifted my head to peek out, it was still dark, but I could sense a human presence. 'Is someone there?' I whispered.

'Yes, I'm here,' a small voice whispered back.

'Are you okay?' I asked her, and after a pause we took courage and crawled out of our hiding places. We held each other, trembling. Bedding and clothes, books and bags, shoes and toothbrushes were strewn all the way to the dormitory door. I closed my eyes to keep out the image. Just two of us in my dormitory had not been abducted. I was confused, and I did not know why I had been spared.

News of the attack spread quickly at daybreak. The whole of Gulu was awash with misery when families learned that two other schools, Gulu High School and Sacred Heart, had also been raided that same night. Parents arrived at

St Mary's, hoping to find their children. The girls were gone, almost all of them. Taken into the bush outside Gulu, without a trace.

Then the wailing for their lost girls began. 'How did a dozen armed boys break into a school without anyone hearing them?' one angry mother demanded. Most already knew the answer: the rebels were trained in guerrilla tactics. They could crawl through the bush on their bellies like snakes, with their guns by their sides. It would not have been hard for them to move undetected through the grounds of a school.

'Why didn't the soldiers respond? Did they not care to risk their lives for civilians, even when they are innocent children?' another mother asked.

'The rebels are brave in the dark, and cowards in the daylight,' scoffed another parent, spitting on the ground. 'I want my daughter back!'

Sister Karla wrung her hands in anguish. 'It was not me,' she said, trying to explain how she had been used to deceive the girls, but her words fell on deaf ears. No parent could find comfort.

I wandered around the periphery of the crowd in a daze. My closest friends were gone, and I had no idea where they had been taken. A man came up to me and called my name. Beside him stood a woman I did not know.

'Alice, we are here to take you back home,' he said.

I shook my head. 'Home? My home is in Lira Palwo,' I said, confused. The stranger and his wife had been sent to take me to the home of my nephew, who still lived in Gulu, right beside Gabriel's old place.

The school closed immediately. I gathered what I could— my mattress and suitcase with a few clothes in it—and we left in a taxi for the town centre. There was no time to salvage books or other items from the jumble on the dormitory floor.

I spent that night in Gulu, sleepless and numb, my eyes locked on the door, imagining the rebels might return. The next day, I borrowed some shillings and boarded a bus bound for Kampala, then another to Jinja. I found my way to Gabriel's home by asking stallholders at the local market. In the south of Uganda, it seemed like the war did not exist—northern Uganda itself did not exist. The suffering north of the Nile crossing was well out of sight and, because so little news came south, Acholi were out of the minds of most Ugandans.

I arrived without warning. '*Lok ango?*' Pauline inquired in a soft, concerned voice, when she gathered herself from the surprise. Grace and Faith had squealed when they saw me.

'How am I?' I echoed, unsure of myself. I took a deep breath. 'I am glad to be here.'

Gabriel and Pauline did not know all the details of the attack on my school, and were eager to hear them, but I could not muster the energy to start talking. I flopped in a chair and closed my eyes. The story would have to wait.

The raid haunted me—even in Jinja, far from Gulu and the north. For the first few nights I slept in short bursts, waking abruptly, frightened by the faces I saw so vividly in my dreams. At dusk on the first day, when Pauline turned on the lights in the small house, I moved swiftly to switch them off. 'They'll find us,' I said, as I jumped up from my seat. I was annoyed with her for putting us all at risk.

'You are safe here now, Alice,' Pauline reassured me, as she reached out to hold me. My limbs were stiff and heavy. I could barely remember the lightness of life in Lira Palwo before the war. It was as if I had left my spirit behind in the village, and now I was just a body—a shell—alive in the flesh but dead inside. With each move, I had lost a bit more of myself, and I worried that there was nothing left to lose.

After our evening meal one night, Gabriel and I sat together, sipping our black tea on the sofa. He was a thoughtful man, and I knew that he could help me make sense of what had happened to me. I relayed the events of the raid, and he listened.

'Why was I spared? There were only six girls left of seventy. Why did this happen to all my friends, and not to me?' I looked at my brother, pleading for answers. 'I feel that my escape was purely God's grace.' I turned to face Gabriel. 'I don't know why the rebels chose not to burn the building down—that is what they do. To me, it feels like a miracle.' Gabriel nodded his agreement.

'Gabriel, how can it be that our own Acholi people can do this to each other? We speak the same language when we beg for mercy, but they do not hear us,' I asked my older brother in despair. He listened attentively, placing his teacup onto the table nearby. He touched my shoulder and looked at me lovingly.

'It is not fair, I know,' he said. 'We can only trust that God will protect us, and in the end he will be the judge of those who harm the innocent.' His words soothed me, as they had since I was a small girl, when he still lived with us in the village.

That night I lay in bed, thinking about his words and my position in the world. *I will survive. Revenge is not an option. Anger will not help me. I have no control. I will have to live without answers.* Finally, after many disturbed nights, I slipped into a deep sleep.

10

Living with the Enemy in Karamoja

'Alice, Alice, I have good news. I'd been thinking about how you might stay in school, and I've found a place for you,' Gabriel said as he burst through the door of the living room. His expression—like a hunter arriving home with prey—made me smile.

'That is wonderful news, Gabriel. Where is this school?' I said, elated at this break in the tedious pattern of sitting, chores and trips to the market during the weeks in Jinja.

'It is a very good school in Moroto. In Karamoja. I'll be able to take you there next week so you can start right away,' he replied. 'You can stay with our good friends, Philip and Florence, until a place comes up for boarding.' Gabriel had started a new job driving a truck for World Vision in north-eastern Uganda. Each week, he made the arduous twelve-hour journey between Jinja and Moroto to deliver food supplies.

He turned and left the room to find Pauline and the children. I fixed my empty stare on the back of his head as he left, digesting what this news meant. I could feel my spirit sinking into a deep hole.

No, no, no, please not there. Please don't make me go there. The vast region of Karamoja, which bordered Acholiland to the west and Kenya to the east, was the last place I wanted to live after my close encounter with its cattle-stealing warriors, the Karimojong who had beaten Baba and stolen our cattle.

Later in life, friends would ask me why I had not resisted the move to Karamoja. In truth, I had no choice: in Acholi culture, Gabriel had the authority of a father, and I had no right to argue with his decision. Gabriel's experience of the conflict had been so different to mine: to him, Karamoja was a place of beauty, and their attacks on us arose from a struggle to survive.

That night, as I lay in the dark, the memories flooded back. I could picture every detail of the naked warrior standing over me as if it were yesterday. I remembered the sound of his voice, the scars on his chest, his nakedness. I cried quietly until my mind escaped to earlier times: the smell of shea blossoms, dipping my mother's maize bread into shea honey, playing in the garden as the mothers dug up yams. *But if I went home, what would I be going back to?* I did not even know who was still alive in my village. Without money, I could not afford to travel home on the back of a truck, or to buy food for the long journey. Deep down, I knew there was no other choice for me—I had to cling to my studies, even if the location was not ideal. Finally, my body willed me to sleep, and I escaped my unruly thoughts.

I was seventeen and had only reached my second year of high school. I tried not to dwell on this, but at times I could not avoid thinking how it could have been so different. There were good schools in Jinja and Kampala, much better than regional schools, but they were also more expensive. When I'd recently raised the subject of returning to school, Gabriel had replied, 'Alice, I'm sorry—there is not a spare shilling to send you to school here.' Now he had found a way forward, and I could not be ungrateful.

I kept my disappointment close to my chest, reminding myself how lucky I was to have survived the raid in Gulu. We did not mention it in the home: as a fortunate survivor, I stayed silent and moved on, even when I heard of several good friends being rescued. There was no sign of my other dear friends. My life was calm now, and I had lived in peace, helping Pauline with the washing and cooking, and caring for my young nieces and nephews.

The next week, Gabriel and I set out from Jinja in his old truck, with its cargo of bags of rice, flour and sugar piled high. The Acholi had a civil war to deal with, but the Karimojong had their own problems: the challenge of poor soil and recurring drought. They were starving to death.

I sat silently with Gabriel as the truck rattled and jounced on dirt roads with deep welts that formed during the rainy season and were forged deeper from heavy use in the dry. There were times on the way when the dry landscape was so familiar that I could have been back in Acholiland. After the first six hours, from Jinja to Mbale, the roads got even worse until the last 160 kilometres when, for five hours, Gabriel carefully picked his way around impossible corrugations or waited behind other trucks as they found a path through.

We exchanged words, but none that came close to conversation about the dread I felt inside at inching closer to Moroto.

'Alice, you'll see how beautiful it is in Karamoja,' he said, looking out the window. But soon it was so dark that we could not even see the trees by the road. We were too tired for pleasantries and spent the last few hours in near silence.

Florence welcomed me like a mother, leading me into their little house and offering me some rice and beans. They were Acholi, but had lived here for many years. Her husband, Philip, had studied at Moroto High School and then trained as a primary-school teacher.

'I'll be back to see how you're going. I'm not sure when,' Gabriel said, as we waved him off the next morning. Afterwards, I sat alone in the middle of the compound, under a leafy edurkoit tree, where elders would have settled disputes and celebrated for centuries. I took several big breaths to calm myself down. *I will get through this,* I tried to convince myself.

That first morning in Karamoja, I awoke to a thought: *That man, the one who raided my village and nearly captured me, could be here.* A knot formed in my stomach, rolling and rolling, and it got tighter with each turn, making me nauseous. I could not bring myself to get out of bed to face this day if it meant walking the streets of the town, where Karimojong tribesmen roamed.

'Alice, you must leave for school in twenty minutes,' Florence said with a gentle chiding tone, passing me a cup of sweet tea.

'Thank you, aunty,' I responded, and felt my stomach roll again. I had to get up.

Moroto High School was right in the middle of the town. Until two years before, it had been an all-boys school, and there were still only six girls in the whole school when I arrived. My feeling of isolation was made worse by my age, four years older than my classmates, and the fact that I towered over most of them.

'You are too old to be in Senior 2. You could be the teacher,' one of the boys taunted in Swahili, a language I barely understood. I scowled back and turned away. But even the nastiest of them refrained from mentioning the knots of scars all down my legs, knowing not to step over that line.

They were everywhere, the Karimojong men. They were on the streets, with guns, wearing bright plaid blankets swathed across their shoulders. They were in the school, in the shops, standing on corners, in houses nearby, scaring me more than the uniformed rebels I had seen in Gulu, or the government soldiers who had barged through the village. I could not hold down my food, I found it hard to sleep, and I could not unravel the growing knot in my stomach. *Why didn't he just let me stay in the north? At least we shared a language with the rebels,* I wondered, with growing bitterness towards my brother. Then I remembered stories that I had heard about girls who had been stolen by the rebels—I might not be alive at all had I stayed. This made me feel a little better.

For the first year, I walked to and from school with two other girls who lived nearby. 'You must always go together,' Florence said on the first morning I left for school. 'Moroto is a dangerous place.' There were gangs of boys here, and policing was weak, so I vowed not to go out alone.

'So it's true, then?' I asked one of the girls, blushing, and looked to the ground as we walked. It seemed to me that young girls in Karamoja were as vulnerable as young girls in Acholiland.

'What's true?' she said, turning to face me.

I kicked a clump of grass in front of me. 'That the boys here steal the innocence of the girls they like, to claim them as their own,' I said.

She nodded and screwed up her face. 'It happens.' I felt the knot in my stomach tighten, as I had when Mama warned me about boys before I turned twelve. I remembered her words, and the stern expression on her face as she said them: 'You must not let them touch you, no matter what they promise you.' I had filed those words away and now felt like the right time to remember them.

One night, I stayed behind at school to rehearse for our school play and did not leave until it was almost dusk. I was not worried, as I was with my two friends and most of the route was along a main road, with just one section of trees and shrubs between the school and our homes. 'Let's stay together,' I said, reaching for the hands of the other girls as we approached the bushy area.

'Yes, we'll be safe as a group,' my friend agreed. We quickened our pace to a fast walk, stiffened our backs, and then moved onto the dirt path that took us into the thick bush, remaining alert.

We had not made it far when a shiny-bodied boy with a wooden stick in his hand emerged from behind a bush, staring us down. Then another and another stepped out, until six boys with sticks surrounded and closed in on us. I could smell alcohol on the breath of one boy, and my heartbeat quickened. Soon the boys were on us, brushing their hands over our bodies, touching our breasts, pulling at our clothes, bringing their sticks down on our backs to try to subdue us.

'Stop. Leave us alone,' I yelled, pushing my hand into the face of one boy and striking another across the chest. I would not surrender. I was strong, and large for my age. My instinct was to kick out as hard as I could when two of the boys grabbed my arms to contain me, and to bite into their flesh if I could. I heard the rip of fabric and knew it was my school uniform.

After ten minutes of fighting we were tiring, and the boys smelled victory. One of them stepped back, unbuckled his belt and unbuttoned his trousers, while the others held me and restrained my friends. I briefly closed my eyes as nausea set in, before opening them and screaming, as long and as loud as I could. I screamed until I had emptied every bit of oxygen from my lungs, and then I gasped for more air so I could scream again. I screamed loud enough for soldiers in military barracks nearby to hear, and within a few minutes I heard the thud of boots on the ground and saw two soldiers with guns, which they pointed at the boys. I cried out in relief at the sight.

'Stop right now or I'll shoot,' one of them yelled in Swahili. My attacker grabbed his trousers and pulled them to his waist, while the others dropped their grip on us and froze. Then all six boys turned and ran away into the dark bushes, without looking back.

The soldiers were kind to us. This surprised me, because in Acholiland I had seen soldiers who were crueller than the boys. They looked away while we pulled our torn uniforms back into place and waited until we had calmed down before walking each of us back to the safety of our homes.

This incident rocked me for days, to the point of wanting to walk away from school right then. How could I possibly pursue my studies when I saw danger everywhere? This event confirmed that it was not just in my imagination. I couldn't share my fear with Florence or Philip—it just wasn't what was done in my culture. I kept it to myself.

More girls arrived at the school, and I made a close friend, Leah Achen. She also spoke Lwo and, like me, was tall for her age. The teachers frequently confused us, with our similar names. We shared everything, yet competed ferociously. We jostled for position in geography and English, and both hated mathematics.

Because of the influx of girls, the directors decided to arrange a disco on the first Friday of each month, so the boys and girls could mix in a social setting. It came as a decree at the school assembly: 'You must all attend the dance.' The girls trembled at the thought of what lay ahead.

'I will not go,' I declared, but it was not optional. When the first Friday night came, I watched in horror as the boys got drunk, struggled over the girls and forced them to dance. Then, the boys locked the dormitory so the girls could not escape back into their own safe domain. Each month followed a similar pattern. The boys felt free to beat us with their hands to get what they wanted, and few of us escaped without some form of unwanted advance.

The teachers turned a blind eye. Some of the young boys drank alcohol made of sorghum for breakfast, and also at school, right under the noses of the teachers, who were powerless and often too frightened to stand in their way. The boys were physically strong and unruly, and they could not be disciplined.

*

I often passed a flat-roofed concrete building with a simple cross above it on my way to the main part of Moroto. On school days, the door was bolted shut and there was no sign of life. But one Sunday as I wandered past, the door was wide open and a sweet sound—a choir of female voices—floated out onto the street, carried by an electric piano and the whooping sound of ululating that told me these people were happy. The hymn was one I recognised from my childhood days in Lira Palwo: *Kwake Yesu Nasimama* ('Here On Jesus Christ I Will Stand').

I closed my eyes. For a few precious moments, I was that child again: in my best floral dress—large yellow daisies—skipping all the way to the church each Sunday, part of a gaggle of sisters and brothers, half-siblings, nieces and nephews. I stood and soaked in the moment. I could once again feel the tranquillity of my life before the war started, its simplicity, when we lived together as a contented clan. I wanted to cry with the happiness of a homecoming.

'Will you join us?' someone said, and I jumped. A young woman stood alongside me, beckoning towards the door. I mumbled a 'yes' and sat in the back row.

I was as drawn to this little church, run by the Scripture Union, as I had been to the flames of the *wang oo* at night in my home village. It felt like I'd been stripped to nothing in Karamoja, and that here, with these people, I could recapture my life. I needed a place to belong, and wise words to carry me along. I was soon a regular at the services, my faith growing every week. That year, my health improved and daily life seemed less of a struggle.

Late in September 1991, a teacher called me from my class. It felt ominous. I left my books and bustled from the room to see a grim-faced Gabriel. I hadn't seen him for a long time: he had been in the south and then north into

Acholiland, and was only now resuming his weekly trips to Karamoja. He stood before me with his head bowed and his hands clasped over his chest. I knew before he opened his mouth that it would be the news I had long feared, and felt a sickness in my stomach.

'I have some bad news for you,' he started. *No, please no.* I tried to keep the words at bay. We both held back. I saw an apology in his eyes. 'I wanted to tell you in person, but I can't stay long.'

'Has he gone?' I finally asked, knowing the answer.

'He and Mama were living with us in Jinja for eight weeks so we could care for him. Our father was in great pain from his cancer,' Gabriel said, stepping forwards to put his hands on my shoulders. 'He asked me to go back to Lapilyet to die, to bury him beside his hut. I have just returned.'

I could not return to class that day. I had known this day would come, but I was not ready when it did. I held myself together, standing motionless as Gabriel climbed into his truck and continued on to Kotido. Then I ran to a quiet corner of the school compound, where there was an old mango tree, and let my tears flow.

God, give his soul rest, I prayed, finding solace in the goodness of his life. *It is final.*

'I did not say farewell, and I was not there when they buried him in the village,' I later told Leah, grieving afresh to think of this cruel blow. In peaceful times, Acholi never missed the funeral of a loved one, no matter where we were.

'He knew you adored him,' Leah replied gently.

I looked at my friend and smiled half-heartedly. 'You know what he told me when I left him? I will never forget his words. He said, "You know one day soon I will die, but if I die you are not to worry so much. The most important thing is your education. You have to study."' I pictured his earnest face as he sat on the chair outside his hut, his voice so deliberate. It lifted my mood to think of this moment and the pride I felt in my dear Baba.

Leah said nothing. I was lost in my own thoughts, reminding myself why I stayed in Karamoja—*education is my future*—and coaching myself to finish. I would make Baba so proud.

11

Crossing the Line

For all the news I heard from my Acholiland home, Karamoja could have been another country, not the neighbouring district. We had no phones and no radio stations, and I only caught wind of events through Gabriel, who dropped into the school unannounced from time to time on his way to Kotido. He had a new job as a driver with the United Nations' World Food Programme (WFP), and had moved his whole family into a UN-owned house in Kotido.

'The news is bad,' was usually Gabriel's opening line. He gleaned his information about the latest ambush, battle or mass abduction from other truck drivers after they crossed the Nile at Karuma Falls and made it safely to Kampala. Even when his words stirred up a deep anxiety in my belly, making me feel sick, I had to know about my homeland.

The violence in the north was like the April rains: torrential and relentless, flooding the district with muddy rivulets that coursed alongside the road, sweeping up anything in their path. The fighting sometimes subsided, the LRA rebels sliding into the landscape, as invisible as air. In these times, the rebels took themselves far away, sometimes going over the border into Sudan, while the government sought to negotiate a peaceful end to the conflict. But it seemed that the rebels always poured back into the district with renewed force, without warning, sweeping away innocent people in their indiscriminate ferocity.

After April 1991, when the government launched a campaign called Operation North, it became even harder to hear any news about the conflict. Acholiland was isolated from all outside contact while soldiers screened civilians, trying to flush out anyone they thought might be collaborating with the rebels. They arrested politicians, clergy . . . anyone they suspected of opposing them. Then they mobilised Acholi civilians into 'arrow groups' and armed them with spears, arrows and machetes, so they could serve as a grassroots force to back up the National Resistance Army (NRA) in their fight against the rebels.

The move infuriated the rebels, who retaliated like a disturbed nest of stinging ants, escalating their attacks until the conflict became more vicious than ever. They began maiming and mutilating—cutting off lips, ears and noses—and they abducted boys and girls at a frightening rate. The boys were given guns and trained to be killing machines, while the girls carried all the rebels' goods from camp to camp and endured daily rapes by rebel commanders. As the backlash reached its peak, government forces withdrew, leaving the Acholi completely unprotected—easy targets for the LRA. The rebels only backed off when the government disbanded the 'arrow groups', and slowly people returned to their homes and villages.

*

My second year in Moroto, 1992—when I was reaching the end of my teen years—was easier than the first. Leah and I signed up for the school volleyball and netball teams, always covering each other on the court. We shared our lunch and our deepest thoughts. We competed fiercely in our commerce class, though Leah excelled and went on to do a diploma in accounting.

I made several other friends among the small group of girls at school, especially in my final year, when I moved from Philip and Florence's home into the boarding school so I could focus on getting good grades. But Leah was the closest friend I had found since my early school days. Like me, she had stayed in school when several of the other girls in their final two years had succumbed to the bullying. They had left at the end of term and had not returned. Leah and I joined forces against the menacing boys. We had learned how to scare them off in their own language, and they now kept their distance. Our voices were our best—and only—protection from the daily harassment.

After the first year, when I had suffered from fear and anxiety, my second and third years brought a healthier state of mind, though I could not say I was happy. My spiritual life had given me the most relief. Church—and the community involved in it—gave me courage. It was run by kind Italian missionaries, who invited me into their home for delicacies I had never seen before, such as tinned mackerel and Italian biscuits. In this environment, I could set aside my problems and feel more positive about my future.

Just before the end of the school year of 1993, a teacher arrived at the dormitory door while I was reading after school. 'Alice, your brother is here for you,' she said. I scrambled off my bunk and out the door, where Gabriel stood under a tree nearby, resting against the wheel of his truck.

'Come, Alice, gather your things,' he said, walking towards me with a smile. 'I have a place for you in the school in Kotido, and you will live with us.' It took me a few minutes to absorb his words. I wasn't expecting to be removed from the school, and in such a hurry. I looked around the school grounds as I gathered myself. I was more settled than in my first year here, but I would be happy to put the boarding house and school dances behind me.

'Thank you, brother,' I said, growing elated. I gathered my few belongings, said a sad farewell to Leah and the other girls, and jumped into the cabin of Gabriel's truck. I murmured a prayer as we pulled out of the school grounds. *Thank you, Jesus, for sustaining me through this time. Amen.*

We crawled along the main road of Moroto, with its line of rickety shops and men standing on the corners with plaid cloths slung over their shoulders. *I will be fine if I never return.* I was close to finishing Senior 4 (or Year 10), and then I had just two more years until I was through my secondary schooling.

I gazed out of the open window as we headed north on the Kotido road, my arm propped up against the window frame, and my face in the wind to stay cool. The landscape was fresh to me now, and I smiled as I thought about starting life afresh. In my unhappiness I'd not appreciated the beauty of Moroto: the rounded tops of the hills, and how imposing Mount Moroto was, standing like a ghostly guardian above the town. I thought about all I had missed in my family during these last two years. I turned to Gabriel, finding comfort in his familiar profile, the beads of sweat resting on his high forehead and rounded nose. I had many questions that were best asked when we were not facing each other.

'How was it when Baba died?' I said. I had imagined it many times, my father lying in the big thatched hut, the paraffin lamp beside him with a small arc of light on his kind face.

'He did not die lonely,' Gabriel said, glancing at me before he fixed his eyes back on the rough road ahead. 'Peter and Doreen and others from the village were all there—I arrived the next day. He died a happy man. It was a blessed release from his pain.' Peter was one of our half-brothers, the son of Baba's third wife, Julie Lapogo, and close to us.

I imagined their concerned faces around him, radiating love for a revered chief and father. *Oh, to have been there.* 'I don't even know how old he was,' I said, my voice choking.

Gabriel shifted gears and then switched into information mode. 'He was certainly born before 1900. He told me he ran away from Arab slave-traders at the end of the 1800s.'

'Ha, I've never heard that,' I said. It made me sad to think that his life had started and ended in times of fear and flight, like foul bookends to all the goodness that came between.

'He was a very good man,' Gabriel said, nodding his head slowly. We slipped back into a comfortable silence.

After three hours we arrived at Gabriel's new home, a compound of staff huts rented for them by the World Food Programme. The WFP was a lifeline in the region, delivering vital food supplies to parts of Karamoja where people were starving. Gabriel and Pauline themselves now had two more mouths to feed: Moses and Daniel had been born barely a year apart. The older children jumped all over me, and Pauline swept me up as if she were my mother. My younger brother, David, had come to primary school in Kotido in 1990 and now joined our happy extended family from his boarding school.

In Kotido, I rose in the morning with a happiness that I thought I had lost forever. '*Icoo maber*', I greeted the smiling faces around me, knowing I'd be answered in my mother tongue.

'*Acoo maber, waya,*' the children chimed, ready to play with their aunt.

If I needed warmth, I could find it in Pauline's open arms. I could chatter with my nieces, and wrestle with my nephews. When I walked the streets, Acholi were everywhere, as many people had brought their children to Kotido to finish their education when the schools in Acholiland closed.

Here, I caught a glimpse of my old life: the house filled with Acholi friends coming and going, nights sleeping peacefully by the fire, sweet potato made sweeter with honey, the love of my family.

*

Pauline was gliding busily around the little kitchen when Gabriel came through the door one evening in my second year in Kotido. I was close to finishing Senior 5 and preparing to move up to Senior 6 (the last two years of secondary school). I sat at the table with my schoolbooks spread out, eager to finish my homework before dinner so I could relax with the younger children. Gabriel greeted his wife, who beamed at the attention, and then he turned to me.

'Edward has asked me to bring you to the city. His wife, Rose, is sick and in hospital, and they have no one to look after the girls,' he said. I exchanged a panicked look with Pauline and turned to Gabriel. My second-eldest brother, Edward Nyeko, had escaped the conflict in Acholiland many years before and now lived with his wife Rose and his children—seven-year-old Lucy, five-year-old Diane and baby Rachel—in the low sprawl of the capital city, Kampala. I hardly knew them.

'But Gabriel, I cannot leave school now,' I said, shaking my head in disbelief. 'I'm so close to finishing. I have my final exams in four months.'

'I know, I know. It is unfortunate,' he said. His face softened. 'Our mother is too old to look after Rachel—she is only six months old and needs to be cared for, as well as the older two. Edward says there is no one else who can help,' he said, opening his hands and lifting his shoulders.

I stared at him long and hard, then turned and left the room, fuming. I found a spot behind the house where I gathered twigs to divert my anger. It was so unfair. Gabriel had pushed me towards school, and now he wanted to pull me out for Edward? I ripped the twigs apart, tossing the pieces onto the ground. *I will become just another Ugandan girl who desperately wants to finish school but cannot.* I lowered my face into my hands and grieved the end of my education as fervently as I'd mourned my father's passing.

That same week I left Karamoja by bus, with a heavy heart. When I'd arrived four years before, I could never have imagined I would be so sad to leave. In fact, many times in my first year I'd daydreamed about this moment—it had always been happy. I stared at the rolling hills, remembering my mother's pain in the garden. Without saying a word, her message had been clear: work hard at your studies or you'll do physical work your whole life like me. Now, my own family held me back.

As we flew past huts and goats and boys by the road, I fought my growing resentment. All I knew about Edward's situation was that they'd lost a son, Allan, the year before, and now Rose was sick too. Edward had left his job as an accountant to care for the children and had no money for support.

'*Two jonyo,*' was the only explanation I heard. Tired disease. The more formal term, HIV/AIDs, was never raised in any conversations, as if this incurable affliction fell from the sky like rain. Every family had been torn apart by it: in every home, in every village, people were dying slow, painful deaths. It was decimating Ugandans as much as—or even more than—the guns of the rebels, but no one talked about it. Even leaders of communities did not talk about HIV/AIDS, out of embarrassment or fear of being isolated, just as they did not talk about girls who were being abused.

As the bus spewed its dirty fumes through the outer communities of Kampala, my mood shifted. The ramshackle huts sitting side by side and the aimless wandering of young boys and girls by the road's edge made me think of the three little girls who would greet me at the other end of this long journey. *They deserve a chance in life, too.* I felt a rush of warmth towards them, and set my heart on bringing some happiness into their sad lives. Soon afterwards, I sprang through the threshold of my brother's small brick house with all the energy I could muster.

'Who is this one?' I smiled as I scooped up the baby girl lying naked on the mat and held her against my shoulder. 'This must be Rachel.' Edward nodded and shot me a proud, fatherly smile. I flung my arms around Lucy, the eldest, who had come up to me, and grinned at Diane, who stood shyly by the doorway. She had been a baby, and Lucy a toddler, when I'd last seen them.

I looked beyond them to the mess of dishes piled up, dirty clothes in rough piles, flies on rotting bananas. I smelled the fetid scent of neglect. When I turned back, I caught Edward's look of desperation and wanted to cry. 'How is Rose?' I asked, stepping closer and touching his shoulder.

'I fear she is not long for this world, Alice,' he replied. His body wilted. His first wife had also died, leaving him with two older boys who were past school age and had moved out, and now he faced further heartache. It felt right that I'd come.

I plunged headlong into the role of fill-in mother. I picked up a small plaid blanket from the mat, bent over and with both hands placed Rachel into the small of my back, balancing her as I lashed her into a cosy cocoon. I went to work washing the beans and rice for our dinner. Afterwards, I started to work my way through the mess. I scrubbed the dishes and stacked them on the shelf, swept the concrete floor and threw out rotting food. That night I fell into the deepest of sleeps, without dreams or nightmares to disturb me.

We formed a daily routine. Edward took Lucy and Diane to the hospital in the morning to see their mother while I cared for Rachel, and later in the day I visited as well, taking time to bathe Rose and to hold a cool towel to her burning forehead.

Over twelve weeks, I watched Rose shrink from a sickly-looking mother to a bony shell, and I saw the light in her eyes fade. At the end she could not even summon a smile for her babies so we left them in the care of a neighbour. She was dying in a sea of other emaciated women and dust and coughing. One day I came into the crowded ward to find a white sheet over the slightest of bumps: Rose had gone. Edward had waited for me, unsure of what to do now.

'I will stay as long as you need me. I will raise these girls as my own,' I told him. I'd grown as attached to Rachel as a natural mother, spending hours carrying her on my back as I went about my chores. For all this time, I'd been the one to feed Rachel her bottle, to rock her to sleep at night in her tiny sling, and to comfort her when she woke through the night.

It wasn't just Rachel I'd grown to love with the intensity of a mother. I'd been swept up in the daily lives of Lucy and Diane, who now went to school. 'What did you like most about school today, Lucy?' I asked one afternoon, as we sat on the front step of the house.

'I like to read. I am learning to read and write in Luganda,' she said before squatting beside me and etching letters of the language spoken in the south into the dust with her finger.

'Very good, Lucy,' I said, putting my arm around her and laughing. 'If you can read and write, you can learn anything. But you must also learn these things in Lwo.' I pledged to teach the girls about their Acholi heritage. I would be their school of *ododo*.

*

The news from the north had become more distressing. A new wave of violence had hit in 1994, after President Yoweri Museveni rejected the terms of a special peace agreement. He would not agree to the time frame for the rebels to put down their arms, instead demanding an immediate ceasefire. An Acholi leader, Betty Bigombe, had spent many months and many meetings brokering this agreement with the rebels, putting aside fears for her own safety, only to have it fail.

Retaliation this time came in the form of large-scale massacres. The worst of these occurred in April 1995 in the village of Atiak. Later, I heard stories of the LRA forcing villagers to eat each other, and the rebels feeding babies into the mouths of mortar guns to be shot into the air—and knew they could be true. As the war progressed, there were no boundaries to the LRA's barbarity. It was horrific, and a long way from the relative peace of life in the south.

*

If I'd learned anything through these past few years, it was to expect change. This time it came in the form of Edward's new job in Masindi, a town on the road to the north of Uganda, but south of the war zone. Edward was bright: he was among the first accounting students in the country to work with computers, and this had landed him a job as a financial administrator with the Kinyara Sugar Works. With a job, he could afford to pay for child care and move his children to his company home in the future.

Edward employed a young girl from the neighbourhood to take on all the tasks that had consumed my days. He released me from my motherly duties as abruptly as I'd begun them. 'You can return to your studies,' Edward said with a wide grin, the day the news came through. He was a gentle man—tall, with a straight back. At times, when I looked at his dignified stance, I imagined my father as a young man. I was happy that his life after Rose was already taking shape.

The next day I was back with my books, picking up where I'd left off just before Senior 6, my final year of high school. I entered into a frenzy of study, oblivious to the noisy play and young people around me. Meals became a distraction, and some nights I forgot to sleep. When the time came to catch the bus back up to Kotido to sit the final exams, I was as ready as I could be, and confident I would pass.

In March 1997, an official-looking note arrived by mail, delivered to my room by a bright-eyed Lucy. 'Mama Alice, here is your letter,' she said. 'Can I open it?'

'No, Lucy, I will,' I said, lifting it out of her hand and flicking my hand. 'Off you go.' I turned it over, pulled the flap up and slid out a single page. I took a deep breath and scanned the contents. I had passed, and though I would not have the fanfare of walking onto a stage with my classmates in Kotido, a warm satisfaction flowed through my veins. I was 23 years old. Girls from the village might have four children by this age. I leaned back onto my pillow and sighed. *Baba would be proud.*

It wasn't long after this that Edward arrived to collect the three girls. His shining face at the door told the story: his life was getting better. He had remarried, and with a new wife to care for them, the girls could live with him in Masindi. I scrambled to pull Rachel's clothes together, while Diane and Lucy gathered their favourite things.

'Diane and Lucy, be sure to take your good dresses for church,' I yelled towards the bedroom. I passed the door and saw Diane sitting on the edge of the bed with her eyes closed. 'Diane, what is wrong?'

'I feel dizzy and a little bit sick,' she said. I put my hand to her forehead and could feel its warmth.

'It will be good for you in Masindi, where the air is clear,' I said, trying to raise her spirits. 'You'll like it there.' I put out my hand to support her off the bed. She had a bus to catch—there wasn't time to be sick.

Rachel tugged on my skirt. 'Mama come, too,' she said, her big eyes pleading.

'I'll come another day,' I replied, smiling, even as panic overran my thoughts. *What will I do here without them?*

I watched them walk out of the house and down the street towards a *matatu* bound for the bus stop. Edward had a bounce in his step and clutched the bags, while the younger girls trailed hand in hand, with Diane plodding last. I felt the life drain from me.

I should have been happy for them, but I could not shake the fact that I was alone again, with just a yearning where the girls had been. I turned back to the house, to a lonely room, to a life empty of their squeals or the daily tasks of cooking and caring for them.

Within a month of the family leaving Kampala, Diane had died. HIV had presented itself as a cough and quickly taken hold. I cried when I heard, but they were empty tears. I was consumed with my own loneliness and loss. Had I known about depression and its symptoms, I might have sought help—but I did not. That knowledge was still to come.

12

Beyond School

In a way, I never left the school of *ododo*. Whenever I made big decisions in life, I returned to the words I'd often heard at the water point as a little girl: 'Wait, and you'll find a way through any problem.'

I had reached a point where I was desperate. I hoped my life would change, but I didn't know how to make that happen. I wanted to pursue further education, but I knew that I could not ask my brother Gabriel to pay for my school fees—he had five children to support. Edward had also been stretched by medical costs. Yet I craved the wisdom that I found in my schoolbooks and classrooms.

It was hard to see a worthwhile life ahead when I filled my days with meaningless tasks: fetching water, tidying the kitchen and sitting around with friends who, like me, were without direction. After Edward left with the girls, I moved in with my half-brother Peter in Bugolobi, an area close to the centre of Kampala. At first I had been shocked by city life, particularly how impersonal and fast it was. Simple things were stressful—such as getting a taxi, being understood in English (as I spoke no Luganda) and finding my way home without money by walking for hours. There were no gunshots, but in the early days I was often gripped with fear. Later, I relaxed and enjoyed it more.

Some days, just to pass the time, I jumped on a *matatu* with a crowd of other commuters, heading to the Owino market in the centre of Kampala. I joined the leisurely crowd straggling along the side of the road, before entering the labyrinth of a thousand stalls that sweated under the cover of plastic sheeting. The brilliant reds and tangerines of the spice mounds brightened my mood. I needed to be with other people, even strangers.

One day, as I wandered past stalls of second-hand clothes, I met the eyes of an older man passing me in the opposite direction. I took a second glance: I knew that face from St Mary's in Gulu—he was one of the teachers who'd arrived at our dormitory soon after the raid. 'Hello, sir,' I said, reverting to my shy childhood self, though I was such a different person now. His face brought back the memory of my tragic last night at the school, which I had never talked about.

'Hello, Alice,' he said, as his face lit up in a big smile. 'It's good to see you. How has your life been since that terrible night?' His hair had greyed, but he was still slender and young-looking for his age. Sweat ran down his forehead from the oppressive heat. People pushed past us in the narrow laneway, but we kept talking around them.

'Um, it's been fine. I finished my advanced levels in Kotido,' I said. I felt awkward. Seeing my teacher reminded me of how I'd lost all my books in the chaos of that night—and how I could have lost my life. In my mind I saw the faces of my abducted friends, and I sucked in a stressed breath.

'I'm pleased to hear you've continued with your studies. What now?' he asked. His interest was genuine, so I decided to be mostly honest in my response.

'I'm not able to go further with my studies. I have no money, and I'm looking for work,' I said. The last part was not strictly true. I hoped for work, but a 24-year-old high-school graduate from the north with no employment experience was hardly attractive to an employer. I had no idea what I could do.

The throngs of people kept coming in the airless passageway, bumping us as they squeezed past. 'Move on,' an angry man said, but we ignored him. I dabbed at the sweat running down my cheeks like tears.

'Alice, you are a bright girl—you should take your studies further,' the teacher said. 'You should contact Peter Okot. Do you remember him from Gulu? He looks after the scholarships program set up by Father Roberto.' He told me where to find Peter before the crowd swept us along, abruptly ending our conversation.

'Thank you, I'll do that,' I said, as a group of determined market shoppers separated us. I kept going with the flow of people, buoyed by this valuable piece of information.

Father Roberto was one of the hundreds of Italians and other foreigners who flocked to Uganda as missionaries before the carnage of the Idi Amin years. Doctors and nurses, clergymen and women, humanitarian workers and negotiators came to work with non-government groups in the north of Uganda. Some had stayed, while others, such as Father Roberto, returned home and continued to send support.

I arrived at Peter Okot's office the next morning and sidled up to the receptionist to explain myself. 'I escaped the war in Pader district, but had to drop out of school,' I said, before she interrupted me.

'You must write it down for the application,' she said. At that moment, Peter Okot came out of his office and walked towards me with his arm outstretched.

'Yes, the scholarships are for young Acholi to study social work and teaching—those who have come through the war. Age is no barrier,' he said, with a firm handshake. My heart sped up as he explained more about the scholarship: it was for a diploma course in social work and administration at the Uganda Institute of Social Work and Community Development in Kampala. The scholarship was for 550,000 Ugandan shillings—US$220 per month—to cover the cost of the course, living expenses, transport and lunches. My eyes were as wide as the moon. It was generous beyond my imagination. I had never received an income, and most people in the north lived on much less than that. Even outside the conflict, many Ugandans survived on less than US$2 a day.

I knew this was tailor-made for me, and it seemed within reach. Soon my letter—written with the assistance of a friend who had better English than me—was on its way to Father Roberto in Italy.

Dear Father Roberto,
I am writing to you about a scholarship for further studies.
I survived the war in the north and was able to escape to
the south. But for four years I stayed at home in the village
without school, and after that my school was attacked.
I have dropped out of school three times and now I am

24 and have only just graduated. I know about the
problem of staying in school.

If I'm able to do this course in social work I will return
to Acholiland. I want to work in my own community and
help other students like me.

Sincerely,
Alice Achan

When the receptionist summoned me to Peter Okot's office several weeks later, I knew it was good news. In the *matatu* to the city, I sat wedged between a mama with a baby on her lap and a man with alcohol on his breath, but hardly noticed the discomfort. I hadn't felt this way since my blue-sky day as a fourteen-year-old, when for a short while the fighting had stopped.

In May 1998, more than a year after graduating from high school, I returned to the classroom. I walked into a new and unfamiliar world, where students wore jeans and T-shirts, and chatted with each other like old friends. I hid behind my books, aware that my conservative long skirt and blouse marked me as different. Yet from the moment the teacher opened her mouth on the first morning, I was hooked. I consumed every word as if it were served up just for me, even though he addressed the whole room as one.

I looked forward to the topic on gender studies late in the semester, as it was well beyond my experience of life. I had made some friends in class, despite my long commute across Kampala, and talked with them as the teacher started to speak.

'Today we are going to learn about gender and how being born male or female affects life in Uganda and other societies,' she said. Her voice was powerful, her presence taking hold of the room and silencing the chatter. I was excited to think that people spent their time considering these things and looking for ways to bring about change. I focused, unblinking, as the teacher spelled out in an unemotional, academic manner the issues that women in Uganda faced, and the consequences of treating women as inferior in society.

In my own naive way, I had fought the system that worked against girls in my culture. I'd made it clear—and Baba had supported me—that I would not marry a man chosen by an aunt, or put up with a husband who took a second or third wife, as my parents' generation had. Nor would I expect to have a bride price, where my worth was counted in head of cattle. I had seen the suffering that these traditions could bring to women, and I knew that I would take another direction. My instincts had steered me, but until the teacher stood in front us in the college and gave them a framework, they had been random.

She outlined the details of the new constitution of Uganda, which had been changed three years before, in 1995, to give women more rights. I learned that women could now inherit land and money, where before only men could; that legally, girls could no longer be expelled from school for getting pregnant; that adultery would be treated equally for men and women under the law; and that, by law, women had to be included as leaders in the districts.

I knew from my own childhood that a legal document could never address all the issues: I had seen how being female worked against women at every stage of life within my own large clan. Like others, I'd seen it as a normal part of our society. Subservience was passed from mother to daughter, and it kept girls toiling in the garden—instead of in the classroom—after they reached a certain age. The men owned the women, and if they wanted unprotected sex, it was their right. An older man could buy the virginity of a young girl for a few shillings. I had also seen how, in a war, there was no protection for girls and women—rape was the enemy's best weapon. I now saw my mother's tears as a silent warning against these things, and her strength of character became my model.

I wasn't sure how to respond to the teacher's words. I was aware of being uninformed, but I was too engaged to stay silent. I shot my hand in the air. 'Miss, you have described my life,' I said, with an embarrassed laugh. 'I have lived through these things, and never before fully considered the implications of being a woman in northern Uganda. We were happy to stay alive and not be taken by the rebels. How can we change this situation?'

'Thank you for your question. This is a good time to ask some of the young men in the class how they see the role of men in our country,' she said, diverting attention to a group of guys sitting near the front. They shifted in their seats, before one bravely put up his hand up to reply.

'I think men are the bosses in Uganda, and we have it very easy. I never had to cook or clean or go to the market as a boy. We are like princes,' he said, without apology. He paused to think. 'It's not right, but I'm not sure how to change this, especially in the villages,' he said, looking to the boy beside him for support.

'What role does education play in changing the status quo?' the teacher pressed, drawing more students into the conversation. For the next hour, passions ran high. Every man and woman in the class—me included—had a view on the power of education.

I left the classroom feeling lighter than air. This was a pivotal moment, but for now I had no power to cause change. It would be some time before the full significance of what I was learning would be brought to bear on my life and work.

*

I'd heard news of a ferocious rebel attack in Alebtong, the village we'd moved to from Lapilyet in the early days of the conflict. I could picture the scene as clear as day: deafening shots, pots dropped, a child's hand pulled, screams, smoke, hearts racing. I tossed and turned all night with worry, knowing that my mother, sisters and other family members had stayed there long after I'd escaped. I tried to find out the details from a distant relative who'd escaped to Kampala.

'I'm sorry, I don't know who survived,' my relative said, lifting her shoulders. 'I heard they are in Masindi now.'

'Ahh, that is good,' I said, with a sigh of relief. At least they were away from the fighting. Masindi was well south of any trouble, and teeming with Acholi.

As soon as my course finished, I found a poorly paid internship as a recruitment clerk with Kinyara Sugar Works in Masindi. Edward worked there an accountant, so I would be able to share his company house. On the bus north, I ignored the rickety shops by the side of the road and the military trucks that sped past us. My mind raced ahead to the reunion with my mother. I laughed aloud to think I'd see the girls again, and then remembered that Diane would not be there. I thought of the terror my mothers and sisters had faced. *None of the men in my family were there to help.* Charles had moved away to Pajule, and Gabriel still lived in Karamoja. I imagined a bedraggled entourage of women and children dragging themselves on foot towards Lira. I saw them waiting on the dirt verge of the road, begging their way onto passing buses and trucks. This was how we travelled in the war.

When I arrived at Edward's home, they were all there: Mama, Aduk, Doreen and a room full of subdued children, some not even born when I left the village eleven years ago. I noticed sad eyes and runny noses, and bulging bellies telling of constant hunger. *What have they seen?*

'Mama! You made it,' I called when I saw her. It had been such a long time, and I had heard so little about her since leaving the north. She looked older, and I could see the dirt on the cloth wrapped around her head. She had lost a tooth, but her face lit up in a radiant smile when she saw me. Her high, angular cheekbones gave her the same regal look I remembered.

I glanced at my soft hands, so clean and plump, and then at my mother's. Hers were like knotted twigs, thin and worn. I curled mine into a ball. How different our lives had been. She had never aspired to finish secondary school, gain a scholarship, have a job or choose where she lived. Given the chance, could she have done those things? I felt a stab of guilt. It had broken my heart as a young girl to see her cry. Now I had failed to make her life any easier.

She motioned for me to sit on the sofa beside her, holding out a glass of cool water. I sat and wrapped my hand over hers, feeling its bony fragility. 'Oh Mama, I have missed you so much,' I said, my eyes filling with tears. I wasn't sure where to start. I looked at the weary faces in the room.

'Where is Maa?' I asked, when I realised my grandmother was not with them. Two years before this, in 1996, my mother had travelled by bus to Anaka, west of Gulu, to bring Maa back to live with her. By that time, Maa was blind and had no one else to care for her.

Mama sat back and closed her eyes. When she sat up and looked back at me, her speech was rapid-fire. 'There were more than two hundred rebels in the village that day. They were everywhere. They were running from hut to hut with torches, lighting everything they could find. Everything was alight. There is nothing left,' she said. She shook her head and turned her eyes towards the window. 'We cannot even find your father's grave. I have never seen anything like it in all my life.' I looked at her face and saw deep, anguished creases.

'What about Maa? Where is she?' I asked, taking a deep breath.

Mama sat motionless in her chair, her eyes fixed on a crack in the floor. Edward broke the silence when he bustled through the door. He looked at our mother's face and knew what we'd been talking about. 'I'm sorry, Alice, that you did not know,' he said. He looked at Mama and nodded. Our half-sister, Aduk, carried in a tray laden with cups of black tea and placed it on the small table in front of us.

Mama took a sip of her tea, and sucked in a deep, wheezy breath. My sisters sent their children outside to play, and they pulled chairs into the circle, as if by the fire.

'We could hear the rebels' guns, and knew they were close by,' Mama said, her voice and hands shaking. 'We chased the children into the bush, so they could not be caught.'

I wanted to block my ears and not know. As Mama talked, I could see my Maa, sitting by the fire in the village, feeding me a feast of exotic stories. I had to know.

'Maa was in her hut, resting, so I said, "Come, let's go to a safer place,"' Mama said. I squeezed her hand. 'But she refused; she would not move. She pleaded with me. "Lucia, I'm tired of running and don't want to go anywhere. Leave me here to sleep." She would not move with us, not even to the tree,' Mama said, pausing.

I held my breath. *Of course, she could not run. She was 86 years old and blind.* In past raids one of the mothers had guided her to a quiet place where she could sit and wait. She was old and useless to the rebels, and was rarely disturbed. The rebels strode past her as though she were invisible.

'They didn't have to burn everything,' Mama said, before she broke down and sobbed. I slid my arm across her skinny shoulder as I fought back my own tears.

Doreen picked up the story. 'Someone even told them, "Stop, there's an old woman in that hut," but they didn't stop. They had torches and set every hut alight. I heard her call, "Please don't burn me, please don't burn the house." It was too late, the roof fell.' Doreen's hands fell into her lap, and her shoulders collapsed in defeat. 'They were angry with us—our huts were empty, and we had so little for them to eat.'

I heard Mama mutter 'murderers' before she dissolved into Edward's arms.

We came back to the story many times in the weeks that followed. I learned that they had found Maa's charred remains once the embers had died down. They had buried her in a small grave with a handful of family to say goodbye.

The rebels were still in the area, so there was no time for grieving before they gathered the children and fled.

*

I settled into a routine of working and noisy family life in Masindi. I revelled in the familiarity of my mother and sisters being close by, and the *posho* made by Mama in the way I remembered as a child. She made us sweet potato and beans with such love that it took me back to our lives before the war. I could have lived this way for a long time, but it was not to be.

Doreen came to my room one morning to announce that they were leaving. 'We will go back to our homes in Lira Palwo,' she said. I bounced out of bed to find Mama, who confirmed the decision. Doreen had trailed behind me.

'But why can't you stay here, where it is safe?' I said, looking from one to the other, my thoughts in a tailspin. They continued to gather their pots and mats, and to corral the young ones.

'We must go,' my sister said, standing tall, with her shoulders pushed back. I could see that she would not budge. Then she softened. 'What can we do here, Alice? This is not our home.' After all these years away, I understood. They would move back to our family home now and attempt to reclaim their lives, while there was relative calm after the storm of destruction.

They left the following day, my sisters' heads piled high with bags of rice and flour, and household goods such as soap that they could not buy anywhere near the village. They strapped the babies to their backs, so they could carry the rolled-up bedding, while older nieces carried younger nieces and nephews, all looking grim. Lucy, Rachel and I walked alongside them to the bus station, snatching last-minute instructions from Mama on how important it was for Edward's girls to learn Acholi ways. Then, when the worn-out bus pulled away, we stood watching in a solemn line. Little hands poked out the windows. I wiped my eyes with my handkerchief. *Will I see you again?*

Not long after they left, Edward found another job—this time in Kitgum, further north and in the heart of rebel territory. 'Alice, it is not safe for the girls in Kitgum,' he said. 'Can they stay with you? I'll find a young girl from the village to help while you work.' I could not refuse: I would do anything for Lucy and Rachel. I did not want them to end up like the Acholi girls and boys in the cane fields I passed each day on my way to the office, who without education could only get casual work weeding and cutting sugar cane. Mostly they were still there on my way home, after sweating under the fierce sun for eight hours. I knew that they were only paid 2000 Ugandan shillings a day—not even US$1. I would make sure Lucy and Rachel did not end up in this form of slavery.

With Diane gone, Lucy had become unsettled and unhappy. She was a quiet child, and for a time became almost invisible. She was ten years old and had been doing well in school until now, but I worried about her. Rachel, who was almost four, was less aware of each person leaving her world: I had been the most constant presence in her short life. Lucy would remember burying half her family.

'I will hold their lives as tightly as my own,' I told Edward, and I meant it. Each day I prayed that these two—my girls now—would grow into strong young women. I had dreams for

Lucy and Rachel. I would see to it that they stayed in school. I could imagine them at Makerere University, where my brother, David, had just started his journalism studies. I would make sure that being female would not hold them back.

'Lucy, you could be a doctor one day,' I had said. She had a kind and inquisitive nature and would be good with people.

'I will take Rachel to school with me,' she said, looking at her younger sister.

Then one day she came in from school, sat down on the sofa beside me and asked directly: 'Mama Alice, will I become sick, too?' Her little face was crinkled with worry. I paused, leaning back for a moment, before lifting her hand and placing it in mine.

'No, Lucy, you are a healthy girl and will not get sick,' I said. I smiled, but I secretly feared that, like Diane, Lucy had been infected through her mother at birth. She had lost weight over the past few weeks, but I had put it down to her being a slender, active girl.

One morning Lucy awoke with marks on her face, like a trail of bruises someone had punched into her skin. 'Mama Alice, it hurts,' she complained, holding her hands across her stomach. She ran outside to the bathroom, and, unsure of what to do, I let her go. I waited, and when she hadn't returned after ten minutes, I went to find her. I saw her small frame on the ground and swooped down to get her.

'Lucy! Lucy, wake up,' I called, as I laboured to pick up her dead weight and carry her through the door to find help. I prayed as I walked. *Please, God, let her be well. Let her be well.* I repeated my words over and over, in time with my steps, until I reached the local clinic, where I knew a nurse could test her for HIV/AIDS. She rested against my shoulder as we waited.

It was hard to be hopeful. These were not the innocuous sweats that came with the early stages of HIV, but the violent sickness that ushered in the worst symptoms of full-blown AIDS. I recognised these symptoms but had been blind to them in my own home. I had not wanted to know the worst. *What will I do if she tests positive?* I could not bear to voice my fears. *Why don't our people know this disease can come through a mother? Can't we stop this?* Lucy was conscious now, moaning in my lap. I offered her a weak smile and held her tighter.

The doctor called me back to the clinic the following week, on my own. I had not even sat down in his tiny surgery before he uttered the news I'd dreaded all week: 'I'm sorry, it's not good.' I fell back into the plastic chair behind me and blew out a long breath. 'It can't be,' I said, more to myself than the doctor. He waited a moment before talking about the illness, but in my confused state I could not listen, and stumbled out the door. *How do I tell Lucy she has a death sentence?*

She already knew. She had been at the graveside for her brother, her mother and her sister, and I could tell from her silence that she knew it was her turn. Each day after that I rushed home from the sugar estate to see how Lucy was faring, and each day I watched as the disease devoured my niece. The bruises on her body became lesions that spread into her mouth, along with thrush, making it almost impossible for her to eat, and when she could eat she did not hold down her food, no matter how plain or soft. Her ten-year-old body shrank to the size of a five-year-old's, a tiny frame with sunken eyes and hollowed cheeks. I watched the waves of diarrhoea suck out her last stores of energy, while the rashes and sores kept her from lying on her back. Without flesh on her bones, she had no cushioning as she lay, and I could tell from her groans how much pain she endured.

I watched Lucy deteriorate while trying to maintain a positive face for Rachel, whose world shrank to Lucy and me. When Lucy found it hard to talk, Rachel followed me from room to room, needing the company. Finally, I could no longer stand being in Masindi alone.

I knocked on the door of my supervisor's office at the sugar company, and he invited me in. He was a kind man, who knew about Lucy's illness, and that I was caring for her. I sat across from him with my hands in my lap and told him the background to my family and how I had ended up raising two girls. 'Sir, it's hard to be here alone,' I said. 'I must take them to Kitgum. These girls need their father.' He put down his pen and looked at me, nodding his head. His kindness—like my own father's—made me want to cry, but I held back.

'I understand, Alice. Let's see if we can get you to Kitgum on a company truck,' he said, as he picked up the phone.

I had one more phone call to make from the office before I left: to Edward. I hadn't told him about Lucy as it had happened so quickly, and I wasn't sure what to say when I finally got him on the phone. 'Edward, we're coming to Kitgum,' I said, yelling down the crackling line. 'We could be there tomorrow or the next day. I'll find you when we arrive.' That was all I could say.

'Alice, why?' I heard in reply before the line died. There wasn't time to debate our coming. I wondered whether Lucy, in her weak state, would even live to see her father again.

I hastily packed up the house overnight and headed for the sugar company on foot the next morning, carrying Lucy with one arm, and our bags with the other. Rachel scurried behind. As we left the house, I had grabbed my most prized possession—my social work diploma, the proof of my education, which was rolled up and slightly grubby from the dust that swept through the house with the winds. *One day I will need it.* Or was I fooling myself?

Every day there were ambushes on the road to Kitgum. It was ideal territory for the rebels, with thick undergrowth alongside the road, streams for water and a flow of desperate people willing to take their chances. The sugar-company trucks took the long way around, via Lira to the east, rather than risk losing precious produce on the direct route.

I threw our small bundle of clothes, wrapped in a cloth, onto the back of the sugar truck, and then lifted Lucy. I cradled Lucy on my lap, with Rachel alongside. Lucy was as light as a baby, and slept deeply. I took a long breath and braced my back against the mound of cloth-covered sugar bags to shield her from the jolts. I felt vaguely excited, as if on a pathway to resolution.

We travelled for four hours before boarding another truck—part of a convoy with military escorts—from Lira to Kitgum. Men with machine guns sat on the roof, alert for bands of rebels. I scanned the terrain, so familiar yet much changed. It was eerily empty of life. The landscape I remembered—the miles of cultivated land, the straying goats and placid short-horned cattle—had all gone, the land overtaken by weeds and grass and vines, tangles of bush that could no longer support grazing. Most disturbing was the lack of children along the road—it seemed like only yesterday that

I'd been one of thousands, trudging to school in my bare feet, grinning and waving at a rare passing vehicle, carefree with my friends. *If only this land could speak.*

By the time the convoy rolled into Kitgum, Lucy was delirious, sapped of energy by vomiting and diarrhoea. She had not had much water since we left Masindi, and her tongue had swollen so she could no longer swallow. The nurse at Kitgum Hospital plunged a needle into the inside of her elbow for intravenous fluids, without any visible improvement. Rachel clamoured for my attention, but I ignored her pulls at my skirt and her growing wails.

I sent word to Edward to come quickly, and within a short time of our arrival in town he joined us, arriving out of breath from running. For several days we took turns caring for Rachel and sitting by Lucy's side, day and night. Lucy fought to keep going: she wrestled to open her eyes when she heard our voices, aware of us by her side. At times she gasped for air but was too weak to fill her lungs.

In the middle of this, my mother arrived from Pader. She had heard that we were in Kitgum, that Lucy was sick, and had risked her life in a public minivan on the road between the two towns to join us. We were all too tired and sad to be happy at our reunion. We rotated our breaks to preserve energy.

On the sixth day, I left Lucy's side to go back to Edward's home to rest. Rachel had stayed with a young carer, and did not grasp the gravity of her sister's illness. She jostled for the attention she'd been missing. 'Mama, let's play a game,' she pleaded, her sweet face close to mine as I fought to keep my eyes open.

'First let me rest for a while, and then we'll play,' I said, buying time. For those two hours I had peace, and when I awoke I idly played with Rachel on the bed, enjoying the respite from the harsh walls of the hospital that echoed with suffering.

Several hours later, I returned to the hospital to be met with loud wails from the direction of Lucy's bed. 'She's gone,' Edward said, looking up from beside her. My mother stood on the other side, holding Lucy's still hand and crying. There was so little of her left. It was hard to imagine that this waif-like figure was the same girl who had led the other children in their games, the girl who had set up a kitchen outside the house and directed her sisters to copy all they'd seen inside, stirring mud until it was the creamy consistency of *posho*, and pretending little stones were beans.

Other family members arrived, and our friend Florence, and after a few hours they bundled up Lucy's body into a soiled sheet and carried her out. Her spot would soon be filled: in war, hospital beds are more valuable than people.

'We will give her a family burial in Lira Palwo,' Mama said, trailing behind her son, who carried his daughter's body. With Rachel on my hip, I followed as far as the minibus and could go no further.

I touched Rachel's forehead, and the beads of sweat dampened my fingers. 'I should stay to look after Rachel,' I said, looking tenderly at the little girl, trying to make my actions sound noble. I watched the bus leave, feeling hollow. I was back in my beloved Acholiland after years of exile, but felt only despair.

13

Back in the War

My childhood memories of Kitgum returned as vivid snap-
shots as I walked the streets with Florence, a family friend
from my childhood who now lived in this town. Before the
war, the central markets had sprawled across a whole block,
fuelling the senses with mounds of spices in shades of red,
yellow and brown; baskets of dried crickets; tomatoes so ripe
they were about to burst; stores with ladders hanging from
the roof to show off a vast range of bright waxed fabrics
from Ghana; and warehouses with bags of rice and maize
piled as high as the ceiling.

As children, visits to Kitgum were rare, as our needs were
so simple in the village and our food was within easy reach.
Yet on those cherished visits, I had loved riding on the back
of a truck, reaching up to hold fast to the side with one hand
and clutching Mama's arm with the other as we bounced
along the pocked roads.

Now, the market was diminished, the colours duller, and
it was without the array of goods that had made it so exciting

in my youth. Florence and I passed sad-looking stalls, near empty with just an armful of green beans, a few eggplants and a tray of tomatoes on display. The vendors looked bored and hungry. My heart sank at the sight. Then I saw a delicacy from my childhood.

'*Ngwen!*' I grabbed Florence by the forearm before reaching into the basket of crisp white ants and picking out a small handful to taste. She watched my childlike delight and laughed her deep laugh. Florence was one of the wisest women I knew, and one of the few strong enough to advocate for the weak in our community. I had known her for as long as I could remember, from the days when she came to our village home to consult with my father.

After Lucy died, Rachel and I shared a small room in Edward's home, a five-room commercial building still under construction. He was building it with his own hands in his spare time, and planned to develop it into a hotel with ten rooms. Edward had been the most financially successful of all my hardworking brothers. He was known for being generous, often allowing friends and family to stay at his home for several years at a time.

Like all the men in my family, Edward was towering in stature and earned the respect of those around him. He had invited our family friends, Florence Komakech and Edwin Yacobo (known as EY), to stay with him, and they were now as close as family. They had two rooms at Edward's, in return for occasional help with his building project. Florence had known my father from district meetings in Lira Palwo, where she had represented the women of the community. Florence and EY still represented our village on the district council, despite the displacement of most people in their constituency.

By 1999, Kitgum had been overrun with people: military, farmers and aid workers, along with refugees escaping another war in southern Sudan. The streets were filled with refugees from within Uganda, too: hordes coming to town from Internally Displaced Person (IDP) camps near Kitgum. They bought whatever they could afford and whatever was available. Even with less produce, the markets still pulsed with people shuffling from stall to stall, picking up a tomato here and a mango there to squeeze and smell before buying. People seemed content to be there, though the town itself was on edge and carried an undertone of war weariness. Those with money could buy fresh vegetables, while those without had to wait until foreign aid groups arrived with supplies of maize and rice.

I was still to visit one of the IDP camps that I had heard so much about. Three years earlier, the government had started moving villagers into vast 'protected' communities. Florence was quick to fill me in. 'The government said, "We are doing this for the security of the Acholi people,"' she told me over a strong black tea at Edward's place. 'This might be true, but it served them well to crowd everyone together where they could not collaborate with the enemy or grow food for the rebels to steal.' I respected her views, as someone who had remained in the north.

'And their huts?' I asked. 'What has happened to the villages?' I looked at her stern profile in the dark room and knew that this was painful for her.

'They evicted everyone from the villages and then burned the huts down so they could not return,' Florence said, her face grim. 'There could be a million people in the camps now.' I put my tea down and faced her.

'Can we go to the camp today?' I said, suddenly impatient. I had heard enough and needed to see this for myself. My unvoiced question was, *Did I learn anything in Kampala that might help here?*

'Are you sure you're ready for this, Alice? It will be hard,' Florence said, frowning.

'I need to,' I said, standing up to go. I had been crippled by grief after losing Lucy, and now I needed to look outwards.

Florence and I made our way through the centre of town and kept walking until we reached the crammed-together huts that stretched out beyond the town for miles, like a forest of thatch. The air was ripe with the raw smells of human life stripped of dignity, the smells of excrement and decay. Babies cried on the backs of mothers who bent over plastic water pails rubbing clothes, while men loitered between huts. The low level of undefined noise in the background sounded like an orchestra warming up. I walked slowly, taking it in, trying to keep my face neutral so I would not betray the anger seething inside me at the sight of the decimation of my ancient culture. Instead of the proud, productive men and women I knew growing up, who tilled the soil, milled their maize and were close to self-sufficient, I saw people who were trapped and forced to beg for rice to stay alive.

I remembered a childhood where poverty and violence did not exist. We had fruits in season—mangoes lingering on long green stalks, threatening to drop at any moment; rich and creamy shea nuts that we bit into to remove the green outer layer before cracking into the nut itself; and bananas in hands of two dozen. But here, around the camp, the fields were abandoned and the weeds flourished, out of control. For centuries we had known how to care for our land, and now it was a mess.

Women did not seem to care how ripped their clothes were, or how dirty their children were. No one seemed to care. Before the war, we would never have allowed our neighbours to suffer like this. In this way, our Acholi customs and clan system had once served us well as a society. I breathed hard to choke the sobs.

Florence saw my face and reached out for my hand. 'We are Acholi women. We will survive this,' she said. When we reached the outer limits of the camp, I hurried ahead of her back to my room. I sat on my bed and closed my eyes, trying to block out the desperation I'd seen in the camp. *While I was away chasing an education, my people lost everything.* I groaned under the weight of my guilt. Then I heard a soft knock, and the heaviness of the moment lifted. Rachel's sweet voice leaked through the crack: 'Mama, can we go into the garden? I've found a nest in the tree.'

'I'll be right out,' I called, and dabbed my eyes dry before joining her. It was hard to be sad when I saw her smile, with its missing teeth.

The next Sunday morning, I set out from Edward's house to visit a friend who lived on the other side of town, a trek around a rocky hill that dominates the Kitgum landscape. As I skirted the base of the hill, I passed an open-sided hall and looked up to see a crowd of people dancing, many with their hands held high. I stopped, captivated, as a sweet chorus of singing—accompanied by a keyboard and drums—filled the air around me. I had been moping at home, unable to reach out for help, and now I felt a stirring inside. Barely conscious of my actions, I found my way into the crowded church, with its dirt floor and plastic seats, and melted into the back row.

For two hours I floated in weightlessness, my guilt and pain replaced with elation as I joined in with the others, singing songs in our own language, dancing on the spot, feet shuffling backwards and forwards in a slow thump-thump-thump to the beat of the drums. I noticed a woman—the only foreigner—alongside the pastor in the front row, dancing with the ease of a local.

The young pastor, David Livingstone Okello, then stood up to preach, his voice quiet as he urged us not to lose hope. I wondered whether his words were directed at me, then glanced behind me and blushed as I noticed a man with severed arms, the stumps raised skywards, reminding me that many in this community had endured far more than I had. As I listened, my chest felt warm, and I lifted my face to the ceiling. The dark cloud that had rested on my mind lifted, clearing room for thoughts other than my survivor guilt. I whispered *hope*, as if it was a new word to me.

'God is our refuge and strength, an ever-present help in trouble,' David read from the Book of Psalms in his worn-out Bible. 'Therefore we will not fear, though the earth gives way and the mountains fall into the heart of the sea.' He explained how the author of these words, King David, had also had his world fall apart and had sought strength from God. In that moment, I felt his strength. I could not remember the last time I had felt so free.

After the service, I locked on to David. He introduced me to Cathy, his wife of several months, and Irene Gleeson, an Australian who had been in Kitgum for many years. 'Irene runs a school not far from here. I work there during the week,' he said, looking at me, then turning his attention to Irene, the small, white-haired woman beside him. Each week they provided meals and classes for hundreds of children, many orphaned in the war, he explained.

'You are most welcome to join us for lunch,' Cathy offered as she reached out for my hand. Her voice was calm and sweet, her smile warm and embracing.

I wanted to go, but remembered the friend that I had been on my way to visit. 'Thank you, I'd like that, but I can't today. May I come by during the week?' I asked. I slipped away, thrilled to have made new friends.

When we met later that week in her home, Cathy and I found so much to talk about. We sat on two large, padded chairs that dominated the living room, sipping from mugs of sweet black tea and sharing our lives like schoolgirls. I discovered that we were close in age, and that as a fifteen-year-old girl she had been abducted from her village of Kitgum Matidi and taken away to Karamoja to be traded for cows. I shuddered as she told me her story, remembering my own close escape.

'It was worse for David,' she said, looking up at him as her husband came into the room. 'He was taken by the LRA and then imprisoned by the government.'

'But at least I escaped quickly,' he said, trying to diffuse the attention. It was too late: I was now curious about his journey from boy soldier to pastor.

'What is your story of the war, Pastor?' I asked him, knowing my turn would be next.

David settled into his chair. 'Well, my mother ran away to Sudan during the time of Idi Amin, so I grew up with my maternal grandparents. When Museveni took over in January 1986 and the rebels came, I ran far into the bush to hide from them, but there was no food, and there was no food in town either, so I decided to sneak back to our family's land, where I knew there was sweet potato, cassava and millet.' The LRA rebels had caught him, and accused him of being a government sympathiser.

'I was sixteen when I was abducted, and spent four months with the rebels. I ran when the rebel leaders started to fight among themselves, but when I reached safety the government soldiers did not believe I'd been abducted, and shipped me off to prison in the south. I thought I would die from the heat in the back of the truck.' We sat in silence, with just the sound of flies buzzing around us, and a child crying in the distance.

'I heard that the prison we were going to was like a death camp, so I slipped out of the truck while we waited to be transferred. I was filthy. My hair was in dreadlocks, my pants were hanging down and my shirt was ragged. I escaped to the police barracks nearby, as I had an uncle in the police force.' I could imagine the sight. 'What a mess we have lived through,' he said, shaking his head.

'A mess indeed,' I replied. There was a special bond in sharing. Talking about our lives in the war was a way of encouraging each other. I knew I'd been spending too much time at home, unwilling to leave the house. It helped to hear how others had turned their lives around.

David's story took a fortuitous turn when his uncle found him a place at a Christian school in Kampala, far away from the war, where he learned to read and write and do carpentry, and found his faith.

'At first I was angry with God, and wanted answers to why I had been through all this, but then I started being thankful to be alive, and that's when my life improved. I felt so alive.'

He was taken in by an Australian, Jude Jacometti, who raised him as her own son, complete with strict rules about manners. Some years later, as a young man, he returned to northern Uganda to help children affected by the war. There, Irene Gleeson had taken him under her wing, and he was now a key person in her work. Irene had lived in Kitgum since the early stages of the war in the 1980s, gathering orphans and vulnerable children from villages and IDP camps.

Although we were close in age, I soon looked to David and Cathy as more than friends and peers—they were my spiritual parents, who offered advice and prayer whenever I was with them. From time to time, David would arrive unannounced at Edward's place to see how Rachel and I were faring. Cathy often dropped by with small cakes and other treats she had made for her own family. Mostly I sat, while Rachel busied herself making up games with items she had found in the kitchen or outside the house. I cared for her needs—visits to the market, making her meals and changing her clothes—but I was emotionally absent, without the will to entertain her.

'Alice, you can't sit here all day. You must find something useful to do,' David said one afternoon, picking up Rachel as he chastised me.

'But there is no work in Kitgum,' I said, barely moving.

'You haven't looked.' He was right. I was doing nothing with my life. I'd lost the motivation to help as a counsellor, or to approach anyone for any kind of job. I inhabited a dark hole from which I could not lever myself out, and the more I sat, the harder it was to feel excited about my future.

'David, how can a depressed person, who cannot even help herself, help others? That is what I am trained for, but I cannot do it,' I argued.

'Helping others might help you,' he said with a slight smile. He spun Rachel in a circle and then put her down beside me. I looked at Rachel's big eyes and nodded. David could not jolt me out of my malaise, but he managed to get me thinking. *Even if my job is typing, that is better than this life of sitting.*

I half-heartedly put out feelers among some friends, and soon heard of a community-development group that needed someone with my skills. 'They have computers, but nobody there knows how to use computers,' my friend reported.

By the following week, I was working with an Italian non-government organisation called the Association of Volunteers in International Service (AVSI), which was running the first psychosocial counselling services in northern Uganda. Already, they were training volunteers to handle trauma cases in the community, including the camps. The program was run by a lively Italian woman, a trained psychologist named Annette, who immediately got my attention. She had blonde hair—a rarity in the north—and the air of someone who was unstoppable.

It was my job to take the minutes at meetings and type them into the computer. I soon discovered that AVSI was setting up a four-month training program for community counsellors and needed someone to assess the training program in the camps. As I typed this information, I felt the first flicker of enthusiasm that I'd had for many months, and when Annette came to me soon afterwards to say, 'We think you could do this job,' I agreed. I'd watched her carefully for weeks, and I knew that I had much to learn from her. She lifted everyone around her when we needed it, while at other times she was serious, thoughtful and vigilant in checking for signs that we were under strain in our work.

On my first day at AVSI, I'd met another foreigner, a young psychologist named Jeannie Annan, who had come from Yale University in Connecticut to research the effects of war on young people. Until Annette and Jeannie arrived in Kitgum, I'd had only superficial contact with foreigners, but I quickly sealed my friendship with Jeannie by inviting her into my home.

Over six years, Jeannie came to the north many times, and we built a close friendship. Jeannie advocated for the welfare of the staff: higher salaries and access to medical assistance. As it turned out, her greatest gift to me would be teaching me how to write proposals in formats that those outside Uganda would notice and respond to with funding. It was a gift that would continue to grow in value.

The more I threw myself into the work, enduring long and exhausting days in the camps, the better I felt. For the first time in as long as I could remember, my life had meaning. I greeted the dawn each morning with arms open wide.

*

When Rachel fell sick, the shockwaves reverberated around our scattered family. Somehow, we had been lulled into believing that Rachel would escape the same fate as her mother, brother and sisters. I had heard this could happen: that one child could contract HIV in utero, and another might miss out.

There was still no treatment for HIV/AIDS in Uganda at that time, though we heard rumours of experimental drugs that could keep the virus at bay. How could we ever find out where to get them, even if they were available?

We could only pray. 'Let us stand together to ask God to save the life of Rachel,' Gabriel said, stepping in as clan elder. Soon afterwards, Mama, Florence, Edward and others gathered in Edward's living room. We kept a daily vigil by Rachel's side. We prayed and fasted, and fell to our knees as we pleaded, 'God, please save Rachel.' But every day we saw her failing. Rachel was in and out of hospital for six months, and though we all knew she was infected and no cure was available, I believed God would spare her life. I could not bear to let my mind wander to thoughts of life without Rachel, who had been like my own child since she was six months old.

Finally, I left work to care for Rachel around the clock, with Mama never far away. Rachel now weighed as little as when I'd first met her in Kampala, and was as dependent as a baby.

At times, Florence stayed awake all night to tend to Rachel, or curled up with her so she would not wake alone. Florence loved the sweet little girl as her own, often spending the whole day with Rachel on her back, constantly engaging her sick passenger in chatter. When we could no longer care for Rachel at home, she was moved to Kitgum Hospital, where Florence arrived daily to cheer her up.

'If we can make her happier, the sickness will decrease,' Florence said, her strident claim buoying us all. I clung to her hopefulness. Rachel rarely cried, even when we knew her little body was racked with pain. She remained strong and cheerful, until the disease progressed, when her body shrank even further and her frail smiles became fleeting treasures.

At the end of two months of her illness, in April 2000, I prayed, *God, let your will be done with the life of Rachel, that it may glorify your name.* That night I sat with Rachel as she eagerly ate some fried fish—tilapia—that I had prepared. It was the best meal Rachel had eaten in hospital. My spirit soared with each mouthful she took, thinking of the goodness that the fish would bring.

'She is eating well tonight, Mama,' I reported to my mother, who often stayed with Rachel in the hospital at night. 'If she keeps eating like this, she will soon be strong again.' I let out a breath of relief. It seemed like I had been holding my breath for weeks, afraid to relax.

'I want to sleep now, Mama Alice,' Rachel announced at the end of her meal.

By midnight she was still sleeping soundly, and at one o'clock my mother said, 'She is sleeping so well, why don't you take some rest yourself?' I was exhausted. For weeks my sleep had been short and broken as I cared for Rachel. I lay down on a mat by Rachel's bed and fell into a deep sleep. Then Rachel came to me in a dream, as a healthy, laughing six-year-old girl. She ran into my arms, and I hugged her against my chest. For these few moments, I recaptured the happiest times of the years we had spent together.

My dream ended with a scream. I sat up, looking around for the source. I looked for Rachel, in a dazed state expecting to see the smiling face of my dream. As my eyes adjusted to the darkness, I saw Rachel's tiny outline on the bed, lying still. It was three o'clock in the morning. Apart from the wails of my mother, there was silence. I had missed Rachel's last breath.

Without a word to anyone, I scooped Rachel up and carried her out into the musty coolness of the street, where it was too dark to see her face. I had not held a dead body in my arms this way before, and I carried Rachel like a child who was alive, as I would lift her as a sleeping child back into her bed. My body shook with my weeping as I walked. I could not bear to let Rachel go: I wanted to take her home to my bed, to protect her, to will her back to life. The nurses would not allow it. They saw a deranged woman who could not even care for herself at that moment. 'Please Miss, can we take her now?' they coaxed, until I finally released Rachel into their outstretched arms.

I went home after this, curling up on my metal bed, where I replayed the past three weeks, ending with the last few days. I wrapped my arms around my stomach, as if to hold it together. *Rachel ate a decent meal and slept peacefully, and I thought she would recover.* I was not ready for her life to be taken. She still had to grow up as Acholi, to go to school and break down barriers, maybe have a career, to have a full life.

I could not get past the waste of her young life. I looked for blame, and decided to stop going to church. *Why would God allow this to happen to a young child?* I told myself. *There is no need for prayers, because God doesn't listen.*

In the following days, I wished I'd gone with Rachel so that I did not have to stay alive, when I was mummified inside. Once, I tried to console Edward, but I was no use to him. I could not even face the woman next door with the girls who had played with Rachel when she was well. I was sure that to many around us Rachel was just another child who had died, and her grave was just another small one chipped from the dry Acholi dirt, to be forgotten by all but a handful of surviving family. Death happened every day here, often in a much more violent way.

Grief brought with it a kind of madness. I walked the streets of Kitgum alone at night when it was dangerous to do so, and did not give a thought to my safety. I stopped caring about what I ate, and the flesh fell away until my clothes hung from my six-foot frame. I would not partake in family meals, and when my mother said, 'Let us come together to remember Rachel,' I selfishly declined. Others could not join me in the depths of my grief.

I thought of the man in the hut down the road, who screamed at anyone who passed. The war had turned many sane men mad, and I felt that I was going the same way. My grief was like a lion lurking in my head that could maul me at any time. I was both hunter and prey.

Where was my education now? I'd forgotten everything I'd learned about grief in my course—how disbelief could give way to anger, and then the inevitable 'what ifs' and depression; this was all to be expected. But somehow, when grief came for me, I was not ready for it.

I opened my dresser and pulled out my diploma, still rolled up from the day I stood on the stage to receive it. I unrolled it, reading my name neatly scribed in black ink across the middle, and remembered how proud I'd felt.

'What good is a piece of paper in this place?' I yelled at the air before throwing the paper onto the floor.

14

Finding Life in Proscovia

It was many weeks before I could gather myself after Rachel died. I squandered my days at home—often sitting in the darkness of my room—until I could muster the will to go out. Yet I desperately needed money to survive, and knew deep down that working would help.

I arrived back at the AVSI office one morning to a sympathetic welcome, and was soon thrust into chaos. The flow of scared, hurting and injured victims of war hadn't stopped when we lost Rachel. I was quickly assigned cases and bundled into the AVSI four-wheel drive with Annette, to go to the town IDP camp. We pulled up to the outer edge of the sprawl of huts and I paused, my hand resting on the door handle, before I pulled it and climbed out into the rising babble of voices. I placed my hands on my stomach—it churned with stress—as we separated into different sections of the camp.

'Help me, my daughter is dying.' I turned to see an older man behind me, his arm held out as if to touch me. He stood near the entrance of a hut, and when I looked past him, I made out the shape of a slender woman. I bent down to enter the dark interior, and stood in the centre of the room while my eyes adjusted from the bright sunlight outside.

The woman, whom I assumed was the mother, kneeled beside her sick daughter, sponging cool water onto her forehead. The girl's bony hand rested on her mother's leg, and her head fell to one side. The mother looked up at me pleadingly, and I took a step closer to her.

'We'll get you some help,' I said, without thinking. I looked at the sunken eyes, too big for the skeletal body, and my thoughts turned dark. *There is no help. There is no hope. Your daughter will die.* I froze, for a moment wondering if I'd spoken these words aloud. Without another word, I turned around, bent down to squeeze through the door, pushed past the father and started running. I did not look back.

'Madam, help us,' he called after me. I covered my ears with my hands as I ran, ignoring the sharp jags of thatch that caught in my hair, the muddy splashes from puddles and the naked children who only just jumped out of my path. I arrived breathless back to the AVSI vehicle and waited, leaning against the car to catch my breath, until Annette arrived.

'Annette, I cannot do this,' I said quietly, my head bowed. My heart beat like a drum, reverberating up to my head so violently that I thought it might explode.

'Why is that, Alice?' she replied, her full attention on me now. She had a way of focusing that made me feel heard.

'Our job is to care. How can I help anyone when I am barely alive myself? I can't stand to hear all the problems right now.'

A dark poison had filled my core, and it was killing me from the inside out. Like a catalogue, my memory raced through some of the gut-wrenching stories I'd heard in my job: one family had thrown the body of a son murdered by the LRA into the bush, to rot or be eaten by wild animals, believing the enemy would then suffer the same fate. I had sat with mothers who fretted for their abducted daughters, or told me about the nightmares of their children when they returned from captivity. Every day in this job I'd absorbed the anger of those who had lost family, property and livelihoods. I put my head in my hands and stared at my dusty feet.

Annette said very little. Her years of experience had taught her the value of space: when to be silent, and how to express her concern through the lift of an eyebrow and a look so intense that it became a pool of compassion into which people gladly dived. She lit a cigarette and leaned forwards to listen with her whole body. She knew about Rachel's death, but had never heard any details about it or my life before Kitgum.

'I feel useless when I go to the camps. I can't help anyone,' I cried, winding my handkerchief around my fingers. 'No one knows what is going to happen . . . even in ten minutes' time, a neighbour could be killed in front of my eyes. What I'm seeing is impossible.' I did not even try to cover up my self-pity.

Annette nodded, and drew deeply on her cigarette. 'Don't tell me everything now. If you like, I'll come to your home tomorrow and we can talk,' she offered. I wiped my wet eyes and nodded, steadying my breath as I climbed into the cabin of the car to head back to the town centre. I trusted Annette to understand my dilemma. She had cared enough to arrange a weekly counselling session with each member of staff at AVSI, to make sure that we were coping with the stress of the work. She knew how to pull strings at the higher levels and was not afraid to ask for favours.

Annette knocked at the door of Edward's home the next morning, just as I was getting out of bed. I picked up my striped *kikooyi* and quickly wrapped it around my chest on the way to the door, then pulled my hair braids into place. 'Ah, it's early,' I greeted Annette with a yawn.

'Not that early—it's after nine,' she said with a laugh. I ushered her into the stark living area, with its concrete floor and nest of three shabby chairs. The building was only partially built, and unlikely to be finished any time soon. I left to put the saucepan on the fire outside for tea.

'Alice, what has been happening in your life?' Annette asked in her heavily accented English, when we had settled into our seats, each with a mug in hand. It had taken me a while to understand her in the early days, but now I could even manage a few Italian words, such as *ciao* and *grazie*.

'Where do I start?' I said, with a half-smile. A night's sleep had soothed some of the torment of the previous day.

'Let's start with your childhood,' Annette replied, sliding down into the chair to make herself comfortable. She had a warm manner, one that invited sharing, like storytelling by a fire.

'My childhood was difficult, with the fighting and so much confusion. It was hard to feel safe in the village.' Once I started, my story poured out in a verbal rush.

For the first time, I spoke of hiding at night when it wasn't safe in my home; of Gulu and the terror of the raid on my school; of my disappointment at leaving school each time;

and of how unprepared I'd been to raise Edward's girls at the age of nineteen. I re-lived the last days of Lucy's life, then my thoughts shifted to Rachel. I saw her bright smile looking up from beside me at the kitchen bench, asking for more peanut butter. That had been her favourite food.

I paused, and we sat in silence. I looked towards the room that Rachel and I had shared, and imagined her sitting cross-legged, playing with the little doll that I had brought for her from Kampala. Rachel's hair was braided, wound up in two balls sitting high on either side of her head, and her arms and legs were as plump as they'd been before she fell sick.

'Rachel had been my only hope for living,' I said, wringing my hands as if it might ease the pain. 'Rachel kept me going after Lucy died. I had to wake up every day to take care of her.' Annette nodded and waited.

'I wanted to care for Rachel, to make sure that she had a good life, that she went to school. And then she died, too,' I said, reaching for a tissue from the box Annette had brought with her. She rested her hand on my back as I cried. When I stopped, I felt drained, but slightly less defeated by life.

'It's okay, Alice,' Annette said, sitting close to me.

'I can't bear to see more children suffer. *I* don't want to suffer anymore,' I said, sitting with my head in my hands.

'Alice, it's still early in your grief. You must take time out of the office, away from your work,' Annette said, putting her arm around my shoulder. 'We'll keep talking—every day if you need to.' She stood up to go, turning as she reached the door. 'Alice, you will come through this,' she said, her gaze direct and reassuring. I slowly nodded, only half believing it.

Annette came often after that, or I visited her office, for counselling sessions. The rest of the time I was numb to the world around me, and sat at home alone when Edward was not there. I'd taken unpaid leave and had no income at all.

Edward left early for work and often came home late, so it was some time before I noticed the telltale signs of the sickness I now knew so well: he was sweating and tired, nauseous and vomiting after he ate. The symptoms were escalating, and he was growing steadily weaker.

One morning at breakfast with Edward, I found the courage to raise the subject that had brought such grief upon us. 'Edward, I know you are getting sick, too,' I said, placing his black tea and porridge on the table in front of him, and standing close to catch his eye. 'What can we do?'

'Alice, we can do nothing,' he replied, without looking up. 'I have lost those I loved most, and there is little left to lose.' He had closed the conversation while I still had unanswered questions, such as how did the virus—a death sentence— make its way into his family? These matters were still too private, even when our country faced an AIDs epidemic. Would he not fight to stay around for his older two boys, who had now moved to Kitgum to live with him? Edward finished his meal and left for work even though he was sick, in the same stoic way he had faced each member of his family departing our world.

I watched, helpless, as his health quickly deteriorated. Finally, he was taken along perilous roads to Lacor Hospital in Gulu, where he could have better medical care for his last days. When the news came through it hit harder than I expected, opening the floodgates of my despair. Out poured the pain of every loved one lost—Diane and Lucy, Rachel, my father, my grandmother, my childhood, my Acholi identity. I cried and cried. It started me on a road of questioning my own usefulness. I kept asking myself one question over and over again: *Why am I still alive when almost every person I rose for each morning is gone?*

Eventually, I returned to work and, for the next six months, I met Annette twice a week to process my experiences. In each session, Annette asked a series of questions, skilfully drawing out my bitterness and mistrust of people. 'What happened then? How did you feel? What did you do?' Each week she kept me talking, reassuring me that I would come through.

'You know, I was the person in my family who most wanted to die, and I survived,' I said, as my feelings started to untangle, and slowly the confusion lifted from me.

Finally, I was able to tell myself: *It is done, and I have a life ahead.* I then prayed: *God, if you're there, deal with my life. Please give me a new life.*

With Edward's death, I became very strong—as though I absorbed all the strength of those I had lost—and now I craved life. One night, I had a dream so vivid that I could remember every detail when I awoke.

I saw an old rotting tree, its trunk greying and dead, its leaves shrivelled and brown. I saw the tree topple and fall, then out of the prostrate log came a new tree, a sapling with fresh green leaves and life running through its core. That day, I awoke feeling confident, my spirit full of a hope I had not felt for many years. I rose quickly, pulling on my sarong and stretching my arms to the sky. I looked out at the blueness. The day before, I had felt like an empty vessel of no worth; on this day, I was an empty vessel ready to be filled. I was open to possibilities.

*

The AVSI office was a bustling place, filled with people passing in and out, each with a desperate need for housing or food or someone to care. They sat for hour upon hour on a rough-hewn wooden bench along the wall in the entry.

One day, a young girl arrived at my desk, standing silently. I spent many of my days behind a desk, reading reports and processing documents to do with my case load. Her presence barely registered with me. I glanced up briefly before putting my head down again to focus on the stack of paper I was working through. 'What's your name?' I asked, scribbling a note.

'Proscovia. Scovia,' she answered, in a whisper. Then I heard a small whimper and swung my head up again, this time taking a good look at the girl standing in front of me. She was so young, and yet she had a small child by her side. Not only that, she was also heavily pregnant. I put down my pen and sighed. *Yet another child returning from the bush, and there is nowhere to take her.* In Gulu, there was a reception centre to receive boys and girls escaping the LRA, but Kitgum had nothing like that.

'Where is your family? Where is your village?' I asked the girl, knowing that these questions could be difficult to answer when most families in the camps were dislocated.

'I have nowhere to go,' she said. Her voice was so quiet that I had to focus to hear her words. 'When I was abducted, my parents were killed and my village was burned. I've been looking for my uncles, but I cannot find them.' The girl looked at her bulging belly. 'If I go to the village, they will not accept me like this anyway.'

'Then where have you been living?'

'I was staying with a woman in the camp, but I can no longer stay there as she is almost ready to give birth, too.'

I looked at the little girl by Scovia's side, and my heart ached for Rachel. I took a deep breath. 'You can stay with me until the baby is born.' I certainly had room in Edward's house. The boys from his first marriage would eventually inherit his property, but this matter had been pushed aside while we were in a war. With their father gone, they had moved to Gulu to live with Gabriel and Pauline, who had returned from Kotido.

'Wait until I finish work, and I will take you there,' I told her, and the girl bowed her head, took her daughter's hand and joined the others at the end of the wooden bench.

Annette threw her hands in the air when I told her. I was used to her Italian ways, with her emotions so visible. It was a welcome contrast to my own culture, where we pushed down our pain. 'Alice, why do you accept this girl when you have so many of your own problems?' Annette asked, in her heavy Italian accent. She was clearly annoyed at me, but I knew it would not last.

I looked at my feet as I considered my answer. 'She had nowhere else to go,' I said, meeting Annette's eyes. 'It is only for a short time . . . it will be good for me to care for her.' I knew that she could not argue with this, when she had taken on many such impossible cases in this work, including my own.

At first Scovia was shy, staying in her room with her three-year-old, not wanting to make demands of me. But soon, my home was filled with the chatter and squeals of a three-year-old again, and then after Scovia gave birth, the nights were broken with the mewling cries of a newborn. As the months wore on, I found that Scovia and her two children brought a direction to my days, a focus beyond myself and my past.

I decided that Scovia and her babies could stay for as long as they liked.

One day, the baby woke up vomiting. Scovia called out, 'Alice, come quickly, something is wrong with my baby.' I rushed into the room, where Scovia held the newborn. The baby's face was hot and red, and screwed up in pain. I picked her up and held my hand out to Scovia.

'Come, we'll get help,' I said, and we hurried down to the hospital. I knew from Lucy how important it was for the infant to stay hydrated. I wouldn't make the same mistake with Scovia's baby. I left them both at the hospital and returned a day later, when it was time for them to go home. The doctor saw me arrive and sidled up to me, asking to speak to me alone. I was now effectively her guardian.

'The baby will be fine with this medication. But you should know that both the mother and baby are HIV-positive,' he said, with a weary look. Each day, he sewed up many people, and tended to burns and machete cuts. He looked like he'd reached his limit.

'No.' I closed my eyes and bent over, my hands on both knees, my chin on my chest. I had to take this in. After what I had seen in the past five years, I was sure that this was a death sentence. It sickened me to think of another child dying in my arms.

I gathered up Scovia and her babies, not having the heart to tell the young mother this news. After all the trauma she had endured, I could not bring her more pain or shame, or fear of this untreatable disease. *Why did I take on this respon-sibility when I cannot afford medicine or hospital visits? Maybe Annette was right.*

Scovia chattered all the way home. 'I'm so happy that my

baby is better now. The doctor was very good to us.' She reached behind her to pat the bundle tied to her back.

'Hmm, that's true,' I replied. I was shocked by the bad news and did not feel like making small talk. I retreated to my room when we returned home, closing the door to keep the three year old out. I resolved to arrange for Scovia to see a specialist HIV counsellor, a friend through AVSI, who would know how to help her through this. It was too close to my heart to manage myself.

*

One morning I had set out on a mission to get training for Scovia. I approached a tailor on the main street of Kitgum, a man in his late fifties whom I knew, called Muze, who specialised in making the traditional women's outfit called the *gomesi*. It didn't seem to matter that there was little to celebrate in the daily lives of those in Kitgum—Muze still had a steady flow of women coming to him to make them new outfits.

'Muze, would you mind if this girl sits with you and learns how to sew?' I asked. 'I'm willing to buy her materials, and I have a machine for her.' This is how she was able to sit with him each day for the next six months, and how she learned to make the finest *gomesi* for the women of Kitgum. The tailoring had been such a big step forward for Scovia. I had scraped together some savings—just enough to buy her a second-hand sewing machine. I reasoned that if Scovia had a skill, she could earn an income to support her children.

Scovia and I mostly enjoyed an easy relationship, sharing news of our day when I returned from AVSI and she had finished her tailoring for the day. I was impressed with how organised Scovia was as a mother—preparing meals early on days when she worked, staying calm when the babies cried and fussed, keeping their room organised and taking full responsibility for their daily care.

*

In December 2001, sitting at my desk doing paperwork, I overheard a conversation that snapped me from my growing despondency.

'There's a group of Italian doctors at St Joseph's Hospital looking for HIV patients. They are experimenting with some new medications,' my colleague announced. 'Shouldn't be hard to find candidates around here,' he said.

At the end of the work day, as soon as I could escape, I rushed to the reception of the Italian mission hospital. 'Can I see the Italian doctors treating HIV?' I asked, my heart racing.

When a young, tired-looking man appeared, I wanted to throw myself at his feet. Instead, I said, 'I have a mother and baby staying with me who are both sick. Can you help them? Please.'

The next day, I took Scovia and her baby to St Joseph's. By now, she knew of her baby's sickness and had seen the counsellor several times. The drugs they were testing were called antiretrovirals (ARVs). They would not remove the disease, but they had shown startling results in suppressing its advance.

At the same time, the doctors gave Scovia's baby feeding supplements that would help her build natural immunity.

Within four months, Scovia and her baby looked much healthier.

'If they eat well, they should both be fine now,' the doctor told us.

'Scovia's life is such an encouragement to me,' I reported back to Annette, when Scovia and her children had been restored to good health, and she was on her way to being able to support her family. Scovia had met a man who wanted to marry her, and he promised that he would take care of her and her children in Gulu.

'There are many other girls like Scovia. You're good with them, Alice,' was Annette's response. 'I'd like to put you forward for further study.' AVSI had paid for a number of staff from the north to study counselling and other courses at Mbarara University in western Uganda as part of their efforts to build the skills and capacity of Acholi people to help their own.

I was ready to do more. Just that day I had met a girl who had been abducted at the age of seven, and her parents could not believe that this girl with two children was their own child. I could see myself mediating in situations like these. I smiled and grasped Annette's hand. 'Thank you for believing in me.'

15

Return to Pader

I sat with every muscle on alert, my eyes surveying the bush by the side of the road for movement, the adrenaline rushing through my veins, making me light-headed. Within weeks of my conversation with Annette, I was with the AVSI country director on one of the most dangerous roads in the whole of northern Uganda. If we made it through this alive, I would soon be reunited with friends and family during a brief visit on the way to study in Mbarara. The road linking Kitgum and Pader skirted along a range of gentle hills, which provided good cover for the rebels. They swooped down to ambush trucks or minibuses or even convoys at any time of the day or night, then retreated stealthily into the undergrowth. Mostly, they captured the children for the LRA and killed the rest.

At Pajule, about halfway to Pader, we passed the edges of an IDP camp, one of the largest in the district, housing 80,000 people. I had heard that the entire population of Pader district was now crowded into camps, and that the rebels had full control of everything outside—the bush and the remains of the villages.

I sat back, deep in thought about what I might find in my home district. They'd had to build their own huts in the camps, gathering the grass and poles from far away. Florence told me that many people had been killed while collecting materials for the huts, if not by rebels, then by government forces mistaking them for rebels.

'I've been told that Pader is worse than Kitgum, and that in Pader town the rebels have their spies on the streets and even in the trees,' I leaned over to inform my travelling companion. Though nervous, I was excited in a way that made me talkative.

'Is that right?' he replied, nervously keeping his eyes on the bush while the driver drove at breakneck speed over potholes.

'Yes, Pader still has food and water, so the rebels do not leave the district from day to day,' I said, relaying all I had heard from my close friend, Florence, who had moved back to Pader, and others.

I imagined the rebels prowling restlessly around the perimeters of the camp like leopards, ready to attack, to steal food or abduct children when the army guard slipped up, or hapless camp dwellers strayed. I had butterflies when thinking about seeing the remnants of my family, who all lived in IDP camps, either at the Lira Palwo trading centre or in Pader township.

I took a long breath to calm myself as the truck came over the slight rise that led into Pader's main thoroughfare. In my childhood, Pader had only a few permanent buildings and a small central market. We drove down a busy main street that I did not recognise. Military barracks, non-government organisations and thousands in the town camp had swelled the numbers.

'None of this was here,' I reflected, more to myself than to my companion. Even from a distance, I could smell rotting garbage and human filth.

We had arrived in Pader late in the day, and I set out into the town camp that spread out from the main street. I wound my way between huts, ducking to avoid thatch overhangs. 'Can you tell me where I will find Florence Komakech?' I asked curious dwellers along the way as I edged deeper into the labyrinth of huts. Everyone knew Florence: direct, incisive, commanding of respect. She was ferocious when it came to fighting for small improvements in camp life. Florence and her husband, EY, had returned to Pader several months before. I had missed her after she left Kitgum.

Florence sat in her one padded chair, looking frailer than I remembered. A bout of malaria, with its sapping sweats and throbbing pain, had kept her at home for several days and stolen her usual vitality. The fading frames on the walls pointed to an important life in this community: pictures of a younger Florence at official occasions wearing the traditional *gomesi*, with its voluminous skirts and sleeves, standing alongside political and church leaders.

Someone in the camp had given her a ripe pineapple, which she offered to me with a grin, its syrupy juice falling in sticky drips onto the bare floor. She talked me through recent events with the air of detachment that we all assumed when we shared our worst experiences. 'It has been sad here, Alice. Pader is not the district we both knew,' Florence said. She stared at the ground as she spoke, her voice lacking its trademark fieriness.

'I can see that already,' I said, resigned to a long conversation. I mostly listened, as Florence ran through a list of awful events in the district that I had missed.

'The women are so desperate for food, they return to the village to look for cassava and millet, and are killed on the way.'

'It is terrible, Florence.' The stories of suffering were hard to hear. From time to time I shook my head in disbelief at what Florence told me. I owed it to them to listen, no matter how hard.

'Remember Mary from Lira Palwo?' Florence asked. She looked towards the wooden frame of the door, expecting EY home at any moment.

'Yes, she was only a tiny girl when I left the village,' I replied, trying to recall the face of this little girl.

'She was taken as she gathered firewood outside the camp,' Florence said, before moving on to the next case. 'The mother of Josephine was assaulted by soldiers as she drew from the water point.' She frowned.

'Even when there is an ambush on the road to Lira and many people are killed, others will still go the next day. There is nothing we can do to stop these things happening. The mothers are so desperate, they sell their bodies and their daughters' bodies to the soldiers in exchange for food.' Florence closed her eyes, wearied by her illness and painful memories.

'Ah no,' I replied. I could feel it: the stories had filled me up with sadness, and now it overflowed. I closed my eyes, bowed my head and let the tears fall. There would be more stories in the morning.

Eight of us shared the hard floor of Florence and EY's hut that night—eight heavy-breathing bodies, lined up, shoulders almost touching, with snores and mumbles and, once, a stricken outburst from a nightmare. My mind raced with images from Florence's stories. I was still awake after midnight when I heard gunfire, then screams. 'Help, help, help,' I heard, followed by deeper tones of mortars and return fire. We were all awake now. The battle raged with a ferocity that I had not experienced for many years. The smell of gunpowder resting over the entire camp made me gag.

'Lord Jesus, help us in our hour of need,' Florence prayed as we all lay in the dark. 'Please help those poor people who are near the fighting.' We lay in silence until daybreak, well after the gunfire and screams had ceased. As the camp came to life for the day, I walked with Florence to its edge, where a silent crowd had gathered, all peering towards the bush.

'Don't look,' someone called, but it was too late. My eyes had already captured what they were looking at, and I could not erase the image. A young woman lay lifeless in a pool of blood, and attached to her breast was a baby, sucking intently, still clinging to its lifeline. I cried out at the sight.

'Maybe she was caught in the fighting, or maybe she was killed and dragged outside the camp. We don't know,' one of the bystanders volunteered. For a time we all just stood, motionless. No one had the courage to retrieve the woman's body or to lift the suckling baby from her breast, for fear of being shot themselves. We unfroze when the baby's grand-mother arrived, her face grim, and pulled the crying infant from its mother's breast. Several men stepped in to help carry the mother's body into the camp.

'Florence, why have I come back to this place?' I asked as we walked back to her hut. I felt so useless, a mere spectator.

In my shock I'd lost all certainty, even my conviction that I had something to give.

'You're back because you belong here among us,' Florence replied in a quiet monotone. She understood the inner battle between flight and duty. She could have run, but stayed. Could I make the same choice?

16

Back to School

My resolve had returned by the next morning, when I set out towards the IDP camp at Lira Palwo trading centre in search of my older sister, Doreen. She was easy to find on Gabriel's small square of land, and was already well known as she helped those around her, even when her own survival was a daily struggle. In times of peace, there had been five or six grass-thatched huts on the block, but now the land housed fifty small huts, crammed tightly together, with barely a gap between them and the vast IDP camp of 15,000 people.

Doreen had been there for six months, since the soldiers had started rounding up villagers from Pader district and forcing them into camps, as they had in Kitgum and other places. Her face lit up when she saw me climb down from the truck and cross the open space to her hut. 'Alice, you look well,' she cried, trying to push herself up from her mat on the ground under the tree. 'Why have you come all this way?'

'I'm on my way from Kitgum to Mbarara, where I will continue my studies,' I said, reaching out to help her up. 'I'm staying with Florence and EY in the Pader town camp, but I wanted to see you before I leave again.'

I studied her face. The lines were deeper; she looked weary, and she was thinner than the last time we'd met, in Masindi. I looked around at the shrivelled plants that had burned up in the fierce sun, a barren space without tree cover. She shared her hut with all but one of her eight children; her husband had long gone from the marriage. I laughed nervously to cover my guilt at having had an easier time. Since leaving the north the first time, I'd mostly slept in beds and had food to eat. In Kitgum, I lived in a brick house with a concrete floor. I'd suffered emotional loss, but had not endured such physical hardship.

Doreen met my eyes with a sad look. 'I have nothing to offer you, Alice, not even a cup of tea,' she lamented. I felt her shame, in her sunken shoulders and down-turned lips.

'It's okay. I do not need tea,' I said, as my heart broke. It was not okay to see my sister suffering like this. 'Let's walk. You can show me around.' I slipped my hand inside her arm, and we slowly circled the nearest section of the camp. She pointed out the latrines and the meeting place where she collected her rice and water. I recognised some of the neighbours from our childhood—local farmers, the families of our friends, people who had been part of my world growing up, the survivors of attack and disease.

'Have you been back to Lapilyet?' I asked, remembering how I had run from our village to the trading centre as a child. We both looked up the road to the right, past the rows of huts, in the direction of Lapilyet.

'It's not yet safe to walk to the village,' Doreen said. 'It is only safe to stay together here. We have nowhere else to go.'

I quickly changed the subject. 'Have you seen any of our brothers?'

'Peter was here recently from Kampala,' Doreen said, with a genuine smile. 'He brought us some supplies. Salt and soap and paraffin.'

'Ah yes, I heard. Charles and Gabriel are now in Kitgum. They are fine.'

A volley of gunshots rang out in the distance, and I felt a gurgle in my stomach at the sound. The lines on Doreen's face crumpled into a frown as she grabbed my wrist to steady me. 'I'm scared for you, Alice. Why did you come here? How are you going back? There are ambushes every day, and many are dying.'

I was making Doreen uneasy, and my body told me that it was time to go.

Doreen leaned through the window of the old truck. 'You should stay in the south where it is peaceful,' she said. I nodded, while knowing that after visiting the IDP camps, the pull to return—to help—had grown stronger. I would have to learn to manage my instinctive gut reaction to gunshots.

As we drove along, I gazed at the scraggly bush by the road and knew I'd be back. We returned safely to Florence and EY's hut in Pader town camp, and I prepared to leave for Kampala early the next morning. From there, I had a seven-hour journey to Mbarara University, in the western part of Uganda.

*

I arrived at the town of Mbarara the day before classes started, after a long bus ride south-west from Kampala. Five hours into the bone-jarring journey, I had turned to the old woman slumped next to me and smiled. 'Do you think we'll soon reach Tanzania or even Rwanda?' I joked. She looked blankly at me and turned away. A man behind me heard my comment and poked his head forwards.

'We're almost there, but if we keep going, it's only sixty-five kilometres to the border.' The terrain had become hilly and overgrown with vines, and a fog set in as we arrived late in the day.

The next morning, I joined a stream of other young students gliding through the gates of Mbarara University just before nine o'clock in the morning. I had decided to wear my favourite dress, a loose floral one that draped softly across my body and reached my ankles. I was impatient to learn, busting to get past the first week of meeting teachers and other students and into the meat of the coursework: public health, reproductive health and trauma. I sat at the front of the class, my pen in hand and blank notepad in front of me, with a clear mission: to get back to the north with new skills. I scribbled notes until my hand hurt, filtering all I learned through the lens of my childhood, my community and the impact of war. Right from the start, two questions lurked in the back of my mind: *How is this relevant to the north? How does this apply to me?*

From the first day, I had looked forwards to the section on trauma, and I rushed to school in anticipation on the day the course started. When the teacher wrote, 'What is trauma?' across the blackboard, I wrote it in my notebook, and I intended to write down every word he spoke.

'Trauma can come from one event or an ongoing set of circumstances. It can come when our lives are threatened or endangered, and each person will experience these things differently,' he said. 'For example, if someone has had a car or an aeroplane accident they might . . .'

I could feel the sweat on my face and shifted uncomfortably in my chair. I did not hear the end of his sentence. Cars and planes? *Why are we learning about the trauma of airplane crashes and car accidents when we travel by foot and bus, and we don't fly?* He had already failed to answer my question about relevance.

My mind shifted to the camps and villages of the north, and I clenched my fists. I saw the image of the murdered mother in Pader town camp, with her baby still suckling at her breast long after she had died, and my breathing became shallow. I closed my eyes, took a deep breath to recover, and tuned in to the teacher once again.

'In Uganda, we've had systems—traditional ways—that have worked for centuries,' he said, looking directly at me, as if he knew my thoughts. 'But often those systems have broken down, and we need new tools for addressing trauma. While we may not travel by plane, the same *principles* apply.'

I relaxed into my chair. He was right: the rape, murder, abuse and beatings we'd endured in the north could not be erased through our centuries-old means of mediation between clan elders, or cleansing ceremonies, or by each side drinking the bitter root. It was too much.

Over the next few weeks, I learned new names and symptoms for the side effects of drawn-out war on our mental health: depression, anxiety, paranoia and post-traumatic stress disorder. In class, my eyes often welled with tears at our loss—and at my own loss, which I had buried in order to move on. I'd stopped having nightmares about the school raid, but wondered whether they might re-emerge under pressure.

That first day, I had left the class without talking to any other students, lost in thought. *Would I ever learn enough to help those still living in the middle of this war? Would I ever be strong enough to deal with my own anxiety?* I thought back to the one time I'd seen my father cry: when his nephew had died under the wheels of a truck in our district. Within hours, hundreds of family and friends had arrived to grieve, to wail around the body, to bring food and together bear the weight of our pain. *How could a dislocated clan—driven into scattered camps—support the loss of their own?*

It took me a long time to sleep that night. I pieced together some of the times I had felt myself tumbling into a hole of despair, and I thought about what had pulled me out. I had grown up with a father who loved his family and knitted us together, a father who showed us that each child was important, whether male or female; I had grown up without beatings; I had grown up in a family of faith. After an hour of allowing my mind to meander, I took a long breath and rolled onto my side. Life would be fine.

*

I arrived back in Pader in a convoy of military trucks one night in July 2002, my hands latched onto the metal rail of the truck's tray, ignoring the twenty others who shared the same small space. I gritted my teeth and lifted my head to stretch to my full height, without the usual awkwardness I felt when I towered above other women. I then stretched my lips into a wide, defiant smile. *I'm so happy to be here.* And I was quietly pleased that at 28 years of age I now returned to my homeland feeling strong. In steeling my resolve to return to my home, I had lost my fear of death and man.

I climbed down from the truck and found my way back to Florence's hut in absolute darkness, with not even moonlight to guide me. I arrived to a tense hush over the camp, quiet but for the occasional cries of a baby, and a mother's shush. It was the noise of twenty people together, not 120,000. Fires and lamps were snuffed out after dusk, and the hungry mass of people huddled in their huts on alert, not wanting to attract the attention of the rebels. As I slid between the huts, as if through a maze, I could feel the heaviness of expectation—a mortar, a stray bullet, a lightning raid—that hung around the camp.

'Sister, do you have some rice for us?' a woman asked in a near whisper as I passed an open door.

'Sorry,' I replied. I had nothing to give by way of food or medicine. Right now I had only spiritual and emotional sustenance to give. I came prepared to stand with my people, to reassure them that they were not alone, and to cry with them. The words of the teachers in my social-work course echoed in my head: the most important thing in the beginning is to *listen*. This I could do, and had done from my earliest memory of sitting by the fire as a child. This was how I could break through into the pain of those around me. Though I had no plan, my chest ached with this burden. That night, I lay down in Florence's hut and prayed that listening—and a sense of being here for a purpose—would be enough.

The next morning, I heard the subdued voices of the mothers in neighbouring huts, who had woken in the hazy pre-dawn light to set fires so they could give their children something to eat. These women would spend their day in the bush near the camp, scavenging for twigs and anything edible. Soon afterwards, I heard the voices of their children, boys and girls as young as eight years old who filed back early from their night-time sanctuaries. They came from safe sleeping havens in strong buildings such as the district head-quarters, with metal doors and patrolling soldiers. I thought of my own random flights to the bush and felt envy that their night commuting from the camp had a structure and inevitability that wasn't available to me. I quickly checked myself: *I was so fortunate to escape and finish school.*

Soon the camp buzzed with life, a sea of seething humanity, its occupants valiantly setting about the activities that would get them through another day. I closed my eyes and remem-bered the coal-fire smell and rich communal chorus of my childhood. I craved a quiet place to pray, and found a spot under a *kworo*, a large tree with a sweet fruit like a fig, where I sat down with my legs crossed and bowed my head. *Please make this whatever you want it to be, God. Show me what I am going to do, what I will make of this life. Please give me the strength to be here and to do this work.* I was so thankful that in the middle of so much loss, my faith had flourished and grown. I was an instrument in God's hands.

The following morning, I gathered some of the commu-nity and church leaders under the same tree and told them about the vision I carried in my heart for the young girls. 'I have seen how God will bring these girls back to life, like fresh green shoots,' I told them, relating my dream.

There were ten at the first meeting, including Florence Komakech and Bishop Ochola, who had survived through the Amin era, when his Anglican archbishop and other bishops had been put to death. Bishop Ochola was a man of integrity, a respected elder and custodian of our Acholi culture—everybody listened to his words of wisdom. He understood our pain—and the pain of the abducted girls—as he had had more than his fair share of trauma. He had lived through his wife's death, caused by a landmine, just five years before, as she travelled from her village to Kitgum in a minibus with a group of women from the Mothers' Union.

Gabriel's eldest daughter, Faith Lajul—who had been a young girl when we first escaped from Pader—joined us on that first day. She had grown into a beautiful, smart young woman, with strong ideas on how to help the girls. Faith was as close as a sister to me, and the first to encourage me on this path of working with girl mothers.

The first girls we gathered under the *kworo* tree could not meet my eye. Several were pregnant or clasped babies in bare arms. They sat in silence, their faces empty of expression, gazing at the ground. My nerves almost tripped me up, too. My pulse raced as the weight of what I was doing pressed down. *What do I say now?* I coaxed my memory into action. My mind ticked through some of the things I'd learned in my training. 'What is one good thing about today?' I asked in a quiet voice, sitting up straight as I looked at the down-turned faces around the small circle.

The youngest in the group, a girl named Josephine who was just thirteen years old, cleared her throat to answer. 'I am happy that my baby is healthy.' She looked at the new baby she cradled in her arms, and her face softened.

This emboldened others, who shared small and large

mercies: one was relieved to have escaped her captors, while another was happy to have found family members on her return. One was thankful just to be alive.

I stepped up my questioning as the girls responded, hiding my dismay at their stories behind a professional veneer.

'I did not know I would have a baby. I could feel something in my stomach and some pain, but I did not know it was a baby,' Josephine shared with the group. I wiped away a tear on my cheek as I realised that Josephine had not even started her monthly cycle when she fell pregnant to a rebel.

The flow of stories slowed. I looked at the girls around me and saw how much it had taken from them to share. 'Let us meet here at the same time tomorrow,' I said, trying to sound upbeat, though I was also tired. We met daily after that, under the wide span of the *kworo*, removed from the clutter of huts. I sat with them, my arms open, my heart receiving them. I pulled out a Bible that I had been given in Kampala—the only one any of us had—and read the words in which I had often found comfort: 'For I know the plans I have for you, plans to prosper you and not to harm you, plans to give you hope and a future.' They came from the Book of Jeremiah. As I spoke, several of the girls wept. At the end, I raised my hands and smiled, trying to lift the mood. 'But this is good news, girls,' I said.

'It is hard for us to believe that,' one replied. Still, at the end of the session the mood among them was lighter.

Every day, I sat with the girls like a mother, as if by a fire, peeling an emotional onion one layer at a time. Each layer was deeper than the last, revealing more of the crippling pain of abuse, and the fear of what lay ahead for a teenage mother in the middle of a war.

'The day the LRA came to my village I tried so hard to run but I could not escape them.'

'My mother was beaten with a gun.'

'They killed my parents in front of my own eyes.'

'They forced me to go with them, and I was given to a man who was forty.'

'I was forced to be his wife. I was only thirteen years old.'

I bit my tongue to stop myself from crying. *You must be strong for these girls. Crying will not help them*, I silently counselled myself. Sometimes, I wanted to cheer at their cleverness. I heard their stories of escape, how some had taken an opportunity to run away while the government forces and LRA fought bitterly. How they had travelled through the bush for days without water or food, not knowing if they would be recaptured. How, when they arrived at the IDP camp, they were fearful of how they might be received, as Joseph Kony and his LRA commanders had spread propaganda that children returning from the war would be killed on sight.

Late one night, a mortar shell fired from the outer edge of the camp found its way right into the heart of the huts, landing beside EY and Florence's place, where I slept. The rebels knew where the district chairman lived—killing him and his family would be a valuable prize. Within moments of the mortar landing, the neighbouring hut was ablaze and the air filled with the screams of its inhabitants. I grabbed a plastic jerry can of precious water and ran towards the flames that now skipped across the surrounding rows of thatch. I joined dozens of others who were ferrying their cans from hand to hand until the flames were finally contained in the small hours of the morning. The fire had been a distraction:

as the soldiers joined in to fight the fire, the rebels snatched dozens of children from the outer rim of the camp.

The next morning, I plodded through the camp to the *kworo* tree, tired and war weary, while around me I heard the wails of inconsolable mothers. The girls were unsettled and frightened. I put my arms around each girl as she arrived. On days after an attack, I prayed more fervently and willed myself to stay composed.

'What if they take us again?' one asked me.

'They will not take you,' I reassured her, knowing that my words were hollow that day.

Day after day I went to the same tree, the numbers swelling from the original forty into the hundreds. The first girls were growing stronger by the day. 'Today I am feeling better. At least I am able to wake up in the morning and talk with you,' one of the girls said as she opened up in the daily devotional meeting. This was all the encouragement I needed to wake early and gather a group of girls the next day.

Before long, the meeting place under the tree became a reception centre for returning children, though it was just an open space with a mud and grass thatch hut like every other dwelling in the camp. The counselling of girl mothers was extended to include abducted boys, tapping into the deep need within the community.

There were no other services for the children. In 2002, hospitals in the district had closed, and daily ambushes meant that outsiders could not deliver medical supplies. Most international non-government organisations working in the north had evacuated their staff. World Vision had withdrawn from Pader after an ambush on one of their vehicles, the United Nations had also withdrawn, and the

World Food Programme was not yet supplying the camps. UNICEF, the Red Cross and Médecins Sans Frontières came later, in 2005. We had to work with the few resources that we could muster among our own people.

One day, as I sat with my team for the morning meal, an older woman approached, cradling the smallest of babies. Her face wore deep lines of distress, and her eyes were clouded. I put down my plate and moved towards her to see a perfectly formed baby boy, his hand the size of a coin, but very still. I stepped back, recoiling at the thought of being handed a dead baby.

'His name is Opiyo. He was born eight weeks too early,' the woman said as she passed the baby into my arms. 'He is still alive, but will not be able to live much longer.' The woman clasped her hands as though begging. 'Madam Alice, can you please talk to my daughter? She threw her baby away—she does not want it. Please help us.'

'Bring your daughter here,' I instructed the mother, who strode back to her hut and returned with her daughter. The girl, whom she called Min Opiyo—mother of baby Opiyo—looked no more than fourteen years old. When I saw the age of the girl, I sighed. I could understand why she might abandon her baby, even if feeding was no problem. It would be a hard road ahead for this teenage girl. Even in the reception centre, there was not so much as a milk supplement that might relieve the pressure to feed.

'I do not want this baby,' she told me, looking into my eyes with a determined expression. 'This baby is ruining my life.'

'Please try to feed this baby, or it will die,' I spoke in a firm voice, gently transferring the newborn back to his mother's arms. I looked the poor girl in the eyes and saw the fear of a trapped animal—a young mother who could not accept that this newly arrived life she held in her arms was part of her own flesh.

With a sullen expression, she pulled open her ragged shirt. 'He can't take it,' she said, and we watched as the baby responded to the smell of his mother's milk in a flutter of open-mouthed quivers, and then fought to latch its tiny mouth around the girl's nipple. The milk flowed from the baby's mouth, dripping onto the soil in dark streaks.

'Let's try again,' I coaxed the young mother, so that she would keep going with her attempts to feed her baby. Finally, the baby attached himself onto the nipple, the first loud gulps settling to a gentler sucking rhythm as he won the first round of the fight to continue his tenuous life.

After that, I met many girls who rejected their babies for many reasons. The babies brought with them the memories of the way they were conceived: a reminder of forced sex and the cruelty of the father. The babies became the object of the girls' anger and shame. If a baby was sick, its mother often blamed it for the inconvenience and called it names. 'Oh, useless child, your father is in the bush, now you are here, you are sick and disturbing me,' I heard one day and decided to act. I could not sit by and see thousands of innocent babies discarded by their mothers. I sent a message through the social workers, assembling the young mothers within the woven grass enclosure we had built to allow some privacy.

I stood up to speak, shifting from one foot to the other as I gathered courage to approach this sensitive subject. I was unsure of how the girls would take my instruction when I had not come out of captivity with a baby myself.

'I have heard your stories, and I know you have suffered. It is true that most of these babies are not born out of love, but these babies are innocent—you should not take out your anger on them,' I told the girls, who listened intently. I saw a couple of the girls nod their heads, while others shifted their gaze to the baby in their arms. I turned away to let out a big, relieved breath. Their reaction emboldened me in my quest to bring further restoration into the lives of the girls, who had lost their self-respect and dignity in the months and years of slavery.

'Just because these things happened to you, it does not mean the end of you,' I encouraged them. I then explained the importance of forgiveness, and told them that this was how they could move on. It was a hard concept for them to understand. I told them how Jesus had sacrificed his life on the cross for their pain. 'Forgiveness is an act of your will. If you can make that sacrifice, it will bring you peace.'

'But madam, you do not know what I went through. This man arrived in the house out of nowhere, he just shoved me down and started using me, and I felt the pain so badly I didn't know what to do. I felt so bad that I cried all week,' one girl told me. 'These men should pay for ruining us.'

'Yes, there should be justice, but today and right here in this camp, with the LRA far away in Sudan and Congo, there may not be justice for many years. Right now, I am concerned for you and your children.' *Who would administer justice right now, even if a girl could overcome her shame and declare that she was sexually abused?* I kept this thought to myself. In the eyes of the Ugandan leadership, justice for the abuse of girls in war was not a priority while the conflict still raged.

My love for the broken girls grew by the day, especially for the most damaged, the ones that I knew had suffered the most. One of these was a thirteen-year-old girl called Irene, from the village of Paimol, who had arrived at the reception centre wounded and weak, with cuts on her hands from trying to protect herself from the *panga*, and with scars across her back from being beaten by a stick. She had spent just two months with the rebels in the bush, but when she escaped she had fought almost to the death. She arrived from the army barracks, where she had been taken after her escape.

I sat beside her, reaching out to place my hand lightly across her bony shoulder. She stiffened and leaned away, then turned to me with a face distorted by anger. 'Don't ask me what happened. If you want to know, go to the bush and find out for yourself,' she yelled, spitting out the words, before turning away. She found a corner and refused to talk, though each of the social workers tried hard to break through. She would not even speak to any of the other girls. 'My soap is finished, give me some more,' was the most the social workers squeezed from her. She would not even speak to people she knew from her village.

It was two months before she would speak, and this was only when her wounds—caused by the deep cuts of the *panga*—had become so seriously infected that she needed medical treatment. When Ketty, one of the social workers, helped Irene find relief from the infection, she started to build trust with the girl, and Irene began to reveal her story.

She sat calmly and stared at the ground. 'There was a boy in the village that I wanted to marry when I was older, but then the LRA came and I was given to a commander,' she told Ketty. 'He already had a wife. I was not going to be his wife. I fought him whenever he tried to force himself on me.' One day, she fought so hard that she overpowered the commander, but he was able to call for help from other men in the camp. 'They gave me fifty strokes of the whip across my back. After ten I could not stand, but they kept going until they thought I was dead, and then they left me on the ground to die.'

Afterwards, she could not sit up or stand. Hatred seethed inside her, and in her mind she saw herself taking the commander's gun and using her last energy to shoot him. 'My friends carried me back to the hut and hid me from the commander. They helped me stay alive.' Irene's friends told her to escape, as the rebels would kill her if they knew that she had survived. After dark that day, she crept out of the camp and, after walking for many days—in fear of being recaptured, and without food or water—she stumbled into the Pader camp and was helped by the local community. As was usual when children escaped from captivity, she was taken to the army barracks to be questioned about her time with the rebels, but she remained silent. This is how Irene came to the reception centre, so damaged and unable to talk about what she had been through.

'I cannot believe one human being can treat another so badly. How can someone who should be like a father be so evil?' Irene said. After many months of counselling, we were able to reunite Irene with her family. She had been in captivity for a shorter time than other girls, but her anger and shame had swelled, just as her pregnant belly grew, keeping her from fitting back in.

One day I called Ketty into the hut that we now used as an office, to talk about new ways we could help the girls. A tall, light-skinned young woman from Lira, Ketty had trained in Kampala and was the most experienced of the social workers. We'd both observed the range of the girls' responses, which were as varied as their personalities. Some retreated from people, while others embraced freedom; some fitted back into the community, and others were isolated.

'It seems that the older girls, who were with the LRA for five or ten years, find it easier to come home,' Ketty reflected, perplexed. 'Do you think they have managed their anger and learned to look after themselves?'

'Yes, they are certainly strong, the older girls. In the bush, they would tell the commanders what they wanted and needed, and the commanders seemed to listen,' I said. I was proud of these strong girls. 'They are survivors. When they return, they are grateful to be free and don't want to waste any more time being angry.'

When Ketty left, I slumped into my chair. These cases had so many twists and turns, it made my head hurt. Nothing in my training had covered this. I sat for a long time, thinking through some of the inconsistencies. I had been surprised that the girls returning from the LRA were better nourished than the girls in the camps. Then it dawned on me: the girls in the LRA had been sent to steal millet and *simsim* from starving villagers.

I also pondered how to help the *mothers* of the girl mothers, who may have accepted their daughters back, but faced being ostracised by angry neighbours. Just in the last week, we had received a girl with two children, who had been abducted at the age of eleven. Her own mother could not handle the fact that the child she had lost was now a mother herself. She could not stand to see her daughter as a mother, to know that she had not been able to prevent this from happening, to hear the terrible names her daughter was called, or to perceive that her grandchildren were offspring of the rebels. Her grief overwhelmed her, and one day she hanged herself from the roof frame of the family's tiny hut, leaving the young mother—barely into her teenage years—alone to raise the children. *What will come of this girl now, without her own mother to help her?* I sat in silence and prayed. *God help her.*

*

The trickle of children returning from the LRA became a flood as the battleground moved closer to the town. The government soldiers had nowhere else to take them in Pader district, and soon we became responsible for dozens of unkempt—sometimes sick and broken—boys and girls who had escaped or been freed in battle. Each week, girls arrived from the bush days after giving birth, unwashed and smelling, with infections. Some were so undernourished that they had not yet produced milk.

Often the boys were angry and resentful at being brought back from the front line. It wasn't long before rival factions emerged, aligned with the different rebel commanders. A culture of hatred was emerging in our reception centre, when we were trying to rebuild the children with love. 'What are we to do?' I cried out one night, my head in my hands.

David Otema—a wiry man with a wide smile and sparkling, kind eyes—was a young Anglican catechist who was training for the ministry at the small church near the reception centre. He had watched from a distance as we received the children coming back from captivity, and saw how we struggled with some of the wilder ones—the boys in particular. One day, he arrived at the hut door to introduce himself. 'Alice, can I help you care for some of the children?' he offered. I wanted to hug him. He was just the father figure that the children needed: his manner was gentle and his love so genuine that he was soon our best helper.

One thirteen-year-old rebel who had been captured in battle came back so wild and full of rage that he could barely be contained. He fought with every person who tried to talk with him, and had to be under guard at the reception centre.

'Let me go right now! I want to leave this place and return to the bush,' he screamed when David attempted to find out why the boy was so agitated. His hair was unruly and full of seeds; his eyes were wide and red around their rims. He was a product of the brutal LRA tactic of the forced choice: kill or be killed. Making a boy murder his own mother was a sure way to break his spirit and turn him into a heartless killer.

'Why do you want to go back to the bush?' David asked the boy, who carried scars and wore bandages on his legs from the fierce battle that had brought him back to Pader.

'I was promised a high position under my commander,' he said, turning away. 'I would still be there if they had not caught me.' David nodded his head and put his hand on the boy's back. Of course, to a powerless boy the promise of power was a strong motivator. Some of the most senior LRA rebels had risen through the ranks this way. But most boys were just fodder, sent to the front line of fighting to be mowed down or maimed.

Even the other children found him difficult. One day, a crowd of agitated boys and girls surrounded the young rebel, with sticks in their hands, yelling at him. 'You're a devil, and we're going to beat you to death,' one screamed.

'You don't deserve to be here,' called another as he picked up a rock and closed in on the boy. They had been expertly trained in hatred in the bush, and today—despite the love and care they were finding in the reception centre—they wanted this boy and all that he stood for to be dead and buried, so that they would not be reminded of the lives they had escaped.

David strode into the middle of the group with his hands held high to signal submission. 'Stop right now,' he demanded. 'Do you really have the right to take away another person's life?' The group was soon silent, heads bowed in shame.

'Instead of killing, let us pray for this boy,' he said quietly. He approached the cowering boy and placed his hand on the boy's shoulder, a gentle response when the boy anticipated retribution. Then he uttered a quiet prayer. 'In the name of Jesus, we ask for release from the bondage of fear and hatred for this boy.' Soon the other children joined in, asking that the boy be freed from all the torment and anger he had brought with him from his days in the bush.

After that, David held a privileged place among the children: that of peacemaker, spiritual counsellor and father to many boys and girls who were fatherless. Prayer was also how he handled the nightmares that so many of the returning children grappled with each night, when their screams at the horror of reliving a deadly battle, or seeing themselves kill another child, rang throughout the compound. He sat patiently with them through the night until their agitation turned to peace, and they could face the day calmly.

In the daylight hours, the returned children faced the taunts of some in the community who despised them. The children paid for the atrocities committed by the rebels. When they stepped outside the reception centre, the names flew like arrows: rebel, murderer, abductor, whore . . . and a long list of others.

'I'm so scared of these people in the camp,' one girl told David. 'They want to kill me.'

'Stay strong. They will not harm you—they are angry at the war,' he reassured her. I grew angry at the war, too, but I kept it to myself. Every day, people in the camps died of simple and preventable illnesses such as malaria and diarrhoea, and from bullet wounds inflicted during ambushes—illnesses and injuries that easily could have been treated if there were doctors. One hospital still operated in Kalongo, two hours away by road, but it was risky to reach, even with a military escort. A truck could take a sick person towards Kalongo, and return with two dead bodies from an ambush. I grew weary of the endless stream of children arriving, some of whom had been abducted so young that they did not remember where they came from, and I became tired of scouring the camps to locate their families.

Yet I drew hope from the people around me in the camp, who still believed that tomorrow would come, that one day the war would end and they would resume their lives. Each morning, the fear and suspicion of the night before disappeared with the rising sun. I absorbed the hope around me as I walked through the camp each morning on my way to the reception centre. At times my mood seemed to be attached to nature: my spirit grew smaller on the dull, foggy days, and inflated with overwhelming confidence when I rose to see a blue sky. On these days, I would not have been anywhere else.

17

Hidden in the Bush

The girls continued to confide their secrets, about conceiving under force and giving birth in the bush. A timid young woman named Prossy shared her story during group counselling. She told us how, for the first three months of her pregnancy, she had to keep up with her LRA group each day, which was constantly on the move near the Sudan border, staying ahead of the government soldiers.

'Every day there were attacks, and there was fighting around us, and every day we walked long distances and joined raids on villages to steal food. I bled constantly and thought I would surely lose my baby,' Prossy had told the group in a whisper, twisting her hands as she spoke. I wanted to cry as I listened to Prossy that day, but I couldn't allow those floodgates to open. Instead, I took a deep breath and opened my heart as if to absorb the girl's pain. In Ugandan culture, even mothers rarely cry in front of their children. To see Madam Alice, as they called me, crying and broken would have been too discouraging for the girls, and it might have started a flood of their own tears. That thought galvanised me. *If nobody helps them, these girls will live in a state of trauma, and their babies will have no chance in life*, I reminded herself when I thought I might break.

'At three months, I collapsed to the ground with the bleeding. The rest of my group left me to die,' Prossy told the attentive girls sitting in a circle around her. They willed her to keep going, to purge her tale so it would no longer be a dark secret. She brightened momentarily as she told them how some local people had found her and given her a herb that, when mixed with water, could stop the bleeding.

'For one week I lay alone, taking the medicine every day until the bleeding stopped. In that week I told myself, "This baby will survive, this baby will survive," until I believed it.' The other girls leaned in to hear more. Each of them could picture the terrain; they knew the agony of swollen legs and battered feet, and the loneliness of being lost a long way from home. 'My baby kept me alive. I had to stay alive for my baby, even for those days I was all alone,' Prossy said, scooping up her naked daughter from the ground, where she had been crawling, and squeezing the baby against her chest.

She then picked up her story again. After three days, she came across a group of wounded rebels. Her own group, including the commander to whom she had been given as a wife, had moved far away. She stayed with the wounded group for months, until the racking pain of contractions told her it was time. Then, having never even seen a delivery, she left the camp, without so much as water, food, tea or any medication, and endured labour alone. Her bones were not yet fully formed, and unready for such pressure. Prossy had screamed from the rupture of unknown parts, with only the vultures circling above to hear her cries. 'I didn't know what to do, how to push, or how hard. I was so scared on my own,' Prossy said, shrinking back, as if to make herself small. She had exposed herself enough.

I stared past her to the rows of crowded huts of the camp. I could feel a hard knot of anguish in my stomach. It was so unfair. The children we received had been discarded like debris in this brutal civil war; they were the innocents without whose enslavement it could not have been waged.

I still sat down each morning under the weeping branches of the *kworo* tree to pray, as I had from the start, knowing that this was all I could do to gather strength and deal with my growing anger at the depravity around me. Prayer was my release after a twelve-year-old girl arrived one day, unable to sit, with a trail of urine leaking behind her from chronic syphilis. Prayer was my safety valve after the girls told me the rules around menstruation in the more permanent LRA camps. I heard how rebel leaders told the girls, 'You are unclean at this time. You must not touch any common food or utensils, or sleep in the same bed as your husband. You must stay in your hut, and you will be beaten if you break these rules.'

I hated the thought of a man's ownership of a girl's body, and of a girl being allocated as the wife of an older man as soon as her monthly cycle started. The bleeding itself—*Am I dying?*—was bewildering enough for a young girl without the violation that followed.

I knew that the boys had also suffered. Boys had been raped, made to rape and kill, and made to trudge like pack-horses for days. But I wondered whether there might soon come a time when the sheer numbers would overwhelm me, and I would have to focus my efforts on the girls, leaving the boys to others.

*

Around this time top-level meetings were held to discuss how to make peace with Joseph Kony or how to shut down the LRA, but few people knew the depths of the human tragedy in the north, even within our own country. Dangerous roads and physical isolation had made our plight mostly invisible to the world. For months I struggled to provide the most basic food, relying on an inconsistent supply of *posho* from the soldiers to feed the children. Then every three months, small amounts of relief food—beans, flour and cooking oil—started arriving through the World Food Programme. It wasn't until representatives of USAID and UNICEF turned up two years into my work with the girls that we found a way out of our constant hunger. Our board had decided to formalise the work by 2002, taking the name Christian Counseling Fellowship (CCF) for our community-based organisation (CBO). Later, CCF would be registered as a national non-government organisation.

Cornelius Williams was a child-protection specialist from Sierra Leone who ran the UNICEF office in Kitgum. He arrived one day in a dust-encrusted white four-wheel drive with the recognisable black UN letters barely visible on its side. He stepped out of his vehicle, adjusting his balance after being jogged from side to side on the rough road. It gave him a moment to take in the children in rags and how undernourished they were, and he paused to gather his thoughts. 'What supplies do you have?' he asked, his brow furrowed as he walked through the reception centre.

'We only have soap,' I replied. I shuffled my bare feet nervously. I had not dealt with many officials from outside the district and did not want to say the wrong thing.

He shook his head and muttered, 'It shouldn't happen in this country.' I could tell that he was shocked by what he found in Pader.

After he had talked with the social workers and some of the girls, Cornelius sat down with a pen and paper, and started to scribble out his recommendations. 'I'll send you a satellite phone so you can tell us what is happening in the district,' he offered as a parting gesture, before jumping back into his four-wheel drive and taking off in the direction of Kitgum.

'Lord, keep him safe,' I whispered as I watched him go. That night as I lay on my mat to sleep, relief flooded through my body like warm oil. Finally, help was on the way.

A week later, a UNICEF truck pulled into the reception centre, piled high with supplies and skirted by a military escort. The girls ran from every direction, squealing as the driver and his assistant unloaded bundles of second-hand clothing, long blocks of blue soap, brightly coloured mattresses and blankets, bags of rice and medical supplies. I cried as I stood and watched our world transform from dismal need to a celebration. My heart was so filled with gratitude that I thought it might burst. Someone cared.

As the driver prepared to leave, he handed me a box. 'Mr Williams asked me to give you this.'

I pulled out a big, black satellite phone the size of a clay brick, and nervously turned it around in my hands. 'What I am meant to do with this?' I laughed, trying to hand it back.

'Ask the boss. You can call him now,' the driver replied, hopping into his truck.

It was only a day before Cornelius made contact. 'Alice, can you tell us what is happening right now?' he had asked on the first day I answered the shrill call of the satellite phone to find him on the other end.

'There have been abductions in Patongo,' I reported. 'There were seventeen children involved.'

'Make sure you inform me when there are children in the barracks,' he demanded. UNICEF was concerned about children spending more than forty-eight hours there on their return from the bush. Some of the girls had reported that the soldiers were sexually abusing them, or interrogating them to find out about LRA movements. Even more worryingly, some were being sent back to help find the rebels.

'I certainly will, but I'll need to work out this phone,' I responded. I held the phone in front of me to take a closer look, before hearing a faint voice and quickly returning it to my ear.

'Never mind, I'll call you,' Cornelius promised. By early 2005, he was calling at least twice a day for updates on what was happening in the camp, where the rebels were, and on which roads the ambushes had taken place. For almost a year, until MTN, the South African mobile phone network, set up a mobile-phone network in the north, the crackling line of the satellite phone was possibly the only point of contact between the district of Pader and the outside world.

Every day, I trudged up the hill from the IDP camp to the low brick buildings and tents of the military barracks. The barracks were high enough for the soldiers to occasionally sight groups of LRA rebels as they approached from the safety of wooded areas, and close enough to hear the steady low rumble of the people clustered below them in the camp.

The bored soldiers at the barracks gate greeted me civilly, waving me through security. I looked around the barracks for newly arrived children, and on the days I found them I strode into the office of the commander to get answers.

'What is the problem? Why are they still here? When are you going to release the children to the reception centre?' I demanded, rudely forthright for a woman in our culture. I had a sense of being commissioned for this, built for this time, and was not about to back down. Most days I was received favourably: the soldiers were cooperative and helpful. But as my contact with outsiders grew, some of the soldiers became belligerent towards me. They were angry that I was telling people outside Pader what was happening in the barracks.

One day when I visited the barracks, a soldier grabbed the camera that I held in my hand, which UNICEF had given to me to help with reporting. He held it high and prepared to smash it to the ground. 'Stop! Why are you doing this?' I yelled, grabbing the camera.

'You are reporting on us,' he replied. 'UNICEF called and complained to our commanders that we are mistreating the children.'

'I'm only reporting what I see on the ground. In any case, when the children get out from here, they will tell everyone what is happening anyway,' I told him. 'They are telling me everything right now when they leave the barracks.'

Back at the reception centre, I picked up the satellite phone to call Cornelius. 'Do not believe them if I am shot and they blame it on the rebels,' I warned, as crude insurance.

'They will not harm you, or everyone will know what they are doing,' he reassured me. After our satellite calls, Cornelius wrote reports advocating for the children.

When outside support came, it came thick and fast. It was still too dangerous for UNICEF people to travel frequently to Pader, but one day a military helicopter descended into a clearing near the reception centre, disgorging two women from UNICEF and a group of high-profile people from the United Nations, who, like Cornelius, talked with the girls and then visited the commander at the barracks. Soon afterwards, in May 2005, the country head of UNICEF, a Kenyan named Martin Mogwanja, arrived in a fleet of UN four-wheel drives with a military escort.

This was not a symbolic visit. It was a risky mission—one that made the pages of the Kampala newspapers—as a military escort did not ensure a safe journey in northern Uganda at that time. The UNICEF country director came ready for action. 'We will stand with the children of northern Uganda,' he declared. He met with the staff and children at the reception centre, with district leaders and with military commanders.

'Let us talk about what you need to do your work,' he said, when we retreated under the mango tree at the reception centre to get into the details. 'We will send two big tents. One can house the girls, and the other the boys.'

'Yes, and could we also build some grass-thatch huts to provide shelter for the girl mothers after they give birth? They will need privacy and a place to rest, and we can take care of them. There is nothing for them in the camps,' I ventured. The whole day was like a dream to me.

Before the delegation left, the list had grown to securing the food supply and medical care, and to hiring a vehicle to reunite the children with their families. There was even provision to send the children home with a small amount of money—50,000 Ugandan shillings, around US$20—to start a small business or for the girls to buy personal-hygiene materials, such as sanitation pads. My hand shook as I signed a memorandum of understanding for almost US$100,000 in assistance. My team was now right at the heart of the reunification process, and on side with the military, who agreed to immediately release any children they captured. An unexpected inclusion was staff wages. After three years of unpaid work at the reception centre, I could now afford a small stipend for myself and the staff; I also hired five local social workers and brought Sister Margaret from Gulu to train them and help manage the girls' counselling. Other non-government agencies followed UNICEF, with the World Food Programme (WFP) soon arriving with a shipment of supplements for the mothers and babies.

'Thank you, Mr Mogwanja, for putting your life at risk to support us,' I said as I stretched out my hand to farewell the man who had saved our lives.

'I hope you will come to Kampala soon to speak to OCHA,' he replied.

'I will come,' I said. I wanted the world to hear first-hand reports, and the UN's Office for the Coordination of Humanitarian Affairs (OCHA) was the best possible avenue. The news reaching the south was mostly based on rumour and speculation. Even journalists had not been able to gather news from Acholiland.

Having support made me bolder and more determined not to be intimidated. 'Maybe we could get together?' a rogue soldier said with a leer when I visited the barracks soon after the UN arrived.

'I'm not here to be dated, I'm here to work,' I bit back at him with a ferocity that surprised me.

Soldiers came to the reception centre, too, guns slung by their sides, looking for children to question about the movements of the rebels. On these occasions, I met them at the makeshift gate, standing tall, holding my hand up to indicate that they could go no further. 'Firstly, if you want to enter this place, you must get rid of your guns and change into civilian clothes, and then you can come in to discuss this with me,' I said. 'Secondly, you cannot ask the children where the rebels are hiding. These are my rules. These children have been through enough.'

The rumours soon started; I heard them through my friends: 'Some people think that you are too close to the soldiers. They say that maybe you find favour in the barracks because you are sleeping with soldiers.' At this, I threw up my arms in disgust. The rumours were too absurd to give them oxygen. Especially when a door had now opened to tell the world of the children's suffering. I wondered if they came from the disgruntled soldiers themselves.

I was jittery as I climbed onto the truck for the journey south for meetings with OCHA, more nervous than when I had arrived in Pader to start my work three years ago, when the adrenaline pumping through my veins had made me feel so wholly alive. We left Pader one morning while it was still dark, in case we were held up on the way, as we had to make it past the game reserve within Murchison Falls National Park—notorious for ambushes—before the five o'clock evening curfew.

I had hours to think about what I would share with the people in Kampala—and hours to worry. Would my presentation do justice to the people I represented? Could I do it without breaking down? CCF Pader was still the only organised community group in the district, and my satellite phone calls the most reliable information, but would I be able to tell the children's stories? As we approached Karuma—the Nile River crossing where northern Uganda ended and I would head over to the south—I saw loose lines of grim-faced mothers and fathers with children on foot, carrying all their worldly goods, waiting to cross to the refugee camp on the southern side of the Nile River. I leaned my head against the truck's metal side. It saddened me to see my own Acholi people so poor that they did not have a few shillings to cross the Nile to safety on the back of a truck, as I did.

Soon the truck rumbled past the edge of the game reserve—now stripped of elephants, lions and any other living creature that the rebels could hunt for food—and my mind concentrated on my surroundings. *Will I even make it to Kampala?* I became aware of where we were and started to sweat. Anything could happen on this road. The game park allowed the rebels to hide in vast tracts of vacant land. My breathing quickened, and I glanced at the faces of my co-travellers to gauge their level of anxiety. The woman slouched beside me seemed calm enough.

I recalled how five years earlier this had been the scene of one of the most ambitious and devastating ambushes ever launched by the LRA, in which the rebels had used petrol to burn a convoy of more than a hundred buses, trucks, minivans and cars, then killed or abducted their occupants. The child soldiers, trained as fearless guerrilla fighters, had positioned themselves in the trees to kill before the government soldiers could see them. The government retaliation had been thorough: boys without identification could even now be detained and tortured, sometimes never seen again, even if they travelled with their mothers.

By the time I made it into the UN offices in Kampala five hours later, I had recovered my courage. I stood up to address a room full of humanitarian workers, some of whom I had met in Pader. 'We are completely isolated, and people are in a hopeless state. They think nobody in the world cares for them. People are dying in the hospital without treatment, there is no food, and people are being killed or abducted by the LRA as they look for food.' I laid it all out for them, sparing no detail of life in the camps and the stories of the children returning from the rebels. 'Mothers have children dying in their arms with treatable sicknesses, babies are dying during delivery from simple complications. We are unable to improve our own lives.'

At the end, there was silence. When I looked at the room of solemn faces, I wondered if I had gone too far. But it was the silence of deep thought, and afterwards many people came to me individually to ask questions.

In the year that followed, I travelled once every month or two to attend an OCHA meeting, as information was best passed on in person. Each time I travelled, I felt well protected—the depth of my passion and my mission for our people outweighed any fear. Only once did I encounter a burnt-out bus beside the road.

In Kampala, the war seemed like a distant irritant to Ugandans that I met outside the OCHA group, many of whom had suffered through the years of Idi Amin. In the south of Uganda, parents also struggled to feed their children and find medical care, so there was not much thought for what was happening in Acholiland.

The tension between life in the camps and the indifference in the south brought me to breaking point. I was too busy to entertain thoughtless questions.

'How is Kony now?' someone innocently asked me on one visit, as if I knew him personally.

I snapped, like an angry young girl from our counselling group. 'Why don't you just go to the north and find out for yourself?'

Another simple question—'How is your life there?'—brought a similar response.

'The situation is the same. What have we done so far that would make any difference?' I answered, waving my hand.

Whenever I visited Kampala, I stayed there for the shortest time possible before making the long journey home to Pader.

'Alice, you do not have to return to the war,' a kind foreign official offered after one meeting. 'I can arrange for you to get a visa to live in the UK, and you can continue your studies.'

I nodded and smiled, but stood firm. 'I came to tell you what is happening, and I must return to the north. The children are depending on me.' I could feel a sickening knot of anxiety rising in my belly at the thought of abandoning the two hundred or more young people who relied on me for food.

The next day, I climbed back onto the military truck for the return journey.

PART TWO

RESTORING

18

Ambushed

By January 2005, I had lived for more than two years right in the heart of the IDP camp, sharing the hut of Florence, EY and their extended family. They had become my family, too. As more children arrived at the reception centre—as more girl mothers returned from captivity—it became harder to separate myself from the stories of the returning children, and harder to process all I heard.

'Please leave me alone,' I had snapped one night when a child had crawled onto my lap, seeking attention as we sat around the fire. I looked at Florence's alarmed expression and wanted to snatch my harsh words back. 'Sorry,' I muttered. I knew it was time to move.

I found a single room, the size of a stable, in one of the new mud-brick buildings that were being slapped up in a hurry near the main thoroughfare of Pader, as international aid groups and government agencies clustered around the war zone. The room was just large enough for a bed, a table and one plastic chair, and opened onto a small verandah where could I store utensils and a gas stove for cooking.

'This will be fine,' I told the owner, setting my jaw in case he sensed my excitement and increased the rent.

For some moments after he left, I lingered in the doorway of my new home, a bundle of clothes under my arm. It was mine. Finally I had a dividing line in my life: a sturdy steel door secured with a metal rod inside that I could slide shut at the end of the day and a padlock on the outside for when I left the room.

I sighed, and leaned my head against the wall. Here, with a door strong enough to withstand bullets, I felt secure. Here, I could retreat into my own thoughts, even if all my thoughts were consumed with life in the camp, where my responsibilities to the girl mothers and their babies stretched me well beyond my capacity.

Several other people shared the row of single rooms, including the employees of a non-government organisation called ACORD, and a busy, slight woman named Nighty who crowded into one room with her seven children. Nighty's husband was a government soldier based in Kitgum, who had rarely come home to Pader over the past decade of the LRA war. Whenever he did, a baby soon followed. Nighty and I quickly became friends, and we were content to sit together in the cool evenings at the end of a sticky day before we prepared our evening meals.

'Do you think this war will ever end? I worry that my husband will never come home,' she shared with me one time, and I realised how much simpler my life was on my own. I often lay awake at night worrying about the girls in my care, but I did not have to ache for my husband or worry that he would die in battle in a distant part of the north.

The youngest of Nighty's children was a two-year-old daughter named Abalo, a sweet young girl who attached herself to me from the moment she awoke in the morning. I prised myself away each day to go to work; when I returned, the little girl was waiting for me, standing near the door with her stout legs and shiny unclothed body. I could not help growing attached to Abalo in all her innocence, often caring for her when her mother was busy cooking or foraging.

'Mama won't give me milk,' Abalo told me one day, her saucer eyes staring up at me from thigh height. Another day, she pointed to a sister she'd annoyed and cried, 'She hit me!' Nothing was too trivial to report to me.

At night, she curled up in my bed to sleep, and when it was my own bedtime, I gently carried her over my shoulder to Nighty's room. When I travelled away to Kampala, I returned with sweet treats for her, unable to meet her wide smile empty handed.

Early in November 2005, Nighty and I sat side by side on the verandah—I could tell by her tapping leg and bright eyes that she had news for me. 'My husband is back at the barracks in Kitgum, and I plan to visit him,' she said with a glowing smile.

'That is so good,' I replied. 'I will look after your children while you're gone.'

I had not met her husband, as he had been away for months and months on end, but she had often told me how she missed him. Her life as a single mother was difficult, with no respite from her daily struggle to feed her family. A soldier's wage did not go far.

The following week, I awoke early to a knock on my door. When I opened it, I found Nighty, wearing her finest dress and holding Abalo by her hand. 'I wanted you to know that Abalo is now coming to Kitgum with me this morning,' she announced.

'Are you sure? I thought you planned to leave Abalo with me. I'm happy to take care of her,' I immediately offered. Any of the girls at the reception centre would gladly look out for her. 'She can play with the other children.'

'Yes, I thought I would, but I will be gone until late and she will disturb you,' Nighty replied.

'I don't mind, she can stay with me,' I told her, shaking my head and reaching out for Abalo's hand. Abalo stepped towards me and wrapped her tiny arms around my legs.

Nighty pulled her back and looked at me with a serious expression. 'She should come or she will never know her father.'

It was decided. 'Ah, I understand,' I finally conceded.

We walked together out to the main road, making small talk about Nighty's plans for her time in Kitgum, and what she might bring back from the market there.

'Have a good visit. I will see you this evening and have some food for you when you return, even if it is late,' I offered. I watched as they climbed onto the crowded private minibus, crammed with a dozen or more people from the Pader town camp who, like Nighty, were all travelling to Kitgum for supplies, or to visit the bank, or to see relatives. Then I turned and wandered over to the office nearby to start my day's work at the reception centre. Within minutes, I was consumed with requests to sign papers, questions about the girls, appeals for meetings from visitors, and clan matters.

At ten o'clock in the morning, a boy arrived at the office, short of breath. 'There has been an ambush on the Kitgum

Road, just outside Pader,' he informed us. My mind went straight to Nighty and Abalo. I sat down at my desk, picked up my pen and rolled it around in my hand, trying to gather my thoughts. We were all so helpless when bad news came through. But I could not sit still or focus on work, so I hurried out of the office to find out more.

When I reached the main road, I saw a young soldier ambling along, his gun slung casually over his shoulder. I stood right in front of him, blocking his way. 'Have you heard news of the ambush?' I asked, trying to hide my anguish.

'I saw a vehicle on its way to the health centre, coming from that way,' he replied, pointing in the direction the van had travelled. *Oh no.* I felt a stab of panic. The news could not be good, as ambushes by LRA rebels always ended badly.

That day, Patrick, a South African who for many years had lived in Kitgum, happened to be in Pader district drilling water wells not far from the town. I caught sight of his truck parked on the street as I hurried towards the health centre. Patrick had helped us many times in the past, ferrying children in his armed four-wheel-drive truck to be reunited with their families in remote villages.

'There's been an ambush, and I think my neighbour and her child were involved. Can you please help me?' I pleaded, leaning into his open window. He readily joined me.

The health centre was just a simple room near the main road. I stepped through the doorway, my hand over my mouth and nose to keep out the smell of burned skin as I surveyed the scene in front of me. An old bed covered by a soiled sheet lay along one chipped wall, while rudimen- tary medical equipment and a single shelf of basic medicines and bandages sat alongside another. My stomach churned as I took it all in: charred bodies, bloodied bodies, those who had not made it. I looked for Nighty, but could not see her. Then I looked at the mounds in the corner, now covered by stained cloths, and wondered if Nighty might be among them.

It took me some moments in the dark room to see Abalo in the corner, her face screwed up in a howl, her body shaking. I walked over and fell to my knees, reaching out to comfort her as I had done so many times, but I could not hold her without making her pain worse. Parts of Abalo's body were burned to raw flesh, her skin melted, her stomach and face an unnatural red. I was both horrified and relieved: she was alive, the only survivor of the twelve or more passengers, I would later learn. I was at a loss to know what to do.

Patrick had survived as a foreigner in the war by making fast decisions and keeping his nerve. He was only steps behind me at the clinic and soon assessed the unlikelihood of anyone getting proper medical care. When he saw the little girl, he moved without hesitation, carefully lifting her, screaming, into his arms and then into the truck.

'C'mon. We'll go to Kitgum,' he called back to me, and I climbed up beside him, before he careened out of Pader in a cloud of dust, ignoring potholes and not waiting for the military to give him the go-ahead to travel on the road. All the while, I prayed that we would not encounter rebels on the way, though I was sure that if we did, Patrick would use the stand-up machine gun bolted to the back tray of his truck. I cradled Abalo in my arms, unable to soothe her pain.

On the way to Kitgum, we passed the scene of the ambush. The minibus was a smouldering, burnt-out wreck, and I could see by the blood and remnants of charred clothing the very places where the bodies had been left by the roadside. When the LRA had attacked, a local villager had been hiding in the bushes, fearful of being caught. He saw the whole ambush take place and later revealed what had happened. A swarm of armed rebels—children not even in their teens, with big guns—stepped onto the road in the path of the van. They ordered the passengers out of the minibus and murdered them one by one. They killed all but Abalo, who escaped their attention. The villager then watched as the rebels torched the van and the flames swept into the surrounding bush. Abalo was too young to understand the danger of fire, and just wanted her mother. When she reached the roadside and her mother was not beside her, she ran back into the flames near the van. The villager watched helplessly as the little girl pulled at her mother's clothes, crying for help.

When the man saw that the rebels were briefly distracted, he ran from his hiding place and rescued Abalo from the flames by putting her back on the roadside away from the burning van. Then he hid again, for fear of also being killed by the rebels, who were still nearby. For thirty minutes, Abalo stood screaming in pain before a soldier emerged from the bushes near the road and rescued her.

It was four o'clock in the afternoon, some six hours after I first heard about the ambush, when Patrick lifted a whimpering Abalo off my lap and carried her into the emergency room at the hospital in Kitgum. My heart sank. There had been other ambushes that day—there were other children near death, and adults with burns and bleeding body parts. But Patrick's imposing presence attracted attention, and we were ushered into a room ahead of others, to see a stressed-looking Italian doctor. He took one look at her burned body and started to sway before collapsing into a heap on the concrete floor.

A nurse ran to his side, turning to us briefly to explain. 'I'm sorry, but he has been here all night and is exhausted,' she said, putting a cool cloth to his forehead. He had also worked all day treating burn victims, as well as a baby who had arrived with its intestines visible and who had died soon afterwards. The nurse then began treating Abalo, though the hospital had none of the equipment to properly deal with burns, and pain relief was inadequate.

That night I stayed in the hospital, lying on the floor beside Abalo, worrying about what would become of her six siblings. Neighbours might care for them today, but what about tomorrow? I made a mental note to ask about Nighty's relatives. When the little girl woke in the morning, her face was so swollen that I thought she was going to die right then. The nurse came into the room and tended to Abalo. 'We have tested her, and she is HIV-positive,' she said, casually. I closed my eyes, bent on erasing the fear from my thoughts. In the car the day before, I had not hesitated to touch Abalo. The blood from her wounds had smeared across my hands and onto my arms. I shifted my attention back to her survival. I returned to work in Pader and visited Abalo when I could.

Patrick had ways of getting things done. After Abalo had been in Kitgum for a week, he marched into the hospital and told me, 'She's going to Gulu Hospital, where she'll receive better care. I've arranged a chartered plane to fly her there.'

It made sense, as Abalo had family in a village not far from Gulu, and they could care for her over the many weeks she would spend in hospital, and as she came through the danger of infection. Her father could not care for her, as he would have to keep fighting for as long as the war raged. I was not capable of caring for her—I had to return to work in Pader. I could not even visit her while rebel movements made the road to Gulu impassable. I cried as she was lifted into the ambulance bound for the airstrip, knowing her life would be hard, her scars painful, and that she would never return to the row of rooms in Pader. I later heard from friends in Gulu that she had been through months of skin grafts, and that she had been taken in by an aunt.

The ambush overshadowed every good thing that year—all the progress—making 2005 one of the worst years of the war for me. For many months after the ambush, I fell into my old thoughts, believing that this work in the north was too difficult for me, too unrelenting, and that it wasn't worth all the pain.

I felt the force of the community backlash soon after the ambush. Anger rose quickly among the families and friends of the victims, who had all come from the Pader town IDP camp. Shortly after the ambush, a young boy escaped from the LRA, arriving at the reception centre seeking protection. Word travelled quickly through the camp that the boy—barely in his teens—was part of the rebel group that had murdered the minibus passengers. A crowd gathered outside the reception centre, calling for the boy and other escaped children to be banished from Pader—or worse, killed.

'Let's burn the reception centre and hang the children!' one of the ringleaders yelled within earshot of the frightened children in our compound, who were just on the other side of the fence. Some people beat the air with their fists, while others waved sticks above their heads. The more noise the protestors made, the more their numbers swelled. They could easily push through the flimsy twig fence or our make-shift wooden gate.

'Please, run to the barracks and ask the commander to send help,' I said to one of the staff members, who slipped out the back of the reception centre without being noticed by the crowd. Twenty minutes later, soldiers arrived. They stood between the crowd and the gate, guns by their sides, and held up their hands to calm the crowd as I stepped out to speak with the angry people.

'Please go back to your homes. More violence will not help,' I pleaded. 'The children here are victims, too.' But my words only inflamed their anger, and as they swarmed like an angry bees' nest outside the reception centre, my bravado began to wane. I understood their anger. The images of the burnt-out minibus and a screaming Abalo were still raw in my mind.

'Yesterday, this child killed our people, and today he is back and you are providing food for him and keeping him alive,' yelled a woman I did not recognise. I kept my mouth shut, as I knew that some of what she said was right. When the minivan was attacked, it was the child rebels—the young boys who seemed barely big enough to lift the guns—who had been ordered to fight the UPDF soldiers who arrived on the scene. Senior rebels and commanders had directed the ambushes from a safe distance. The boys were dispensable—fodder—as rebel leaders could always capture and train more teenage killers. In the middle of our grief and anger, it was difficult to remember that these boys had been stolen from their families, forced to kill loved ones, and made to maim and mutilate strangers. In the beginning, they had not willingly participated in these kinds of acts. But I did not say any of this to the people gathered around me as I stood among the soldiers.

'I appreciate that you are angry, and understandably so. This is personal for me, too. I have lost dear friends as well, but the answer is not to hurt these remaining children,' I said quietly, trying to calm the mood. I did not want to make excuses for what the children were doing with the LRA, but I wanted to protect those who had found their way home and now had a chance to be reintegrated into their families. These young rebels had been captured or seriously wounded in battle, had surrendered to government soldiers, or been drawn home by a skerrick of conscience or a childhood memory. Some had to be extremely brave to return after all they had done under the influence of the LRA.

The incident prompted an intense dialogue between the district leaders, church leaders and community members to bring the crisis under control. Finally, after some weeks, the community settled back into its grim existence of hunger and grief.

*

Each week, more children returned to Pader, flown in—up to twenty at a time—on chartered Eagle Air planes, as the roads were too dangerous between Pader and the reception centres in Kitgum, Lira and Gulu. I would wait with the social workers at the end of the red-dirt airstrip on the outskirts of Pader for the plane to bump down the runway and swing around near where we stood. When the propellers finally came to a halt, a procession of solemn-faced children in oversized second-hand clothes would step nervously down the stairs. Their deadpan faces and hesitant steps reflected their trauma. They were uncertain of what to do, where to look and how to respond to the row of adults who lined up to greet them. Each had a plastic bag with all of his or her worldly goods, and a rolled-up foam mattress given to them by the group who had received them from the bush.

We tried to reassure them. 'You're very welcome back in Pader,' I told each young girl or boy as I shook an outstretched hand, or offered a hug, before they moved along the line to the UNICEF representative to be ticked off a list, and were then transported to the reception centre in a UN four-wheel drive. It was the end of one difficult journey and the beginning of another rocky road to recovery.

Working at AVSI in Kitgum for four years had been my first exposure to non-government organisations (NGOs) and foreign aid workers. I had seen how attuned many visitors were to our needs, and how willing they were to open doors to their networks outside northern Uganda.

Until 2005, Pader had been considered too dangerous for most aid groups to establish a support base, even as Gulu at this time was overrun with those doing relief and aid work. We had worked in isolation for three years, doing what we could without financial or other resources. Yet slowly, it was becoming more secure around Pader, and we sensed that there was growing support from outsiders. When they came, they were surprised at how many people were still in IDP camps, and that the government was not acting quickly to improve living conditions. The CCF Pader reception centre soon became the first point of contact for international visitors.

Small amounts of support kept us alive. One of our earliest outside friends was an American woman named Carol, who worked for USAID in other parts of Uganda. When she heard about our work, she was moved to make craftwork to sell to fellow expatriates living in Kampala, donating 50 per cent of her profits to CCF Pader.

My friends from AVSI brought milk and sugar to supplement the beans and *posho* from the World Food Programme in Kitgum. The WFP delivered food once every two months, but the reception centre often ran out before the next delivery arrived.

When we worked in isolation, my role was clear-cut. For those first three years, I had intense daily contact with the girls, at least fifty in the reception centre and up to one hundred and forty in the camp at any given time. From 2005, life shifted again. I found myself losing daily contact with the girls, and I missed it. As my role started to evolve, there was much more paperwork, administration and management of staff and supporters. I realised that the relationships I was building with foreigners would be a lifeline for us all. The difficult daily decisions, such as releasing the vehicle to take the children back into their villages when rebels could ambush them and abduct them once again, weighed heavily and kept me awake at night.

The only relief during this time was the news that sexual violence against girls had lessened in 2004 and 2005. The rebels had been too busy moving from district to district, and within ours, to set up more permanent camps where the girls might be abused daily.

David Livingstone Okello, the young pastor who—along with his wife Cathy—had cared for me during my time in

Kitgum, became an important source of personal strength. His Australian employer, Irene Gleeson, had founded an organisation called Childcare International some years before. Childcare was also rescuing and educating young children who had escaped from the conflict or suffered in the camps, and had been doing so since the start of the conflict. Even when the road between Kitgum and Pader was at its most deadly, and when David struggled with his own past as an abducted child in the LRA and dealing with the many children in his care, he still came each weekend to pray with the children, and to offer advice and support for the work. UNICEF came to Pader once or twice a month, and sometimes I travelled back to Kitgum in their armed truck or on a chartered flight for a reprieve from the work. The Livingstone family home in Kitgum became my refuge, a place where I could rest. I was treated like their own child in their home, though they were not much older than me.

So much of what we were doing to help the girls in 2005 was experimental. The counsellors were inexperienced and underqualified, and they were all still learning the skills they needed to work through the complex issues thrown up by the returning girl mothers. In these sessions, I avoided bringing up negative memories of the war, which quickly distressed the girls. We introduced music, dance and storytelling, and in the process discovered that some of the girls were very good storytellers, as might be expected in a culture with an oral history passed down through the generations. We asked each girl to share a story from her childhood, or simply something she felt good about. Though we often sat in silence as the girls struggled to find one good thing about themselves to share, we usually broke through.

'I am happy that my feet were strong enough to bring me all these miles home.'

'I like the way my hair sits.'

It was enough.

The words of one girl stood out: 'I'm blessed to have this child because as hard as it is to have this child, sometimes when I feel lonely and I see her smile, I know that I am not alone. It makes me feel so good. I'm proud that I'm a mother, even if I'm young.' It delighted me that the young girl's positive thoughts about her child and being a mother spread like wildfire among the others. Maybe some of these innocent babies had a chance in life.

Towards the end of 2005, a research team came to northern Uganda from the Human Rights Center at the University of California, Berkeley, to interview the directors and formerly abducted children at seven reception centres in Gulu, Kitgum, Lira, Pader and Soroti; they were assessing the impact of the war on the children. I welcomed people when they came, but I never knew what to expect in support when they flew in and just as quickly flew out again, back to their peaceful countries. With my limited experience, I could not comprehend what their lives were like in the United States, or how a human-rights centre in faraway California came to be connected with the war in Uganda. On one such visit, I met the centre's director, Eric Stover, at the reception centre in Pader. During the course of our conversation, Eric asked me what I wanted most for the children. Without hesitation, I said it was to create a secondary school for the girls who had left the LRA with children and, for various reasons, were unable to return to school in their communities.

Armed with this information, Eric approached the president of the MacArthur Foundation and the head of its human-rights program, Mary Page, who, in turn, asked Eric to form a team to assess the needs of former child soldiers in northern Uganda. Months later, Eric returned to the region with Marieke Wierda of the International Center for Transitional Justice and Erin Baines of The University of British Columbia. In their subsequent report, Eric and his colleagues recommended that the MacArthur Foundation fulfil our wish and fund the establishment of an academy for young women who had escaped the LRA with their children.

The visit from this group of North Americans was a turning point for CCF. We could start to think about bringing education and training to the girls returning from the conflict or left in the villages. Eric Stover was in his early fifties at the time, a university professor who had investigated war crimes and worked with survivors in a number of countries. I came to value the connection and enduring friendship far more than any money Eric and his colleagues might bring. Their bright minds and caring hearts brought a boost of energy to CCF, and to me personally.

The researchers had already found that more than a quarter of the households in the IDP camps were headed by girls and women, so when the team came to the reception centre and I shared with them the vision for an educational facility and skills training centre for young mothers, the idea found fertile ground. I learned that the MacArthur Foundation saw the reception centre as a natural starting point for a pilot program to train girl mothers in income-generating activities. They were just as interested in academic pathways, and were able to offer fifty secondary-school scholarships.

This was the beginning of a series of relationships that would pave the way for girl mothers to be educated. I was relieved beyond words. It felt like rain had finally fallen on the seeds that we had been planting on behalf of the girls for the last three years.

CCF's main activity that year was reunification, the sensitive moment when an abducted child is reintroduced back into his or her own family and community. We could never just send a child back to the IDP camp without weeks of preparation. That would be too cruel, knowing that he or she could be ostracised, could be called a rapist or an abductor or a rebel, or could even be killed in retaliation.

First, a social worker visited the family and explained what they knew of the child's history with the LRA and the circumstances of their return. Then she gathered the elders of the community to discuss how this child might be accepted. By the time the official reunification came, the path had been smoothed as much as possible. On the day we took the child home, he or she arrived with a set of pots, basic cooking needs, sleeping mats and a bag of maize to share with the community.

Not all reunions were successful—often we still needed to intervene on behalf of the children. In some cases, if their families would not accept them, the girls came back to us. By now, a number of non-government organisations—UNICEF, World Food Programme, Save the Children, World Vision, War Child and Caritas—had returned to Pader to help. With the steady flow of children, we needed all the help we could muster.

By the end of 2005, my optimism had returned, and I felt hopeful that many more Acholi children would soon be home.

I only had to look around me to feel better. I remembered the dream that had awoken me all those years earlier—an old tree with brown leaves, a fallen tree without life, and the green shoots of fresh leaves growing out of the grey—and my skin tingled. I now saw life around me where there had been nothing—the girls alive with the promise of new friends and lives beyond the war—and I knew that I would press on.

19

2006: The LRA Retreats

As 2005 rolled into 2006, people in the camps were ready to explode in desperation for the war to end. Florence arrived at the reception centre one day, fresh from a meeting with government and military officials, sweating with the exertion of hurrying back in suffocating humidity. 'The government is starting new peace talks with Joseph Kony and the LRA commanders,' she said, panting, before breaking into a wide smile.

'Will they be held in the north?' I asked, head to one side, curious about how it would work. Maybe this time a solution was within reach, but I would not yet be swayed into a hopeful mood.

'No, the talks are to start in July in Juba, and the new government of South Sudan will mediate,' Florence explained. 'They've called a ceasefire.' South Sudan had also been through a long civil war, and peace talks had only recently brought a fragile autonomy. Previous talks between the Ugandan government and the LRA had limped along, mostly ending in walk-outs.

'I hope it works this time.' I studied the lines of Florence's war-weary face. She wanted peace badly, but never as much as the parent of an abducted child, who ached for their precious one to be returned, and who knew that every rebel ambush and every government victory left more children dead on the battlefield. The news of the peace talks brought an outbreak of cautious optimism, with ready smiles and bursts of thankful song among the women in the camp.

Early in the year, a delegation working on the peace process came to Pader from Kampala for a consultation with women in the IDP community. Like the young mothers I met with every day, the older women shouldered unimaginable pain: sons and daughters dragged from their own hands, the fortunate women receiving them back but broken. Each craved relief, eagerly leaving the tedium of daily chores to be with other women and hoping for the chance to voice her concerns. The Kampala team had arranged for plastic chairs, which they lined up in rows in a shaded clearing in the heart of the camp. The clearing soon overflowed with women who had questions to ask and who did not mind sitting on the hard ground once the chairs had been filled. They vied to be heard, their hands shooting up for attention; they called out questions, and shook their heads when they didn't like the answers. There was so much to say, and this was a forum to vent.

At the back, a woman as frail as a fawn—with a bulging belly—rolled to her side on the mat to stand, her friend standing first to pull her to her feet. She waited for a lapse in the discussion and then raised her hand to take her turn. Her voice shook as she spoke, her pain visibly raw as tears rolled down her face. 'Four of my children, a boy and three girls aged eight to fourteen years, are being held captive in an LRA camp,' she told the meeting, holding her pregnant stomach and trembling. 'I am pleading with you. We have all seen atrocities, but I am willing to forgive Kony and his fighting forces on condition that the child in my womb will never see abduction and torture.' Then she sat down, gently lowered by her friend, her shoulders heaving as the tears took hold.

The woman's words entered my heart like a switchblade—short, sharp and unexpectedly painful. In her desperation, this woman would overlook the suffering of her captured children, who had not been spared, to spare the one in her womb. Anything to end the suffering of the war and to raise her child in peace. The word *forgive* challenged me the most, uttered from the mouth of a woman whose heart was in fragments, a woman who, having lost four children, would surely not be expected to forgive. The meeting was silent now—the woman's words carried the weight of her own experience, and there was nothing more to add. *Our freedom depends on it,* I thought, a revelation so loud in my head that I looked around to see if anyone had heard me. I had known this, but in this moment I received it as a new understanding of the true cost of our freedom. If we could not learn to forgive, and in time to move on, we would be waging another type of war forever.

In recent times, the villages and camps around Pader had been overrun with rebels. There was more food for them to steal, fewer military than the more populous centres, and more scrub in which to run and hide. With a ceasefire and peace talks on the way, the LRA had agreed to withdraw its rebels from the district. It became the topic of every conversation in the camp and at the water point: the rebels will go.

They came out of their hiding places like white ants, a trail of untidy, uniformed men with AK-47s slung over their shoulders, marching nonchalantly along the side of the road that would lead them to the north-west. They were retreating into the wilderness of the Garamba National Park across the border in the Democratic Republic of the Congo—days and days, maybe weeks, of walking—while their most senior leaders headed further north to Sudan for the peace talks. The rebels had been brazen, some even hiding within the camps, and now they were equally defiant in their departure. We didn't know if they were going for good, or would be back if the talks failed.

Intrigued, I stood with the mothers and children near the reception centre to witness their retreat on the road out of Pader, my mouth agape. The crowd buzzed with a mixture of sadness and excitement. It was hard to be hopeful in the midst of so much loss. These talks were different to the others: they were to be held outside Uganda, with a 'referee' in the 'boxing ring', an adjudicator who could possibly mediate a fair outcome. I felt a spark of hope. *Could this be different?* I drifted with this thought, only to be pulled back by a shrill voice.

'They're taking the children with them!' a woman cried out, as a procession of hundreds of barefoot children with pots and bags of rice on their heads—human packhorses—passed by. I felt sick as I saw children—some pre-teens—being marched into the bush with the adult rebels. We had been sure the children would stay and we would be able to reunite them with their families. They would now be thrown into the negotiations as bargaining chips.

'Release our children,' someone called out as a group passed them.

'Let them stay,' another person shouted, and then spat on the ground in disgust.

'My son is with them,' I heard a mother scream, and turned to see a woman with her face skewed in pain, running behind the rebel group. The mother pulled her son away from the other boys, shouting, 'My child is not going, and if you want to shoot me for taking him, then shoot me.' She shepherded the young boy away, towards her home in the Patongo camp, planning to hide him until the rebels had left the district.

I discovered that soon after this, rebel emissaries found the mother. 'Where is he?' the rebels had questioned the mother at gunpoint, barging past her and dragging the hiding boy from the hut. 'You're coming with us.' His mother fell to the ground, inconsolable, and her wails rang out long after he had gone. While the LRA fought around the camps and villages, she had kept alive the hope that her son would make his way home, but now he was going far away, far from recognisable landmarks such as the Kalongo Hills in Agago district, which might have guided him home.

I seethed as the children left. Then I marched up the hill to the barracks. 'Where is the military commander?' I asked, then barged into his office. 'How can this be so? Why was there no provision made to allow the abducted children to stay?' I asked. 'They have been through enough.' I could feel my jaw tightening as I waited for his answer.

He shrugged. 'The LRA has negotiated safe passage for its rebels to cross over the Ugandan border into Congo, and that includes the children who were with them,' he replied. He remained unapologetic, fixed on his orders to allow the rebels to retreat with the child soldiers.

'It is negligent of the government to allow the children to go away again when they could have stayed in Pader district with their families,' I argued, but my words fell on deaf ears. Under the ceasefire agreement, parents had no power to protect their children. *How could outside negotiators, the government and all those involved in the peace talks allow this to happen?* I railed at anyone of influence who would listen, without effect, while the mood in the camps plunged to a new low. We were powerless to stop this injustice.

But the children were resourceful. Hundreds seized the opportunity to escape the LRA while on the march, arriving at the reception centre in large numbers during the weeks after the ceasefire, battered and bruised, emaciated and wounded. They returned with feet ripped by thorns, and they came shyly, carrying the heavy burden of their shame of being killers or teenage mothers, not sure of how they would be received. Most were unaware that the government had introduced an *Amnesty Act* in 2000, which exonerated children from prosecution for war crimes. Even so, and even after the ceasefire, the children faced interrogation at the barracks: Which commanders have you met, and where are they right now? Where do they plan to go next? How many were in your group? Did you ever see Joseph Kony? Mistrust built over twenty years did not evaporate with one announcement.

One day, a soldier arrived cradling a near-dead girl, her body limp and her arms like sticks on either side of her tiny frame. He presented her like a trophy to the social worker at the reception centre. 'I found her alone, lying under a bush. She was a long way from the road or any camps,' he explained. 'We found a group of girls that day. She must have been with them.'

'What is your name?' the social worker asked as the little girl's eyes fluttered open and then closed again. She was dehydrated and suffering from malnutrition, too weak to respond to the social worker and other adults who crowded around her.

She regained consciousness after the social worker had held her upright, tipped water into her open mouth and spoon-fed her some *posho*, but she did not speak to anyone for several days. 'She has appeared from the bush, so let's call her Atim,' one of the carers suggested. Atim was a name given to a person born out of Acholiland, or in the wilderness.

'Where is your family?' I asked when Atim was stronger.

'I don't remember,' she answered, then went quiet, her face troubled.

'Can you remember how old you were when you were abducted?' I asked her, trying to establish her age now. She looked to be twelve, maybe thirteen, but it was hard to tell.

'I was five and my sister was seven,' she replied. I had to look away. *Who would steal a girl at such a tender age?* It was unusual for the rebels to abduct a girl so young, one who could not walk far or quickly, and was so far from sexual maturity. But nothing surprised me in this war. Girls could escape after months, or spend a decade in captivity.

'And were you with a commander?' I was almost reluctant to ask for fear of what I might hear.

'Yes, I called him father. He was good to me,' she answered in a whisper. At this, I felt a rush of relief. Perhaps this waif-like figure had not been violated. Perhaps she had escaped just ahead of puberty, when she would be put into sexual slavery. Still, she had many other hurdles to overcome.

'Can you remember anything at all about your family?' I asked.

'I can only remember the water point where I fetched water with my mother. I was collecting shea nuts with the older girls when the LRA came.'

The team had already reunited hundreds of returning children with their families, so I could not understand why Atim's case eluded them. Parents arrived at the reception centre daily, asking the girls who had returned, 'Have you seen our daughter with the rebels?', and I had seen both joy and devastation at the answers. I had witnessed the highs of 'Yes, I have seen her in Congo, and she is well,' and the lows of 'I'm sorry, she was shot last year in a gunfight with the UPDF.'

I had learned to temper my own reactions in order to continue the work. At times a child would be returned to a distant aunt or uncle—in Acholi culture, this was enough. Many people still upheld their family responsibilities, even in war.

With Atim, the team ran out of avenues. They had already decided to wind up their search and find any home for Atim beyond the reception centre when Daniel, one of the social workers, made a last-ditch attempt while talking with people in the camp one day. He casually asked about a certain water point using the description that Atim had given, expecting another dead end.

'Yes, that's where we used to go before we moved into the camp,' a man nearby piped up. 'It's about twenty kilometres east of here.'

'We have had a girl with us for one year who came from this village. We've been unable to find her parents. Do you know who this girl might be?' Daniel asked, pulling out a photo of Atim. The man's eyes lit up, and Daniel could now see that the face in front of him—a man who had been the village pastor before moving to the camp—bore a strong resemblance to the face in the photograph. 'That is my daughter! She was taken eight years ago. Praise God! We have prayed every day for her return to us.'

The next day, he arrived at the reception centre with Atim's mother, who ran into the compound and lifted the tiny girl into the air with a clenched hug. She then placed her down again, and thumped her bare feet on the ground in mock dancing, her arms up, a deafening trill cutting the air as she ululated in sheer delight. The tears ran down her cheeks as she gathered up her lost child again.

Atim stared cautiously at the couple. Almost two-thirds of her life had been spent with the rebels, and these two people with wide smiles, though familiar, were like strangers to her now. When her mother offered her a gift of peanut butter that she had crushed by hand, the little girl shook her head.

'Look, this is where you lived once,' her mother said, extending her skinny fingers, which held a dog-eared black-and-white photo of a group standing in front of a small hut. Atim's stare flickered in recognition, and I saw her shoulders relax. A small seed of hope in my heart made me believe that Atim would be fine.

Later, I took Atim's parents aside. 'We will need to be patient with her. It is a lot to take in, and it might take a while for her to accept you after what she's been through.' They were undaunted, taking their daughter to their hut in the IDP camp, determined to pour eight years of love back into the five-year-old they had lost.

*

One day in April 2006, I had a call from Erin Baines, the Canadian researcher who had been part of the visiting team the previous year. 'The UN want you to go to New York immediately to report firsthand on what is happening in the north', she said matter-of-factly, as if this was something I did every year. Erin was based in Gulu, now the hub for relief work in the north, its streets crammed with NGO trucks and new, swish restaurants catering to foreign tastes. I had built good working relationships with Erin and others, including the UN representatives who were now based in Pader and Kitgum. This had freed me of the obligation to make regular trips to Kampala to report on the movements of the children.

'I do not have any travel documents, or a passport,' I told Erin, my voice tentative. I had never travelled beyond the borders of Uganda and had been too busy to consider the world outside my country.

'It's fine. We'll make sure you get a passport in time,' was Erin's reply. 'This is a great opportunity for you and CCF. People will be interested to hear what you have to say. Oh, and you won't be alone. Michael Otim is going, too.' At this, I relaxed. Michael Otim was the project coordinator for the Gulu District NGO Forum, and I knew him quite well.

Soon afterwards, I travelled again to Kampala, armed with my visa application and a letter of invitation outlining why I was applying to visit the United States, and whom I planned to meet. It didn't seem real. *Am I really going, and if so, what am I going to do there?* My thoughts were in turmoil. How was I going to explain to these people outside Uganda the situation in the north? It seemed to be a long way to go to tell people in another country about our misery.

I confided in my niece, Faith, 'I'm not sure how this will benefit the lives of the children in Pader. I have no idea what I will be doing.'

'But you will be our voice. People do not know what is happening. You must tell them,' Faith replied without hesitating. Back in Pader, the buzz of excitement around my impending visit to New York grew each day, until the second week of May, when I was due to travel south to fly from Entebbe on 21 May.

That morning, I awoke to a soft knock on the door. It was my elderly neighbour, a stooped, leathery woman who lived with her family in the hut right behind my mud-brick room. I knew her hacking cough and gravelly voice well. 'Alice, when you go to visit these people, please tell them what we have been through here,' the woman said with tears in her eyes. She then placed a small plastic container into my hands. 'This is for the kind people you will meet,' she told me. I looked down at the gift and felt a lump in my throat. I held a cup of rich golden honey, fragrant with the scent of shea blossom, more valuable than gold to Acholi people at this time, and certainly beyond the means of this dear woman.

The responsibility of representing my people weighed on me, but I stayed firm as my sad-looking team and girls at the reception centre, Florence and other friends lined up for their turn to say farewell. I was like a soldier leaving my home to go into battle on their behalf, but I was now waging a different war, entering terrain more unfamiliar than Congo or southern Sudan. A knot of fear lodged itself in my belly as I steeled myself not to weep until the bus left town. Soon I was rattling along the long road that would lead me south and to the wider world.

*

This journey required more faith than surviving in the bush or working through situations with the girls. The first descent, into Heathrow, was the most harrowing. I closed my eyes and silently sung myself into a place of peace with an old Lwo hymn that I loved. When the next flight descended into New York, it disappeared into a bank of misty clouds so that I could not see the ground, and I could not think past my thumping, hurting ears. I looked over and saw Michael's eyes closed, sweat resting on his brow, and suspected that he was nervous, too. Around me, faces were unworried—calm and expressionless.

When the aircraft burst through the clouds over John F. Kennedy International Airport, I caught sight of a maze of waterways below, with long sandy beaches stretching in each direction, and became more fascinated than scared. I stared at blocks of uniform concrete, before the plane took us over rows of solid-brick houses—larger than I had ever seen—and then landed in a chaotic parking lot of aircraft with bright and varied livery.

That night in my hotel room, I barely slept. I heard sirens that sounded like howling cats, and when I looked out the window to the street far below, I saw flashing red lights and felt a stab of panic at the sound accompanying them, even though its whine was so different to the blaring horns of dilapidated ambulances rushing to the site of an ambush. For a time I sat on the side of the bed, worried for the people being rescued below, and missing those I loved in Pader. It was unsettling to be alone in this hotel room, where I could not hear the sighs or deep breathing of my friends and family. *It is unnatural to be so alone*, was my last thought before I slipped into sleep.

It was a short walk from the hotel to the headquarters of the United Nations, but my senses were in overdrive. I saw trees that I did not recognise, with the freshest of new green leaves; metal grates with steam and heat curling up that did not burn my skin; loud voices; people rushing; empty stares; angry faces; happy faces; and people talking, sometimes to themselves.

Michael and I strode up the stairs to the imposing entrance of the UN building, resting at the top to admire the long line of flags stretching all the way along the concourse. 'Can you see the flag of Uganda?' I asked, looking for the familiar bold black, red and yellow stripes and the majestic crested crane planted right in the centre.

'It will be here, but I cannot see it,' Michael replied.

'But *we* are here,' I said, with a burst of pride at being Ugandan, pleased that I had chosen to wear my most vibrant green batik outfit, one that I had had specially made for the occasion by a seamstress in the IDP camp. I pulled out the camera that I was given before leaving Pader, knowing that it would be hard for those at home to believe that there was a place on earth like New York. The whirr of the shutter made me smile. In a war where our cameras were confiscated in the military barracks due to security concerns, this was a small but significant freedom.

I did not utter a word as I went through security, for fear I would be stopped or rejected; I was silent as I was led through the cavernous entry, where every cough and footstep reverberated around me. I paused to watch a group of children, laughing and confident and carefree. In my heart, I yearned to see our girls and boys—the ones I dealt with each day in Pader—like this: living in freedom. *Will there be a day when our children have no cares?* I felt my chest tighten, and my body ached with longing for change. Then I hastened to catch up with my American companions, men and women who wore suits and moved with crisp authority. I passed a mural so large that it covered an entire wall, and again I paused. It was a collage of many people, of every race and colour, all jumbled together, though involved in their own activities. On the wall I saw images of suffering, faces full of pain, and I knew why I had come. *Alice, you are doing this for the children in Pader.* I stood tall and entered the meeting room, taking my place at the large round table beside Michael. *This is not about you.*

The first meeting was with OCHA, the UN coordinating group for humanitarian assistance, where Michael and I explained the predicament in the north of Uganda. We answered questions for one and a half hours from the ambassadors of many countries. The session was labelled 'View from the Ground: Acholi Perspectives on the Current Situation in Northern Uganda.'

It all spilled out—no awful detail was spared. 'The war may be winding down, but we are still dealing with the girls who were abducted and raped. We are battling issues around the rape and defilement of girls and women by soldiers and men in the villages, and this month alone, ten children were killed by soldiers who mistakenly thought they were rebels,' I explained. 'We are living in conditions worse than you can even imagine.' My steady gaze met with soft eyes that cared, some with tears, and brows that folded together in frowns as I relayed my stories of life in the IDP camps. Heads nodded when I pleaded for food and protection. Not only had I at last found a group of people who might listen and act, but I had also found my voice.

Afterwards, we were led to a dining room overlooking the East River, where I could see small boats and ferries going back and forth, and cranes on construction sites—a whole flock of them, like strange giant metal birds pecking at the ground. The waiter handed me an oversized menu filled with lists of food I did not recognise. I scanned the page for something familiar and found fried chicken, potatoes and green beans.

'That is so much!' I exclaimed when my meal arrived, as the plump chicken leg was three times the size of those found on our scrawny village hens. 'This is enough for a family,' I laughed. I picked at the chicken, scraping away the creamy white sauce. Its richness—after my usual diet of boiled white rice, maize and stewed red beans—was more than I could digest.

'Alice, you're not hungry after all that hard work in the meeting?' Erin asked, with a smile.

'I'm not used to so much food. My stomach cannot take it,' I said, pushing the plate away. 'May I have some black tea, please?' I shrugged by way of apology, and sat quietly as the others ate.

The three scheduled meetings of the visit turned into many more, and I met a variety of people: a large group of ambassadors to the United Nations from many countries, a special committee dealing with East and Central Africa, the whole of the United Nations ahead of UN Watch, and the Special Representative for Children and Armed Conflict. Among the UN ambassadors was an accomplished Canadian, Allan Rock, who was highly engaged in the first session and would later become one of CCF's greatest advocates.

We were escorted into the New York offices of a number of different NGOs, jumping in and out of scratched-up taxis, and riding up and down lifts where I felt I'd left my stomach behind. I gazed at breathtaking views of buildings of such elaborate design and so high that it made my mind reel to think about how they were constructed. Outside, I followed Erin's every move, watching as yellow taxis and buses and black cars sped past. I dared not move until I saw her take a step forwards, and even then I felt a firm hand on my shoulder more than once.

'Take it easy here, Alice. They don't stop for pedestrians.' I found this confusing, how everyone was rushing to get some-where—I could not imagine what could be so important. Or that so many people could be together in one place and be unconnected, not knowing each other's extended family. Even running and hiding in the bush had not made me feel so alone.

It tired me to try to make sense of this unfair world. My mind traversed between images of the surroundings in New York and where I came from, from the bowl of split peas and yellow cornflour that the WFP meted out each day in Pader to the abundance of restaurants, the hot dog stands and pretzel stalls on corners across Manhattan. *How could people throw away food while my people starve? Are we really living on the same planet?* I wondered, sinking lower into despair. Then I pulled myself up. Bitterness would not help anyone, and here I had found kindness. Back in my room, I slumped onto my bed, exhausted.

The next day when I arrived at the check-in desk at JFK, the airline did not have my booking. I stood peering at the airline official's busy hands on the keyboard to keep the panic from rising. In New York, someone had mentioned the word asylum. It crossed my mind that I might be detained. 'Here is my confirmation,' I said, as I passed the folded page over the counter.

'Thanks. Looks like our mistake,' he offered in a cheerful British accent. 'I'll find you a seat in Business. Enjoy,' he said, handing back my documents.

I felt so small in this place. *What can one woman do?* This question lingered as I started on the long journey home to Uganda, staring vacantly out the window, exhausted, as the aircraft lifted into the pale twilight sky above New York.

As a child, the path had been so clear: my position in the clan would be elevated only when I was attached to a man. Yet at almost 33 years of age, marriage rarely crossed my mind.

'You have to get married—now is the right time,' a friend had told me. 'You cannot do this without a man beside you.' The words still stung when I remembered how I'd been left feeling like something was wrong with me.

I smiled, my face warming at the memory of my strident response: 'I will not marry for convenience, and when I do it will be at the right time, and only to a man I love and want to be with.'

I was traditional in many ways, still preferring long dresses and traditional clothing to the trousers that modern women in the south of Uganda wore, but on the question of marriage I was resolute—the Acholi culture and trying to please other people would not dictate such an important decision.

'Besides, I have no time for a relationship. For now CCF is enough,' I had told my friend. I would not allow loneliness to consume me. I saw no higher calling than to open doors for the girls who were forging their own identities against all odds. For now, my every waking moment would be filled with meetings and problems.

I slid back into my business-class flatbed and slept.

20

Just a Woman

It was July, not long after this trip, when a government soldier arrived at the gate of the CCF compound in his shabby uniform, looking for me. In his arms he held a small bundle of dirty cloth, and he was being careful to keep it away from his chest. 'Where is Alice? I must see her,' he demanded of the guard, before pushing his way past.

In my hut, I heard the commotion and the guard's call for the soldier to wait, so I stepped out to meet him. 'What is the problem here?' I asked, walking towards the soldier.

'Please take this. I found it under a tree,' he pleaded as he hastily unloaded his package into my arms.

I lifted the fold of the cloth to see the tiniest of faces, and pulled further to see a bulging torso with a shrivelled umbilical cord still attached. It was a little boy. 'Oh no,' I groaned, my mind flashing to the probable scene. 'Where did you find this baby? Did you see the mother?' I questioned, wondering whether the girl might be lying helpless nearby, maybe torn and bleeding. I imagined the wave upon wave of heaving pain, getting closer and closer until the crowning moment, when the mother might have tried to suppress the urge to cry out for fear of being killed. Was the poor girl alone as she laboured while gunshots whistled around her? I had heard such a story before.

'I found this baby under a tree,' the soldier told me. 'We were fighting very close to the town. We were looking for the wounded after fighting the rebels,' he said, more relaxed now that he had brought the baby to safety. 'It was a big battle, and there were bullets everywhere. I didn't see whether she lived or died. I think she has thrown the baby and run.'

The baby stirred in my arms, its tiny limbs shooting out in involuntary spasms. I was now aware of his rotted smell, and the dirt mixed with oily blood coating his tender skin. Then he opened his mouth and thrashed his head from side to side, letting out a desperate cry.

'Nurse, please come. We need to feed and clean this baby,' I called to a woman standing nearby. It was the third motherless baby we had received this year while the remnant of the rebels were fighting in Pader district. Some rebels had refused to leave. They kept spies in the camps, and launched bloody ambushes from their hiding places in the bush.

I then turned to the soldier and gave a weary smile. 'Thank you for bringing him to us,' I said as I shook his hand. Even in the middle of a war, and even with an underfed, under-appreciated and seemingly heartless government army, there were acts of kindness, and I was grateful.

Alone in my room that night, I replayed the scene in my mind that was so familiar from the accounts of the girls. I wondered how many girls could not make that last powerful push to release their baby into the world. How many mothers and babies perished this way, when a fierce battle raged and a mother was powerless to hold back the natural force of child-birth. Then there was the most painful of choices: to stay and die, to run with her baby and possibly die, or to run for her own life and leave the baby's fate to providence. I took a deep, wobbly breath that quelled my tears. I had never been asked to make a choice like this, and I determined that I would never condemn a mother who did.

The staff at the reception centre decided to name the baby boy Emanuel Komigum, a Lwo name that announced to the world 'I am lucky'. For two weeks, the nurses cared for the sickly Emanuel in the compound, nourishing him with powdered milk from a bottle, doing all they could to build up his strength, before they realised that he needed more care than they could offer. They arranged for him to be transferred to the intensive-care unit in Gulu, where he had a better chance of survival.

Other girls from Pader had been in the bush during the gunfight. Many had died that day, but some had returned. When I sent out word among their networks about this young mother and her newborn, a verbal report soon came back: 'They think the mother died in the battle.'

The same networks traced Emanuel's mother back to her village, and to her own mother. When Emanuel was strong enough, his grandmother took him home to her village to raise him as her own, without time to grieve. 'I have this baby, but I've lost my own daughter,' she lamented. She had joined a legion of grandmothers raising children who would never know their mothers and fathers.

*

The response to my pleas in New York came swiftly in the form of a Sri Lankan woman named Radhika Coomaraswamy, who had recently been appointed UN Under-Secretary-General, Special Representative for Children and Armed Conflict. When she pulled up at the reception centre in a convoy of UN four-wheel drives with her own Lwo interpreter in June 2006, I knew that she meant business.

'We will get to the bottom of what is happening to the children in the district,' she promised, after shaking my hand. 'When can I talk with the girls?'

'Right now,' I said, my heart racing with excitement that this woman had not just the skill and tact to tease out stories, but also the authority to act on what she heard.

I left Radhika and her interpreter to sit with the girls and women on plastic seats under the *kworo* tree, glancing over every now and then to see the visitor slumping in her chair, or fanning away the sweat on her face, or lifting her hand to her heart in solidarity with the girls who were pouring out their inner pain to her. The stories were now not just about what had happened in the battlefield, but were also about the atrocities that had occurred in the IDP camp that surrounded the reception centre, and in the military barracks.

Radhika's warm manner helped the girls as they opened up to her, and she was taken deeply into each girl's story of abuse. In one interview, with a mother and her teenage daughter whom I knew had both been raped by soldiers in the dead of night, I watched Radhika's body stiffen, and knew that this story would not end there. The soldiers had returned the day after the rapes to taunt the pair, saying, 'Which one of us did it? Are you going to report us?' Of course, they could not be identified in the dark. I was quietly hopeful that there might be justice, or at least a change in behaviour.

After several hours of meetings at the reception centre, I joined Radhika under the tree and sat quietly with her. There was little to say. The woman's face was stony as she absorbed the unbearable pain of those around her. 'I know, it is difficult to hear,' I reassured her, lightly patting her back.

The rest of the visit was spent in briefings with other non-government organisations in Pader, especially those involved in child protection. On her last day, Radhika visited the local military leaders to deliver her findings. From our conversations afterwards, I was sure any abuses would be reported at the top in Kampala or perhaps beyond. I sighed with relief as her UN four-wheel-drive entourage sped off in a cloud of red dust.

The dust had hardly settled when I received an angry call from the local UPDF military commander. 'Why did you report us to the UN?' he yelled into the phone. I sighed into the mouthpiece. It was tiring to be in a battle with the soldiers sent to defend us against the LRA rebels.

By the next morning, the UN had called an emergency meeting in Kampala. I found myself in the middle of all the issues and was physically threatened by the soldiers at the meeting. Afterwards, the angry commander barged into the reception centre, placed his hands on his hips and demanded, 'Alice, if there was any problem, why didn't you call us? You discussed it with UNICEF, and now we are going to have serious problems with Kampala.'

I was quick to reply. 'I know that I have talked about these issues many times, but this time it did not come from me.' I had agitated for months on behalf of the children, complaining about the girls and boys being kept in the barracks for interrogation about their time with the LRA, or being used to track rebels, but it had taken a high-ranked UN visitor to shift the situation. 'It was the children themselves who told the UN what is happening here. I was not even translating,' I defended myself, knowing it was the truth. I defiantly mirrored the commander's stance with my hands on my hips, and stood tall. 'I am happy that the soldiers' dirty behaviour has been revealed, as it must stop.'

Despite my assurances that I was not at risk from the threats of the UPDF, the UNICEF country leader was concerned for my safety. 'Alice, please take today's bus to Gulu, and we will house you in a guesthouse,' he insisted. When I returned after a couple of weeks, the crisis had passed and frayed tempers had settled down. I hoped the children would be safer now.

*

Abalo Alice Joyce was one of the many girls I met at the makeshift airstrip in Pader, where children from the district were brought on Eagle Air flights from other reception centres. In the bush, Joyce was known as Grace Aloya to protect the identity of her family from rebels who might come after them, and she still carried the residue of wariness that had kept her alive in captivity. Her pregnant bulge and toddler clutching her hand quickly caught my attention: she was a girl who needed medical attention and counselling.

'Where were you before you arrived in Gulu?' I asked Joyce after she had settled into the reception centre and joined the social worker for her first interview.

'I have travelled a long way, madam,' she replied wearily. 'I was eleven years old when I was taken, and I am now twenty-one years old.' She paused to let me take this in. 'I was with a group that walked all the way to Sudan, and when we reached Sudan we walked through the mountains to Kenya, and when we reached Kenya we walked back again. Once we came back to Sudan, we stayed in the one camp for eight years. The fighting in Uganda was very bad at that time.'

I glanced at Joyce's scarred feet, which would never recover from such abuse. I had not been to Sudan or Kenya, but I could well imagine the rebels cutting through thick grass with a *panga* for days at a time.

'And how did you escape?'

'I ran after a battle. I walked for many days until one morning I came to a big IDP camp, where I saw an old woman washing her clothes. I was very scared to enter, and wanted to run when she stared at me, but then I saw that she was crying. She looked kind, and called me over to her. She offered me food, but I was too worried to eat.'

'Where is the father of your children?'

'The commander? I think he has left the rebels, too, but I don't want to see him. I must find David.'

'David? Who is David?'

A frown formed on Joyce's brow. 'David is my friend. We met when our groups passed, when we camped together. He came from the same sub-county as me. We have plans together. He told me: "If we make it safely back to our homes, I will marry you and raise these children as my own." I must find him.' She looked past me blankly and then back at me again.

'I'm sure we can find him,' I smiled, musing how even in

the chaos of war, true love could flourish. By the time Joyce entered labour several months later, my spirits were high.

Just a few days before, I had been at a church conference in Kampala and had met a pastor, Christine Pringle from Australia, known as Chris—a woman with the whitest of smiles, wearing a bright flowing dress and a red scarf around her neck—who was now coming to visit.

Chris had prayed for me, and told me: 'Alice, you are not to worry about the direction of this work. Great men and women will come around CCF to support you.' They were reassuring words that I would hold on to long after Chris had left Uganda. When we met, I had been overcome with shyness, the boldness I had previously carried into high-level meetings suddenly deserting me. I had hung back, my woollen scarf wrapped around my shoulders for security, resisting David Livingstone Okello's suggestion that I march up to the front after the session. He'd persisted, and I had gathered my courage to talk about my work with the girls. Within moments of meeting, Chris had turned to David and asked, 'How far is Pader from Kitgum?' She was already flying to Kitgum. 'I will take you to Pader,' David had replied, and it was set. There was no mention that the road between Kitgum and Pader was still dangerous, with weekly ambushes from the rebels venturing down from their hiding places in the rocky hillsides to the north, and deep potholes during the rainy season.

When David's Land Cruiser pulled up with Chris, I could not contain myself. I leaned into the car, beaming. 'Chris, Chris, a baby has been born—come and see,' I said. I led her into the darkened birthing hut, and it took some moments for Chris's eyes to adjust to the room, and for her senses to take in the musty smell and quiet whimpering.

'Joyce, we have a visitor from Australia,' I said, trying to buoy the girl, but at that moment she could barely respond. Joyce lay motionless on a mat, resting in the dark, and beside her lay a newborn girl—just two hours old—wrapped in a cotton cloth.

'It is sometimes hard for the girls to feel happy in this moment,' I whispered to Chris. 'But we will celebrate the arrival of this little girl into the world.'

Chris moved close to the bed and took Joyce's hand. 'Take heart, Joyce, nothing bad will happen to you now,' she spoke tenderly. She turned around to beckon me and I could see the wetness of her eyes. 'This girl is a symbol of breakthrough for women in northern Uganda. She symbolises peace in northern Uganda,' she pronounced. I took a deep breath and nodded. I would remember these words so I could repeat them to Joyce when she felt better.

'Chris, did you know that when a baby is born in Uganda, it is named according to its circumstances? Maybe this baby can be called Christine,' I suggested. 'That would be a good name for this baby.'

Chris laughed, thrilled to be part of such a profound moment. 'And what does your name mean, Alice?' she asked, with a mischievous look.

'Ah, my name, Achan, means born in a difficult time,' I replied, feeling self-conscious.

Chris shook her head. 'You don't have to live under the shadow of your name,' she told me. 'Mercy would be a better name for you, Alice. What is the word for that in your language?' she asked.

'The word for mercy in Lwo is *lakica*. It's a very good word,' I said, pleased at the thought of this new name. We moved on to tour other parts of the reception centre.

'You must see where we plan to build a school for the girls. The Uganda Fund has helped us buy some land from a family who wanted to help with the girls,' I told her, leading Chris to the vehicle and driving a few minutes from the reception centre to a scrappy piece of land with thick undergrowth, the stubs of past cassava crops and a few tall shea and mango trees. I pointed out where the various buildings would be, and explained how we would introduce academic studies alongside sewing, baking and other vocational programs. 'We will build a sanctuary for girl mothers,' I explained.

'How can we help with all of this?' Chris asked, as we traipsed through the bush.

'I have some plans to show you,' I replied. I'd had a dream one night, of a comfortable guesthouse near the school where the girls could put their training into action. I had seen the girls there in uniforms, cooking at a stove, baking rolls and learning how to make beds and how a hotel might run. The dream was so vivid that I could commission plans from the images in my dream. In the office, I pulled out a cylinder from beside my desk and stretched out the paper so we could both see the plans.

'I think we can help you,' Chris offered, thinking of the women in her wide church network who would be excited to be part of this project. To me, it felt like God was going ahead of me, opening the doors, bringing friends and healing the girls, and all I needed to do was remain faithful to what was in my heart.

I had felt the same way when Mary Page from the MacArthur Foundation had travelled to Pader earlier that year, and we had walked around the plot while I explained how the new school would work, where the first building would be, and how I saw it expanding. In my mind, it was already there: a school building, a boarding facility, a school hall, a nursery and a training facility. When Mary walked on the land, she could see it too. She too could see another pathway for the girls, other than servitude in the village.

Four years into the work, my role had shifted into management of the programs, advocacy and dealing with the growing number of people offering support. I was no longer the retiring woman who had spoken only reluctantly at the OCHA meetings in Kampala, but a woman on an unstoppable mission, bold and opinionated on the topics of education and maternal health care for young girls.

'How can you sit here and discuss our situation in such general terms, ignoring the issues specifically affecting women and children?' I challenged in one meeting, impatient that district leaders, UN representatives and international NGOs had not shifted enough focus onto the needs of the most vulnerable.

Now, if I joined a meeting and did not speak, my companions asked, 'What is wrong with you today, Alice?' I was still at times the only woman in some meetings, but I knew others would listen to my opinions.

I had come a long way since the early meetings in Kampala, where there had been a clear bias against—and sometimes outright hostility towards—my questioning. 'Who are you to express this view? You're just a woman,' one man had declared. I could now laugh at my timidity and knew that I would not be so accommodating these days.

Like the pieces of a puzzle, all sorts of resources—funding and people and contacts—were falling into place. I was sleeping well, putting myself at the mercy of the path of faith I had chosen.

Joyce was among the first girls who came to the reception centre for hospitality training, sometimes staying for several days, before returning to her children in the village. She arrived one morning with exciting news. 'Madam Alice, I have found David. He has escaped and is home in our sub-county now,' she said, her face glowing with happiness.

I reached out to squeeze her hand. 'I am happy for you.'

Joyce related David's courageous story. On 3 August 2007, near Juba in southern Sudan, David was part of a group ambushed by government forces. Instead of running with the other young men who came under Bogi, their commander at that time, David fled into the swirling waters of the White Nile. He had learned to swim as a child playing in the streams near his home, something many children could not do. When the government soldiers passed by, he submerged his whole body under the water, with just his face coming to the surface for air, like a large fish avoiding a predator.

Under the flow of cool water, he decided that this was his moment to escape the war. When his own group of LRA rebels passed by on a grassy path close to his hiding place, he once again let his body slide under the current until he was certain that they had left the area. Afterwards, he found a friend from his group who had had a similar idea, and together the young men embarked on a perilous journey home that would take them four months, all while dodging other people. As a twosome, the men could easily travel undetected, walking by night, and hiding in the canopy of a tree or in the heart of a big bush whenever they saw passing groups of soldiers or rebels. The further they walked, the more their hearts warmed; they would not become the cold, hard killers that the LRA wanted them to be. With every step, they regained some of their humanity until finally, on 21 December, the two men arrived at the vast camp of Padibe, near Kitgum.

Not long after Joyce and David reunited, a man arrived at the reception centre accompanied by soldiers. He was a high-ranked LRA commander who had been detained in the barracks to help the military with information, and he had asked if he could locate his wife. Sensing trouble, I had met him at the gate.

'I sent my wife and children back home ahead of me, and I need to find them. I am told they are here,' he claimed, standing tall. It was not unusual for returned commanders to have such a sense of entitlement, ownership even, about the young women they called 'wives' in the bush. I decided to play it carefully.

'What is the name of this person?' I responded politely.

'Her name is Grace Aloya,' he replied. I stiffened, recalling Joyce's tale of the commander who was the father of her children.

'That's not possible,' I said, my voice firm.

The man scowled as he stepped towards me, trying to intimidate me. 'Where is my wife? I know that she is here at CCF. Bring her to me,' he demanded. The government soldiers, who were once his nemeses but were now his guards, stood compliantly behind him.

Not far away, in the large round hut where the girls had their cooking lessons, Joyce heard the commotion and recognised the man's voice. She cowered behind the other girls as the commander's anger escalated, praying that he would not barge in and find her.

'She is not coming with you. If you want Joyce back, then you go and talk to her father,' I shot back as forcefully as his demands. I knew that Joyce's father supported her marriage to David, and he would not allow the commander back into her life.

'I don't ever want to go back with that man,' Joyce had told me. I recalled Joyce's softness when she talked of David, and her plans to marry the young boy from the village. How she still grieved the loss of her mother before she was taken into captivity. With all my heart, I wanted a happier life for Joyce and her babies. If I had to put myself at risk by standing up to soldiers and rebels, refusing them entry to the reception centre and then sending them away, it seemed to be a small price to pay.

'You must leave right now,' I bellowed. With my heart racing, I stepped closer to the commander, raised my arm and pointed to the gate. He snarled and turned away, marching heavily towards the gate, his minions following.

'I'll be back,' he threatened, and I shrugged my shoulders.

21

Building the Dream

I picked up my buzzing phone from the desk and walked out of my office. 'Hello, Katherine,' I said, recognising the number that flashed up as that of a British friend from Save the Children in Kampala. We spoke almost weekly. I tried hard not to sound out of breath as I trotted along the dirt track between the compound and my room, where I would finally relax for the evening.

'I've just been in touch with a young girl from Pader who was airlifted three months ago during the peace talks in Congo,' Katherine informed me. In early 2007, CCF Pader was still the only registered reception centre in the district to receive girls as they returned from the war. It was bursting at the seams, with new girls arriving daily from the barracks. Most had escaped on the way to Sudan.

'She came from Congo?' I asked, frowning as I negotiated the steps to my room.

'She had serious complications from childbirth and is now under LRA watch in Nairobi. It's sensitive. They want her back—she knows too much,' the humanitarian worker told me. 'Her name is Polline—she'll call you.'

'Thanks.' I signed off from the call and sat for a long time on the edge of my single bed, staring at the cement floor and knotting my hands, digesting this information. I hadn't expected to hear of girls coming from the Democratic Republic of the Congo. The peace talks in Juba had not been what we'd hoped, dragging on for months already without resolution. Yet an agreement had been made during the peace talks—as long as government and foreign visitors had access to the LRA camp in Garamba National Park, then the United Nations would allow safe passage to hospitals in Nairobi, Kenya, for badly injured rebels and their 'wives'. Lying on my bed now, my eyes rose absent-mindedly to the room's roughly plastered ceiling. I groaned, wondering how I could possibly manage another damaged young woman. The trail to my office door was already well worn from such cases. Then I took a deep breath. *It will be fine.*

Within days, I answered my phone to hear a lilting voice coming down the line. It was soft yet determined, and notably confident for a girl who had escaped from the bush. 'Hello Alice, this is Polline Akello. I'm calling from Nairobi.' It was the first of what would become almost daily phone calls in the months ahead. In the early calls, Polline's words were carefully chosen—just the facts—in case others heard her. 'A nurse has helped me . . . I will be okay,' Polline told me. I soon picked up on the discreet language and knew that Polline was planning her escape.

'This girl is so clever,' I confided to Stella, one of our best social workers, after a call in which Polline had told me, 'I am calling on my second sim card. The LRA escort gave me one, but it is monitored.'

With a secure phone connection, I could learn more. 'The LRA guy here wanted to keep my passport, but I told him, "No, you cannot have my passport. I am in a foreign country and I need to keep it with me." I gave it to the nurse to keep safe in case he took it from me.' I smiled on the end of the line. I already admired Polline's quick reactions and how she had eluded the malevolent eyes of her minders in Nairobi. She'd never had a passport before, but she knew that the small document she'd been handed before she was airlifted to Kenya was like gold. She was a lone girl up against a network that seemed to be well-resourced, with the money to buy whatever they needed. The peace talks had brought leverage for the rebels, but it now looked like the talks would fail—again—and the war would continue to ruin lives.

'I had a call from Joseph Kony himself,' she told me during one of our conversations, and my stomach tightened. Kony reportedly wielded a strange power over his people. He seemed to know in advance what was going to happen, as if he had a mystical source that told him the future. 'He told me that they are missing me and want me back. But I will never go.' She then told me how, on the day she left Congo in the weakest of states, she had promised that she would come back. Her commander—the man to whom she had been given—had argued that she needed urgent medical care or she would die, and Kony had pushed back, saying that a cunning girl like Polline would plan to escape. 'She won't come back,' he told the commander.

'Of course I will come back here when I'm better. This is my life now. You are my family. What else is there for me at home now?' she had declared, even as she battled to think straight from the pain. This was the opportunity to escape for which she had long prayed. She had taken a deep breath, as though swallowing the agony she felt. She clutched the bloodied cloth that covered the deep slash across her lower abdomen. The bleeding had stopped and the blood on the cloth had dried to the brown of the soil around her. The baby was gone.

At the time, she was not sure that she could hold on. She had hours, not days, to live, and fought with all she had to avoid becoming another Ugandan girl buried in an unmarked grave in the bush far from home.

I listened intently to Polline's story, careful not to over-react to her words. Though I tried, I could not hold back my curiosity about the man who had destroyed a generation of Acholi. 'Joseph Kony. What is he like?' I asked Polline, barely able to utter his name. I knew that Polline had come from the top camp, the heart of the LRA, and that she knew many of the LRA's secretive ways, the disciplines and routines that Kony imposed on his rebels and abducted children.

'People say that he changes all the time, that he can become very thin, or turn into a tortoise. Those things are lies. He's just a human being—tall and brown,' Polline replied, with a defiant edge to her voice. Even from afar, I could hear the girl's confidence blossoming. 'I think the force behind him is an evil spirit.'

Then, almost a year after Katherine's first introduction, Polline's calls became shorter, and I detected a growing anxiety in her voice. 'Alice, I've not told anyone my plan. Only you and Katherine and one or two of her colleagues know. They will surely kill me if they find out,' she whispered.

Behind the scenes, advocates from Save the Children had been in discussion with the Ugandan authorities to smuggle Polline out of Nairobi and back into Kampala, and into their care. My anxiety grew, too, during the longer silences, as I wondered how Polline was faring and whether the LRA's operatives would close in on her before she could get away.

In January 2008, I received a call from Polline. 'I'm here in Uganda, Alice. I'm home in my country,' she said, her voice light and full of happiness. She laughed as she told me how she had escaped in style, on a commercial jet out of Kenya. 'I think I will be safe now,' she announced, referring to the halfway house she shared with other young women, where she would undergo an intensive period of debriefing from the military about her experiences, overseen by child-protection advocates from Save the Children. It would be many months before she would be ready to return north to her home in Pader.

'Polline, we will protect you from the rebels when you come back to northern Uganda. You do not have to worry about being taken back,' I reassured her, before a parting word: 'We will help you find your family and get your life back.' I put down my phone and flopped into my chair.

My conversations with Polline had made me think about education for girls. I wondered whether some of them might have avoided abduction—or been able to escape sooner—if they had been literate and more worldly. I did not have an answer, but the idea of formal education had percolated in my mind from the time the first girls arrived under the tree for counselling in 2002. There were many other girls like Polline, smart and motivated to learn, who had missed vital years in school and would struggle to catch up.

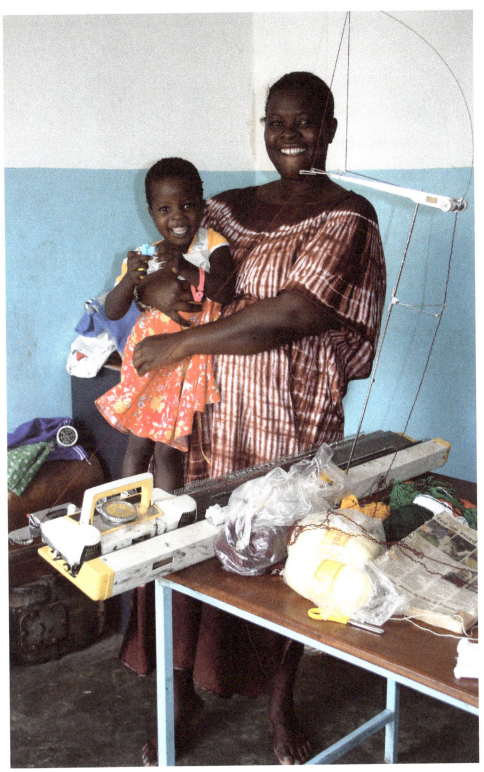

Cathy Livingstone and her daughter, Patience, in 2011.

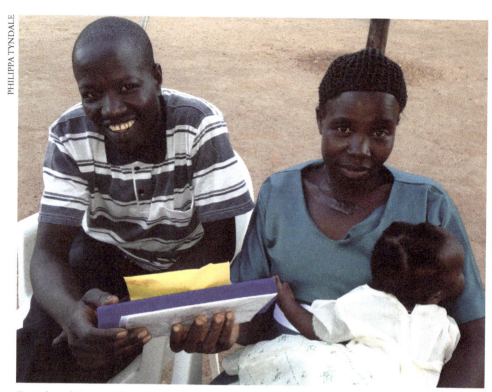

David and Joyce, who met while being held captive by rebel forces in Uganda and Sudan. Separated for years, they both managed to flee their captors and were finally reunited, with Alice's help.

David Livingstone Okello (right), preaching in Kitgum.

An excited group of girls with Alice as she gives them their first sight of an iPad. The school now has a computer laboratory, but access to technology is still limited.

Children in the Pader Girls Academy preschool on the perimeter of the school grounds. It caters to the children of both schoolgirls and neighbourhood families. Beside it is a nursery where the mothers can feed their babies during school breaks.

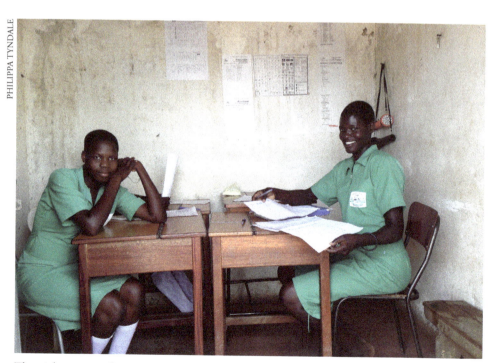

The school grounds—here looking towards the science laboratories—provide a tranquil learning environment for the girls.

The girls prepare for exams in the guardhouse of the school. All quiet corners are taken during exam preparation time.

Washing clothes in the school grounds on the weekend. On Saturdays and Sundays, the trees and walls around the school grounds are draped with brightly coloured sheets and clothes that have been hung out to dry.

Enjoying work in the garden during the twilight hours after homework is finished. The school farm supplements the school's food supply.

The formidable Pader Girls soccer team. The girls love the physical activity and spend hours training in the school grounds.

A young girl at Pader Girls Academy participates in early-morning prayer. The girls rise early each day for personal reflection and spiritual refreshment, which take place in the school hall or school grounds.

The girls find peace and freedom from their troubles when they pray.

A group of girls practise worship songs during Sunday morning devotional time. Music and dance are favourite activities in the school curriculum, and they are the most natural forms of self-expression for the girls.

NIKKI DENHOLM

The mothers share their breakfast of maize porridge with their babies and toddlers. When it's available, they'll add milk.

NIKKI DENHOLM

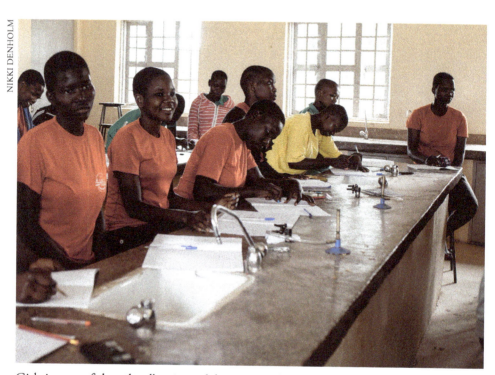

Girls in one of the school's science laboratories. Science is a compulsory subject under the national curriculum.

In the classroom, during an internal exam at the end of term one. The main national exams are in November and December.

A young mother and her little boy after class. The girls often help each other with the babies after the day-care workers leave for the day.

Alice with two of the students in the classroom. They are eager to share their experiences with Madam Alice when she is at the school. If they do well at school or in sport, or they have a complaint, she will hear about it.

A mother and her baby. CCF established Pader Girls Academy as a peaceful place where vulnerable girls could resume their disrupted education. Some students had lost seven or more years of school and arrived at a mature age.

A group of Pader Girls Academy students at play. Alice and the team were determined that pregnancy or motherhood would not be an impediment to learning. Pregnant girls are not accepted into other schools, and that's usually the end of their education.

Mothers and babies gather after class. Girl mothers now make up a smaller percentage of the school than when it opened not long after the conflict ended.

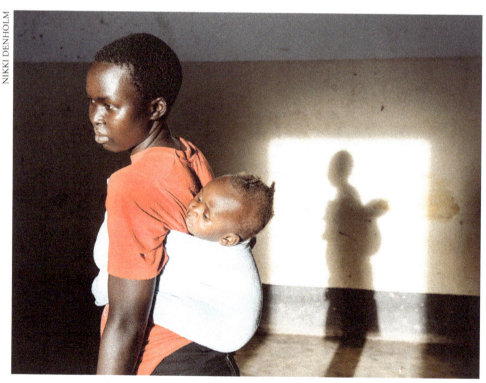

A quiet moment for mother and baby at Pader Girls Academy. Alice's school brought hope to teenage girls experiencing post-war trauma and interrupted education.

A tailoring student in the school's vocational stream. Secondary-school academic courses are only available to those who've finished primary school. Many girls learn tailoring as a way of building a livelihood. Some of them have come through a scholarship program that provides a sewing machine to start their small business.

A Pader Girls Academy girl shines. The school aims to build confidence and healthy self-esteem in the girls, and to empower them through their education.

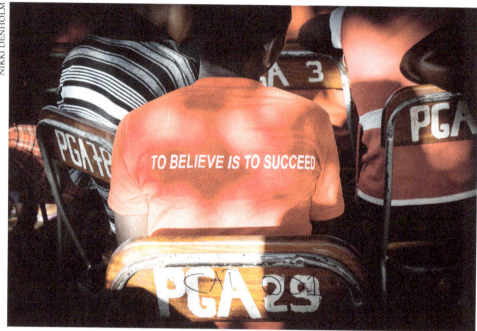

The school motto. Many of the girls in the school had lost hope of ever studying again and are thankful for a second chance. From the beginning, Pader Girls Academy teachers have been trained to manage the special needs of the girl mothers and war-affected students.

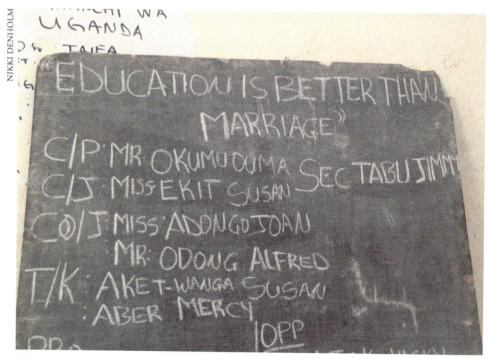

The topic of a senior-school debate: *education is better than marriage*. Whenever they can, the teachers stimulate conversations with the students around their personal life choices, challenging them to believe that they can achieve more through education.

A student stands proudly outside the school hall. Since its opening in 2008, Pader Girls Academy has provided a safe and attractive environment for learning. This motivates the girls to value their school and their education.

The whole school gathers for assembly under a large tree. Although the school hall can hold all the students, the favourite gathering place during the dry season is outside, where it's fresh and open and the children can run around.

NIKKI DENHOLM

Chris and Bernie from C3 Everywoman, with Alice and the Seeds of Love, a group of Christian women in the community bringing spiritual and practical support to struggling families.

NIKKI DENHOLM

Sisterhood. The school aims to create friendships and to provide an environment where the girls support each other, so they can overcome trauma, build self-esteem and discover a love of learning.

Already, a stream of girls had come through vocational training. The South African High Commission had donated sewing machines for International Women's Day 2006: a dozen Singer sewing machines, with foot-propelled treadles and wooden tops, which did not need electricity and could withstand the heat and dust. A group from C3 Church Sydney had visited fabric warehouses in Kampala on their visit that year, and donated rolls and rolls of bright batik fabric from Ghana to make into dresses that the girls could sell or wear. Twenty girls, all mothers with babies, had learned to sew under the instruction of a woman from Kampala, and four of the twenty were now excellent trainers themselves. Other girls had learned to bake bread and cakes to sell within the camps or to the foreign aid workers who were coming in growing numbers. It took just a few shillings of income to improve a girl's life.

But it gnawed at me that there was still no element of formal education, other than random classes in English and writing. By the time I met Polline, the urgency of my desire to make this happen was like a drum that would not stop beating in my head. I was bursting with ideas for this imaginary school. We would create an environment for the girls that would be everything I had not experienced in my own education. These girls would not be bullied for being old, or beaten for being slow at maths, or excluded from learning because they were pregnant or had babies. In the school of my dreams, girls would be nurtured by their teachers, and learn that they are equal to any other person. I took up the cause of formal education with anyone within my sphere who would listen.

Our community of loyal foreign friends had grown over these years. Some had been with us from the first days working under the tree. As I became increasingly strident in my advocacy for girls' education, I found willing ears, starting with Eric Stover, one of our earliest friends, from UC Berkeley, who had long been a strong ally and voice of support. His work in human rights had led him to conclude that denying a girl an education amounted to a violation of human rights, and his findings reinforced what I knew from my own experience.

The North American group of researchers who had first come to Pader in 2005 had returned several times since, and as a result the MacArthur Foundation had helped to set up a trust for vulnerable youth called the Uganda Fund. The group had spoken with the girls at the reception centre, who had given them a clear message: 'We want to go back to school, but we can't because we have babies.'

Our plan for a special school for girls with babies fell squarely into the Uganda Fund's mandate. My own board at CCF heard my passionate pleas, and I was able to easily win their support. 'These girls can't wait until we have money in the bank—they need to be in school right now,' I stated.

'What would we call such a school?' Florence asked, with her usual degree of enthusiasm. 'It must show that we are serious about this matter. What about the Pader Education and Training Centre?'

'Or the Pader Learning Centre?' I mused. But I was unconvinced by both of these names: neither embodied my aspirations for the girls. I sat back to consider what we hoped to achieve.

'What about calling it an academy?' Florence said, sitting up to make her point. 'There are not many of those in Uganda. It tells people that our school will be excellent, and the girls will be so proud to do their studies at such a place.' The name Pader Girls Academy said it all.

The seed of this idea grew quickly. CCF signed an agreement with the Uganda Fund in December 2006, allowing us to pay teachers salaries as we recruited them, and for the first time in five years I also had a steady income—US$400 per month. In the early months of 2007, local workers dug the first trenches of the school's foundations into the unpliable red soil on the land they had cleared.

The local authorities had been harder to convince about a school for girls, as they drowned in the overwhelming needs of a war-ravaged Pader district. I had already trekked up to the office of the District Education Officer, Wilfred Opimo, to float the idea of a special school.

Mr Opimo sat behind a big wooden desk in a newly built office block on the hill looking across to the camp. A fan buzzed in the corner, while piles of paper sat like sentinels in front of him. This was a new precinct of Pader, a clump of administrative offices built by foreign governments during the reconstruction program, and where the World Food Programme had built its vast grain-storage facility, with a high barbed-wire fence and guards to protect the precious food supplies.

Mr Opimo's face wore the weary expression of an overworked and under-resourced official. Daily, he was swamped with requests from every direction. He was expected to reconstruct a broken education system in the middle of a broken community, without clear policies and without funding. The specific education of young women was not high on his list of priorities.

Still he greeted me warmly, and motioned to me with a beckoning nod, which said, *Please share your business.* I was well known in the administrative offices, always pushing for change—better child protection, and better resources for health and nutrition—but the money simply wasn't there.

'There are at least ten girls whose schooling in the village finished in Grade 1, and they are ready to progress right now. They are talented and need to be continuing their formal education,' I started. I told him how one group of girls excelled in English, and they now needed a more structured program to take them to the next level. 'These girls are clever, and they are ready to learn.'

'Yes, I remember meeting them,' he replied, his face brighter. For several months, Mr Opimo had come to the reception centre one Monday each month to address the girls as they finished their sewing training, often admiring the beautiful skirts and bags they had made with their own hands. He nodded his approval. 'What about the babies?' he asked with knitted brows. 'It is difficult to keep the babies with the girls. The mothers will never be able to study.'

'But Mr Opimo, with respect, if a girl is capable of going into the garden to tend vegetables all day with a baby strapped to her back, then surely she can study with the baby?' I argued, driven by the memory of my own deep longing to learn during the bored years I spent in the village after my school closed. I sat up straight and looked Mr Opimo in the eye before delivering my rehearsed speech. 'What kind of generation will we have if girls like these, with babies through no fault of their own, cannot be educated? These are the girls who would give Pader a very good record, and I want to open a school for them so they can go beyond tailoring and baking. These girls could study right up to Senior 4 and even do professional studies.'

Afterwards, sweat tumbled down my brow and onto my cotton blouse, but I kept my hands clasped in my lap as I waited for his response. The fan whirred noisily, and children chattered outside the window.

'I am handcuffed, Alice. It is a lot to ask when we have so much to do,' he replied, with an apologetic shrug, wilting into his tiredness.

I was undeterred. 'I need to do this,' I informed him, as I stood up and stepped away from his desk. I then turned briefly to deliver the last word. 'It's fine—I will find the money for a school myself.' I later heard that after I left, one of the local councillors, who had heard the conversation, came to my defence. 'You should let Alice do what she wants to do. If she wants to do it, she'll get it done,' she told him.

*

Polline's stories of captivity unfolded like a book, chapter by chapter. Each chapter was a layer in her heart, a knotted scar of painful experience. Yet so much of her experience was still fastened shut.

'Alice, my child is buried somewhere in Congo, not even in my land,' she had told me. I understood that this was one of the chapters still closed to her. I had learned some of the headlines: that Polline was abducted from her village of Ajere in 2004 at fourteen years of age, that her experience had left her with deep trauma, both physical and emotional, and that she had been airlifted from the LRA camp to seek medical care in Kenya during the peace process.

Late in 2008, Polline nervously boarded a northbound military truck in Kampala, on her way to be reunited with her family in Pader district. She had sounded strong when we spoke the night before she left. 'I will not let my experience with the LRA steal my future,' she said, barely able to contain the excitement in her voice.

She reached Gulu, where she would rest to break up the arduous journey to the north. There she found a lighter atmosphere and the streets teeming with people on foot, now that the LRA hold had been broken. The crowds included many former child soldiers, who had been processed through the large military barracks in Gulu and then released into counselling by non-government groups such as World Vision, UNICEF, Caritas and Save the Children.

Polline joined the throngs, barely able to believe that she was back in Acholiland, with the smells and sounds that she had missed for so long. She smiled as she scanned the faces she passed, revelling in features that were so familiar. Her gaze settled on a boy's face that she recognised. She could not place him until his eyes found hers and his smile turned to a look of dismay. Then she remembered him, though it had been four years since she had last seen him.

Then, he was a young soldier with a gun too big for his skinny body, who arrived at her family's home—one of three isolated huts—as she hung out her washing to dry in the sun. She even remembered their brief exchange of words.

'Where are your parents?' he had demanded.

'My husband has gone to the village and will soon be back,' she had told the boy, hoping he would leave her alone if he thought she had a husband. She held onto the thin wire clothesline to steady her shaking hands.

'Ah, you are just a girl. I do not believe you,' he had responded, and he reached over to grab her by the arm with a firm grip, pulling her as she struggled to free herself. He herded her, under the threat of his oversized gun, to join a large group of boys nearby. She was the only girl taken that day, marched with the boys to a larger group of sullen-looking children and then into a mindless pattern of daily plodding and lugging for hundreds of kilometres, ending up in the camp of Joseph Kony's rebel group.

It unnerved Polline to see her captor in Gulu, free and laughing as if he had never robbed or killed—until his eyes locked onto hers, and he folded. He hesitated, looking for an escape route, then took a few steps and stopped, turning back to face Polline. They stared awkwardly at each other, neither knowing what to say. He looked nervous and ashamed, his body tight, as if ready to run.

But Polline caught his eye, fixing him with an intense stare as she took several long strides towards him. She had rehearsed what she might say on this day, but had not expected to deliver her words in person, and so soon. Now she stood in front of him, so close that she could smell his sweating body. She paused to take in his face and its boyish stubble, and to remember the words that she was determined to say if she met him again. Her face softened and she gently shook her head. 'Don't be scared,' she reassured him, trying to smile. 'It is okay—I have already forgiven you.'

He staggered back, as if she had struck his face. 'Right now I see you as my own brother, and I am your sister,' Polline told him, her voice steady. 'You did not choose to take me any more than I chose to be taken.'

'Are you sure that you have forgiven me?' he asked, incredulous.

'I am speaking right from my heart. I have forgiven you,' she replied firmly. 'I don't need to hold you in my heart, because holding hatred will block my blessing from God.

I don't want any more enemies.' She paused to let the words take root.

He lifted his shoulders, and she saw his face become clear. He nodded his gratitude and bowed his head to Polline before walking away to join his friends. Polline watched him go, smiling at her own strength, then bounced away in the opposite direction with her head high and a lighter step, liberated. *I am free indeed,* she told herself.

Her greatest fear, much more than seeing her captor, was whether her family would welcome her home. She had heard of many girls who had come home to accusations and shame. But Polline's family received her with squeals and a crush of hugs, calling on the rest of their clan to receive their lost child. She could not yet tell them what she had endured all these years. She simply soaked up their much-longed-for love, expressed in a welcome feast, a gentle touch when she was near and eyes that danced when they met hers.

I heard all of this much later, in the village of Ajere, as we discussed her time in Kampala and her return home. Polline was taking me on a journey, too. Her forgiveness challenged me: what was I holding onto that needed to be swept away?

Polline's eyes lit up when we talked about the future of her education, though we both knew that she was not quite ready to jump that hurdle. That night, in the sanctuary of my own home, I thought about many of the stories I had been told, and the meaning of the word 'brave': it is facing the world boldly when you're a young girl returning from captivity, and facing each day alone with children born of rape. Brave is forgiving the man who raped you, and choosing to move on so that brutality does not define the future course of your life. I had never been asked to be that brave.

22

The School of Restoration

I watched my dream rise out of the ground. Every morning I was up with the rising sun and the roosters' crows, rushing to pull on my dress and sandals, to wash down a piece of dry bread with my morning tea, so that I could be on site. Within days, there were piles of red bricks alongside the excavation for the foundations, made one by one from Pader mud by Acholi hands. They were Acholi hands that might have been used to kill or might have been idle, but we set out to use local labour and skills to create jobs in a district that had scant opportunity to make jobs. We wanted the school to benefit the whole community.

Some days I pinched myself: *Were we really doing this?* Some days I could barely believe that outsiders believed in us—me, the CCF team, the girls, northern Ugandans— enough to pay for this school. After the Uganda Fund, others kept coming. I didn't realise that the initial funding might have been the least stressful part, and that bigger challenges lay ahead. We faced a lack of building supplies in the north, and inexperienced builders and project managers who had had little to manage for two decades. I spent my days writing cheques, receiving donated supplies and writing as many letters as I could to people who might help. And pushing the builders to complete the task.

It took eight months for the school building to make it to lock-up stage. We had not been idle during the construction period: we started the process of finding desks, books, blackboards and other equipment for the classrooms that were now taking form. We worked for months on basic approvals from the Department of Education so we could start to interview the girls who would become our students. Our team set out by motorbike in different directions from Pader, so our search could cover three Pader sub-counties. We looked for the most vulnerable, the hidden girls, enlisting their parents into selection committees.

In Patongo sub-county, I sat with a group of parents who showered me with questions. I explained how we wanted girls whose schooling had been interrupted by war and who now had no other options. Under government requirements, girls without primary-school education were ineligible for the academic secondary-school stream and senior exams. It saddened me to discover how many girls had stalled at this low milestone before the conflict.

'Any girls are welcome to come to Pader to learn catering and tailoring, but today we are looking for girls who have a primary-leaving certificate,' I announced, looking from face to face. 'Can you nominate the girls in your village who need this most? Babies are welcome,' I said, to a collective ripple of surprise from the parents.

'What if my daughter had low marks in primary?' one curious father asked.

'It doesn't matter if her marks were average,' I explained. I was careful not to set the bar beyond reach in case it excluded the most needy. 'We just need girls who want to learn.'

It took weeks of community consultation to bring some elders around to believing that teenage girls from their village were worthy of an education. 'This school will just encourage young girls to get pregnant. It will be a breeding place for young mothers,' an elder had scoffed.

I bristled at this. 'That is not true. It will help them see possibilities beyond being a mother,' I argued. He pulled his head back in surprise. It was not usual in our culture for a woman to speak so firmly to an elder. 'If we can show the girls another path, they might not get pregnant at sixteen or seventeen.' During our interviews with girls in their late teens with babies—not all of whom had been abducted—we had heard many similar stories: my boyfriend told me he'd help me if I slept with him; he promised to marry me but he left when I got pregnant.

As the weeks of interviews wore on, we grew tired. I could see the furrowed brows and feel the heaviness that bore down on us when we met at the end of the day to share our findings and the stories of our prospective students: Anna had come from the IDP camp, but before that had watched as the LRA cooked fellow villagers alive and forced others to eat them. Betty had seen her brothers beaten to death with a stake. Christine had escaped captivity while collecting firewood and cassava.

One morning, I pulled the team together to pray for God's strength and wisdom as we made our choices. 'I know that these stories are hard to hear, but we need to believe in order to have the courage to keep going,' I encouraged them, and myself at the same time.

These were not average students, and we knew that we would need extraordinary teachers to manage them from day to day. I nervously placed a notice for the top position in the regional paper. 'Position available: head teacher required to head a girls' secondary and vocational school. Must have a Bachelor Degree in Education, a mature Christian background, strong management skills and an ability to teach in a school with special needs. Must be open-hearted and passionate about educating girls.'

I omitted any particular mention of war-affected girl mothers, knowing that this might drive away the best candidates. These girls had been traumatised and violated, seen violence I could not imagine, and missed out on learning life's lessons from parents and clans. We needed to balance their psychological needs with our goal of providing an education.

Quietly, I was counting on compassion for the girls to override any of the applicants' apprehensions. When a woman named Catherine Anenna applied for the job from her teaching post in southern Sudan, I was soon in contact. In Sudan, Miss Anenna had taught adults, mostly men who as boys had fought for the Sudan People's Liberation Army. She had identified with the struggle of staying in school through conflict, and was not put off by my mention of special needs.

I waited close to the road as the new head teacher stepped off the bus in Pader, recoiling when a cloud of fine red dust engulfed the bus and those standing around it. Miss Anenna had been on the road from Sudan for ten hours or more, so I took her to the room she had reserved to freshen up before inviting her into my office to explain some of the challenges ahead. Miss Anenna paused at the door to straighten the pleats in her skirt before nervously making her way to my desk.

'Miss Anenna, you will find that some of the girls are unruly and won't listen. This is because they have had little instruction in life from their parents. Some have been very badly treated, and they react to all people with anger. Some days will be very hard, but you will see the rewards of your care,' I explained, speaking softly. Miss Anenna nodded.

It was only at the school in the next few days, as the girls started to arrive with suitcases in their hands and babies strapped to their backs, that the full nature of those special needs hit her. 'But there are so many babies at the school,' she blurted out, as she watched the girls arriving over the afternoon. 'Where will they all stay?'

'We want them to stay with the students in the dormitory and not be left in the village where they will not know their mother's love. If the babies are here, we can train the girls to be good mothers,' I explained, half expecting Miss Anenna to turn around and head for Pader township, looking for the next bus back to Sudan.

Miss Anenna stood and silently surveyed the schoolyard. 'Yes, I have seen this in Sudan, and I have handled angry children,' she mused, without looking at me. The girls were standing in small groups, getting to know each other, some cradling their babies or watching as toddlers chewed twigs on the ground. 'It is the same in Sudan. Girls cannot feed their babies in the school, and so they leave.' She pulled her shoulders back and pushed up her chin. 'Don't worry, I will manage,' she said.

'So you know how much we need to care for these girls.' I let out a long breath. We had found our head teacher, one with a shared passion to help the girls.

The recruitment of teaching staff was equally sensitive. 'What is your understanding of the term "special needs"?' I asked every aspiring teacher I interviewed.

'It is a disabled child, or a child abducted by the LRA,' most answered. By the time I made it through the interviews, explaining how these girls would be even more needy than usual, I was sure that we had the right staff. We had chosen eight teachers—two women and six men—who were prepared to go further than the easier option of teaching in a government school, where girl mothers were not welcome.

*

The Pader Girls Academy opened on 15 March 2008, a month behind schedule, and a month into the school year. But the girls did not care. Nor did they care that the day was oppressively hot, that there were few trees to offer shade, or that they did not yet have uniforms. School was an unexpected turn in their lives, and they were happy to be there.

That morning I woke before dawn to a dead silence, shrouded in a mosquito net that I had suspended from a small hook on the ceiling above me. I let my eyes flutter closed and slipped easily into a prayer for the day ahead, gratitude flooding my soul.

I took in a long breath, my chest slowly rising, before expelling the air in a hurry at the thought of embarking on a new adventure. Gone was the daily crush, when I had awoken with too much to do. I knew this would be a good day. I had dreamed of this day, when the teams of noisy labourers and their dust would be gone from the building site, and the girls could finally start their new lives.

The day before the opening, I had hovered nervously in the school's central courtyard as forty-six girls—twenty of them with babies—had bid farewell to family members and filed past me. I knew each girl by name, as I had hand-picked each one. I ushered them through the big green doors into the dormitory, a room filled with rows of bottle-green double bunks supplied by UNICEF. The classrooms and offices were in two side rooms; one office was reserved for the matron, who would dole out medication each morning as part of the school's HIV/AIDs program. At the southern end of the main building was a room with a built-in brick oven where vocational students would learn the secrets of baking bread.

I was drawn to the timid girls, those who looked at their feet and would not meet my eyes. With each one, I extended my hand as if to transmit confidence through my fingers, and coaxed the girl's eyes up from the ground to my smile. The bolder girls were cheeky, playful in their excitement, and already making new friends. Each girl had just one box of possessions she could slide under her bunk, with a plastic bowl for washing faces and clothes, and for bathing the babies.

In the first few weeks, both the teachers and the girls navigated the chaos of babies that could not be corralled; babies with stomach upsets that brought diarrhoea and vomiting, which in a confined dormitory were soon passed on; babies with coughs, colds, allergies and runny noses; babies crying to be fed when the girls needed to concentrate; and who refused to be separated from their mothers, or crawled across the dirty classroom floor. Some days the academic classes spilled out under the few shade trees in the grounds beyond the building, and the babies were ever harder to catch—though they were more content to be exploring outside.

We knew that the girls had many medical needs, from old wounds to injuries and disease, but apart from some of the integrated programs for HIV/AIDS, the school had no resources. Behind the physical illnesses lay the crippling psychological burden that the girls carried as victims, and we knew that healing their pain and trauma could take a lifetime.

Mr Opimo was among the first visitors to the school. I greeted him nervously when he pulled up in his government car, aware of how important it was to keep the District Education Officer on side if we wanted the school to flourish. He surveyed the girls and their babies playing, washing and laughing around him, at first entranced by what he saw. Then his brow furrowed as he remembered his official role. 'Alice, if the Ministry of Education comes, I will be in trouble for this school.'

'Why?' I asked, alarmed.

'You know it is not allowed according to Ugandan law. When a girl is pregnant, she must be expelled from school,' he told me. 'And there must be a fence around the school.'

'Can you please give me a copy of the document that mentions pregnant girls? I would like to see it,' I demanded, my voice escalating quickly in defence.

I pointed to Grace, one of the young girls nearby. 'This girl right here is fourteen years old, and when she was abducted she had just completed her Primary 7. Do you know how much she got in P7? She got a six, one of the best grades possible. And do you know where she got it? From one of the most remote villages in the whole of Pader district. This girl will not go into tailoring and remain there. I believe she will go much further in her studies.'

Mr Opimo stood, staring at the ground. When he lifted his head, he said quietly, 'It is good,' and I knew that I had an ally, however reluctant.

I then made a point of asking my friend Cathy to find a copy of the *Education Act* in Gulu. I read through the pages of the document and could find nothing at all about pregnancy and school attendance. It was blank on the subject. I knew then that this was a cultural and not a regulatory problem, and that the government could not oppose us on the grounds of girls being pregnant or having babies.

After the first month of the school's operation, the science teacher, Nicholas Opiti, knocked on the door of my office. Nicholas was 26 years old and had graduated only the year before from teachers' college in Gulu. Pader Girls Academy was his first teaching job. He had arrived on the first day in a radiant white shirt, creaseless trousers and polished black shoes. He now stood on the other side of my desk equally well dressed, with his hands clasped together, and looking troubled.

It did not surprise me to see him. I had already received the geography teacher, Joan Adongo, and knew of many of the problems that the teachers faced. The teachers were all under pressure to get the girls to the exams, to guide them in how to be more disciplined and more academic, and how to follow the principles of the curriculum.

'Madam Alice, it is too hard to teach these girls,' he said, throwing his arms in the air. 'One girl is so angry that she will not listen to me. With one of the others, I just say, "Please ask for permission to leave the class when you need to feed your baby" and she will cry. I don't know what to do. They did not teach us this in college.'

He paused to gauge my reaction before continuing. 'There is one girl in Senior 2 who was the wife to a commander for nine years. She is rude to me and nasty to all the other girls in class. The girls told me that at night in the dormitory she calls out with nightmares, but during the day she is so angry with everyone.'

I nodded. I had been observing the way that the teachers and girls interacted, and wasn't sure what to do. Many of the girls who came through the rehabilitation process found it hard to see themselves as anything other than victims—it would be a slow road out if they were ever to live in the community or go beyond that.

'Nicholas, I'm sorry. These girls are not like other girls. Some are so rebellious that they don't know how to listen, and some are very shy and feel so inferior that they cannot even speak for themselves. Please remain with us, and I will see what I can do to help the teachers.'

The person I had turned to in the past was Sister Margaret, the primary teacher who had cared for me at school in Gulu, and who had since earned her Masters degree in psychology and counselling. If anyone understood the challenges of dealing with traumatised girls and might be able to train the teachers in how to listen to the girls and manage their behaviour, it was Sister Margaret.

'With these girls, you'll have to find other ways of teaching,' she told the teachers, who sat quietly listening to her every word, grateful for her help. She had aged well. The strands of her hair were now more grey than black, the smile lines around her eyes were etched deeper, but age had also brought a deep and loving wisdom. 'You can't teach the curriculum and expect the girls to learn as other children learn.'

She talked with the girls, too, her gentleness drawing out their fear of failing or of being inadequate or unworthy. The self-esteem of many girls had been trampled in the bush. I stood at the side of the classroom, for a time melding with the students. It took me back to my days as a shy primary schoolgirl at Holy Rosary. How I loved this woman, who had kept my waning spirit alive all those years ago, and who would now do the same for another generation.

The whole school changed after Sister Margaret's visit. The lives of the teachers became more bearable, while the attitudes of the girls became more positive and cooperative.

Nicholas soon reported back to me. 'Remember the young woman who was my worst behaved?' he asked, barely concealing his relief. I nodded. 'I have seen such a change since Sister Margaret has helped us. I have been able to talk with her, and she is opening up to me,' he smiled, as proud as a man who had won first prize in a marathon.

I smiled and patted his shoulder. 'Thank you for your patience, Nicholas.' I was thankful for any progress.

I was at the school every day, making sure that the teachers were speaking kindly to the girls, and talking with the girls about their lives, helping any young woman whose trauma was still raw and visible with how they related to those around her. Whenever I heard a baby cry, I scooped them up and sought out the mother to pacify the child on her breast. My eagerness for the girls' wellbeing put me in the role of mother, teacher, counsellor and protector.

The school had already lost one teacher back to a government-run school, where she could look forward to a pension at the end of her career. On her way out, the teacher had complained that every time a baby came into the classroom, it grabbed books and pens from the girls and interrupted learning. This had prompted us to set up a supervised space for babies under a tree about 100 metres from the classrooms, though the tree was still within earshot of the school building, and the cries of hungry babies were still a distraction.

One afternoon after classes had finished, Miss Anenna arrived in my office. She was dressed impeccably in an ankle-length dress, and her hair was braided and swept up high on her head. 'Excuse me, madam, can we please talk about the school?' she asked. 'These girls have to pass exams, and if they don't pass exams they can't do anything. Let us try to follow the curriculum without the constant interruptions,' she told me, with the confidence she had gathered over several months in her position.

I felt the warmth rise in my face. I met Catherine's serious stare with a long look. 'I know. I am too protective of the girls. I'll try not to meddle,' I promised. 'Thank you for saying this, and thank you for staying.'

I had bought a small piece of land right beside the school on which I intended to build a grass-thatch hut so I could live nearby. But that wet season brought heavy rains, the rivers in the district overflowed, and day after day it was not possible for the women caring for the babies to mind them under the tree. I arranged for builders to hastily finish the hut, and then moved the babies and carers into their new space. I could not have imagined that, after such rain, the skies would then close and not open for two years.

Within four months of the school's opening, the number of students had doubled, and with growth came even more babies. During visits to villages, I had met more needy and capable girls than we could cope with at the school as it was now: I could see how in five years we might be teaching five hundred girls, and I was already planning new buildings. In these short months, a meeting hall had been added to the original building, and another building—a guesthouse and hospitality training centre—was well on the way beside the school. Still, a few girls had dropped out after being summoned back to their villages by families needing help with labour in the fields.

*

Late one night during the early months of the school, the matron woke to the sound of hands clanging on metal, followed by laughing and catcalls, and muffled female voices. Soon afterwards, she heard the shrill cries of babies woken from deep sleep, and squeals that told her this was not an internal disturbance. She wrapped her cloth tightly around her waist and rushed into the inky darkness, to see figures darting from window to window, and hands worrying at the lock that secured the heavy metal door of the dormitory she locked each night after the girls had finished their evening meal.

'What are you doing?' she asked in a voice so stern it pulled the boys up.

'We're looking for love,' one of them replied, his voice pathetically weak and barely broken.

'You leave these girls alone and don't ever come back,' matron commanded, standing tall and pointing to the path towards Pader township. The boys melted into the darkness.

'Are you okay, girls?' she called into the dormitory, where she could see the young women already settling back into their bunks.

I arrived at the school the next morning unaware of the evening's ruckus—there were no outward signs. When the matron pulled me aside to explain what had happened, I shook my head. 'We will get a security fence as soon as we can,' I promised.

Within weeks, a foreign visitor had offered to pay for our fence. We could enclose the gaps between the classroom blocks, the dormitories and the small kitchen, so the girls and babies could live safely. We'd solved the urgent problem of the girls' security, ensuring that they were not the defence-less targets of young boys from the township, but there were many other issues at hand. The brazenness of the night visitors worried me, especially as some of the girls were newly escaped from the conflict and still vulnerable.

I made a mental note: at the next assembly, I would speak on self-respect and how to say no. Deep inside, I despaired. I marched back into my office so no one would see the anger that had set my jaw, stiffened my arms and clenched my fists. *Can any of us solve the bigger problem?* The war had blurred the line between sex and love in the minds of the young boys, so that they were indistinguishable. Often now, when both men and boys looked for love, it meant forcing themselves sexually on the girls. I sighed and moved on to my pile of paperwork.

*

Though my childhood in the north was disjointed, I knew many people in Pader district, and soon many more knew of our school. I heard the names that people had for Pader Girls Academy: the school of second chances and the school of foundation. Some sceptics called it the school for lost girls. My colleagues and I saw it as the school of restoration, where we were concerned with all aspects of the girls' lives: the physical and the spiritual, the emotional and the practical.

It wasn't long before others noticed what we were doing. I had emailed my friends outside Uganda to tell them about the school, and offers of support came back. A young American friend named Veronica Guzman arrived with sixty pairs of underwear for the girls, and left offering to help set up a website for the school.

By mid-2008, War Child UK had set up a new office in Pader, and soon I had met with the two local workers, Matthew and Saidi, to discuss how they might help widen the students' experience and counsel those with a wild edge—those who, in missing school and growing up apart from their families, had missed learning vital social skills. When, in the second half of the year, an invitation arrived from the Minister of Education and Sports in Kampala to join a sporting competition with five hundred children from ten primary schools in Pader district, our friends at War Child UK encouraged us to take up the offer.

'It will build confidence and allow them to integrate with other children. We will pay for them to go,' Matthew offered, and I gratefully accepted. This was the first chance for the PGA girls to mix with young people from other schools, who routinely met to play each other in sporting activities such as track and field events and soccer.

'Any primary-age student wishing to compete for our school track and field team in a district competition should meet outside the kitchen block at 7 a.m. for trials,' the head teacher announced at assembly that week. 'We will take the eight best athletes.'

A wave of excited chatter swept the room. When the assigned time came, more than two dozen girls lined up to race around the perimeter of the school grounds, across clods of dried mud and through long grass in their bare feet. Most were naturally strong and fit from their days of living in the bush, or from carting heavy water from the pump in the village, or walking long distances.

Two weeks later, a minibus from War Child UK arrived early in the morning to collect the eight top athletes in the junior school, a couple with their suckling babies. They had only just descended the stairs of the bus at the sports field when the taunts started. 'What are you doing here? You're the Pader second-hand girls,' one girl in a group from another school called, and the rest tittered. The Pader girls stopped still near the bus, deflated. They had not anticipated cruelty on such a happy day. A teacher with the Pader girls quickly picked up on the exchange and herded them away, then went to talk with the organisers of the event.

By the time I arrived, the girls had been parked in a small fenced-off area, away from the ridicule. They hung their heads in shame, too disappointed to acknowledge me. 'Madam Alice, they are calling us names,' one of the girls eventually said, the tears splashing down her cheeks.

For a few minutes, I waited silently with them. I was too angry to speak and feared what I might say. 'Don't worry,' I finally reassured them, knowing that my response was weak. I felt the ferocity of the insults as if they were directed at me. Soon the girls' natural instinct to fight back rose up among the group, and the conversation turned to revenge.

'We'll show them we are not second-hand girls.'

'We will beat them up. That will stop them calling us names.'

I heard their plotting and stood up to address them, looking at each in turn. 'We are not to fight back in that way. We must not fight with our fists,' I told them with all the authority of my position. 'There is only one thing you can do. You must run faster and show them how talented you are. That will keep them quiet.'

But the name-calling continued that day, especially when they could not summon the spirit to run hard, and into the next day, when they again stepped off the minibus and heard, 'The useless Pader girls are back. Go back to your babies.'

On the second day, the teasing was less potent. Matthew had met them off the bus and taken them aside for a pep talk before the nasty words could crush them. 'Keep going and do your very best. You have to ignore those girls—they are jealous because you are so fast,' he urged, and it was enough to boost their confidence.

In the first race, the Pader entrant flew off the starting blocks, her head down and legs pumping, unaware of anything but her determination to overcome the prejudice with a good performance. Again and again the girls took Matthew's words to heart, and by lunchtime they were leading in all events. They went on to come second in the district overall.

I stood with Matthew as each of the girls mounted the podium to shake the hand of the District Education Officer and receive her red ribbon. I choked up as I thought of what they had overcome to be there. 'I am so proud of our girls,' I declared.

At the end of the day, when we all climbed into the minibus, the atmosphere was electrified with their victory. As one girl broke into song, the others soon joined in, composing the words as they sang. 'It's our first time, and we are second best in the district,' one sang happily in Lwo while the others echoed.

I sat in the front seat beside the driver, contented. Two of the girls were so fast that they were on their way to compete at the national championships. I stared absently into the long grass beside the road as the bus rattled back to the school, while my mind pondered the possibilities. *Where could these girls end up? What barriers can we break down for them?* With a pang of guilt, I thought of Polline, who had done little since her return home to her family village. We'd agreed that she would need some time to recover from her captivity with the LRA before she plunged back into school, but it seemed to me that she'd lost some of the hope she had carried on her homeward journey. With their livestock gone, her family had even less to live on than before the war, and her prospects were low. Yet when I had visited her several weeks before, she had said, 'I wake every morning so thankful for my freedom.' I made a mental note to visit her again soon.

*

Polline was not expecting my white truck to roll up the rough track leading into her village. She was bent over a pot, stirring beans over the fire for the evening meal, when the car pulled up beside her.

'*Apwoyo*, Polline. You look well,' I said, stepping out of the four-wheel drive and walking towards her.

'Madam Alice, it is so good to see you,' Polline called, her face lighting up into a huge smile. She quickly wiped her hands on her skirt and stretched out her forearm to me, the polite way to indicate that her hands were not clean.

'I'm here to talk with you and your parents,' I said before dipping my head and calling into the dark void of the hut beside me. 'Min Polline, Papa, it is Alice Achan from CCF Pader,' I introduced myself and stepped inside, with Polline close behind. 'We have a place for Polline in the school, if you are willing for her to join us.' I spoke to Polline's parents with the respect reserved for elders.

Then I turned to Polline. 'Are you ready to come back to school now?' I said, grinning.

Polline beamed back, before a dark cloud of uncertainty appeared and her smile turned to a frown. 'Will they hate me because I was with the rebels?' she asked, looking to her mother for reassurance.

'No, you will find many others who have been through this, too. Don't worry,' I replied warmly, placing my arm around her small shoulders.

Soon afterwards, Polline walked into the quadrangle with her single cardboard suitcase and rolled-up mattress, accompanied by both of her parents. To her delight, and that of the girls, Polline recognised some of her friends from her time with the rebels.

'Ah, Polline, you have made it home,' one girl squealed, as they embraced.

'Yes, I am here,' she laughed, pushing back with straight arms to take in her friend's happiness.

Other girls now returned from Congo to similar acclaim. Each time, Polline was the first to cry with joy when she saw her, the first to embrace her, the first to hear her stories, and the first to put her arm around the girl and sit with her in a darkened room if she was too traumatised to talk.

Just as she had stood out as a leader among the young girls in the LRA camp, Polline now stood out among the girls in Pader. Only weeks after her arrival, Polline's natural leadership ability had emerged. Already, she was unfazed about addressing the whole school, and rousing the girls with uplifting words at assembly. Even when she chastised girls who stepped out of line—those who swore at the teachers or abused other girls—it only seemed to bolster her popularity. When the time came to elect a new Head Girl of Pader Girls Academy, Polline put herself forward and was chosen with an overwhelming majority by her peers as their leader. She had risen from near death to this position in just two short years.

23

Talking

In the north of Uganda, it was a time to breathe. And talk. I could feel the change in mood by the end of 2008 as I visited family and friends, and went about my work in the community. The government was orchestrating a program to break up the mass camps for the internally displaced—they called it decongestion. Those leaving the security of large numbers in the camps now built their new homes in groupings of five or six mud-brick huts, often in extended families. The huts hugged close together, in close proximity to pre-war villages if the families could not go back to the actual site due to disputes over land ownership.

My sister, Doreen, was in limbo, one of a dwindling number of camp dwellers living in abject isolation, as they were still to find a permanent home. I visited often these days, in my four-wheel drive, and one day when I came, Doreen wanted to talk.

'Alice, we are still a strong group here, the women left in the camp,' Doreen greeted me with fresh buoyancy. She was a different person, so positive compared to earlier times. I looked at my sister, tall and slender like our father, and felt a flood of pride at her natural ability to lead others, no matter what her circumstances.

'The Seeds of Love, we are doing well, Alice,' she smiled, a gap where her front teeth had once been, before the ravages of war. 'Just last week we prayed with a grandmother who is caring for all of her grandchildren. We were able to give her some flour and help her wash the children.'

I was doing what I could to help, with transport and food as well as money for small items. Many of the women had started small businesses selling tomatoes or bananas from their huts, and CCF had been able to arrange some funding for seeds and a machine that could mill flour. The tin hut housing the grinding machine was the centrepiece of the community, a meeting place as important as the well.

Outsiders had tried to make Acholi lives better in the camps over the past few years. As I walked to my sister's hut I could see their efforts, still visible even after most inhabitants had left. I passed a faded sign in English that told me, 'Put children's faeces always in the latrine as they are also harmful.' It reminded me of the people who had cared during the worst of the conflict. It no longer mattered that only a fraction of the people in the camp could read the sign, or that they had continued the dangerous practice of leaving faeces everywhere around the camp. I had seen worse indignities.

I looked across at the few remaining huts and imagined the camp at its crowded peak. I pictured the scramble to receive food when the World Food Programme trucks rolled in every few weeks, the lines of yellow jerry cans and mounds of rice on blue tarpaulins, and the farmers who, despite centuries of tradition, had lost their farming skills after two decades off the land. I could understand the desperation. My own girls—those training in sewing and hospitality—had been kept alive by such handouts.

'We'll all be gone from here soon,' Doreen told me, and it was true. Just as soldiers had razed huts to empty out villages and force whole communities into the camps in the mid- to late 1990s, they now destroyed huts in IDP camps so people could not return.

'Yes, life will get better for all of us,' I reflected, the hope rising within me like a balloon. I welcomed the purging of our dark recent past. When I walked up the hill in Pader, I saw plumes of smoke rising into the blue sky in every direction as fire took hold of weathered thatch. I imagined the families who looked on as flames consumed their wartime homes, and hoped they had better homes now.

In many ways, life in the north was looking up. For many years in the camps, people had been without access to hospitals or medical supplies for ailments as basic and widespread as diarrhoea and malaria. Now, organisations such as Médecins Sans Frontières had set up clinics, and other groups had arrived to test for diseases such as tuberculosis and HIV. Children were being immunised against basic diseases, and malnourished children finally had food.

With the ceasefire came opportunity, a surprising side effect of peace after so much suffering. Foreign NGOs brought staff, and they built or improved accommodation. They operated from foreign budgets that could stimulate trade at the local markets and create jobs and training.

We were already a step ahead. 'There are so many foreigners here now. They have nowhere to eat, and we have girls training in hospitality with nowhere to get experience,' I said to my board at our meeting in the reception centre. 'We could set up a restaurant. I already have a place in mind.' A corner shopfront was available right across the road from the reception centre, on one of Pader's main intersections.

The Mega Ber—meaning 'good table' in Lwo—was open within weeks, with half a dozen bare tables, some brand-new plastic chairs and a fridge that ran sporadically on the local power supply. It soon filled with aid workers—American, British, Irish, Dutch—who were delighted to support a local business and to find a meeting place. However, it was hard to find fresh food in Pader at that time, with so little land under cultivation. The local Pader produce market was a simple row of thrown-together timber stalls, selling a handful of misshapen tomatoes, green beans and eggplants, which locals could not afford to buy in any case. Its vendors sat there all day, hoping for a few shillings in sales to buy more produce to sell. But the larger markets in Lira had all we needed for the delicacies on offer in the restaurant: spicy chicken and rice, stewed beef with potato, vegetable dishes and beans. The bread came straight from the brick oven at the school, where a team of cooking students had perfected the art of baking buns to a uniform tan.

Most days, Grace was among the younger girls scraping leftover food into one bucket and plunging the dirty dishes into another. Childhood polio had crippled her legs, but her hands could move nimbly, and she revelled in her usefulness at the restaurant. Her bright manner and ready smile lifted those around her. Some years ago, someone had crafted a bicycle into her means of transport, allowing her to propel the bike with her strong arms, and move freely on the dirt roads around the town. She had come under my care several years before, but this had not prevented her from being preyed on by unscrupulous men, and she now had three small mouths to feed.

'If you give birth again, I will not support you. Next time you will have to go back to dig in the garden,' I told her in a joking tone, and Grace threw back her head and laughed. At times I felt the intense pressure of carrying the responsibility for so many, but mostly I was thankful for the privilege of standing with women like Grace.

I often sat at a table in the corner of the Mega Ber, greeting patrons from NGOs such as Dutch groups ZOA and MWH, and Save the Children and World Vision, and directing the girls from the hospitality school who ran the restaurant. Occasionally, I slipped behind the floral curtain at the back of the restaurant to visit the dark verandah where the girls prepared and cooked the food over a small coal fire, the dishes piled high beside them. I often sat for hours, updating visitors on local matters, and telling newcomers where to find food and lodgings, how to stay safe and who was who in the district. It helped the school that I was the go-to person on local partnership.

One day as I sat at my corner table, Saidi, a friend from War Child UK, popped down beside me. 'We have the people from Comic Relief in the UK interested in supporting girls' education,' Saidi told me, her face breaking into a wide smile. I smiled back, though quietly baffled.

'Why are they interested in northern Uganda?' I quizzed, shaking my head and laughing at the odd mix of comedy and war.

'We've told them about the children here, and they would like to help,' Saidi answered. 'They are not just comedians.

They are people from the entertainment industry who raise money for good causes.'

'That is so good,' I said, welling up. 'It is just what we need.' In our harsh world, the unsolicited kindness of strangers still moved me.

Before long, a small film crew had arrived at the school to start filming for the combined War Child UK and Comic Relief advocacy project. I flitted from the crew to the girls, explaining and translating, directing and mediating. The cameraman hid behind the heavy camera resting on his shoulder, zooming in on lively young faces, sad faces and tearful faces, adding images to the girls' narratives of life in the war, and placing a spotlight on the power of overcoming.

At the end of this small project, both partners wanted more. 'Please send a proposal for any activity that you think will best support the youth who've been affected by the conflict,' requested the people at War Child UK. It was not hard for us to find a worthy project in education.

'What if we look at the group of boys and girls who were midway through secondary school, in Senior 3 or 4, who were not able to complete their studies because of war?' the head teacher suggested. 'If we give them a six-month intensive course and then allow them to sit for their Senior 4 exams, they'll be able to finish school.'

This set off a ripple of conversation in the room, as it had not been considered before. 'We can then train our own young people as teachers and nurses, and employ them in the community.'

We called this catch-up program Protection of the Community, and I proposed a gender mix of 60 per cent girls to 40 per cent boys, which in turn sparked intense questioning. 'Why are you favouring the girls over the boys, Alice?' a community worker dealing with boys asked me.

'Well, there are hundreds of girls in the district who did not finish Senior 3, that is why I favour girls, and I am not ashamed of it. Pader Girls Academy will take every girl, and we will find other schools for the boys,' I responded. I was sick of being told that it was a waste of money to educate girls, and set out to prove otherwise.

At the end of the catch-up program, CCF had to find other schools to host the girls during their examinations, as Pader Girls Academy did not have the necessary accreditation. At each of the other schools we approached, we were told, 'Yes, we have space for your girls to sit the examinations,' and 'Yes, we have room for them to stay in our school.' That is, until the schools learned that the girls had babies, and then every door slammed shut.

'Why won't you take the girls?' I confronted one of the school principals.

'Because we are not used to handling the babies,' he replied.

'You are refusing to allow them to sit the exams simply because they are mothers? Is that the only reason?' I asked, waving my hands in frustration. 'Okay, I will find outside accommodation if they can sit the exams at your school.' It was hard to accept how few people around us understood the needs of the girls. *These teachers needed education as much as the girls,* I told myself, kicking the ground.

I set about finding huts to rent, transport for the girls each day, and carers for their babies. In total, there were 110 people spread around many different locations. It proved to be an effective three-year program, with thirty-seven boys and girls from the intake eventually returning to their communities with new skills. Of these, twenty-two went through to teachers' training, and fifteen became nursing assistants. In one of the schools where CCF girls sat their exams, they were the best ten students.

'Ah, I am shocked. Pleasantly shocked,' the District Education Officer exclaimed when I arrived at his office with the news. Back in my own office, the staff met to pray and give thanks for the girls' winning scores.

I had also taken an interest in another group of young people, those who went into vocational training—mechanics, hairdressing, secretarial work, welding, metal fabrication and catering. Twenty-eight young women came through catering training and left the school with the basic tools they needed to start a tiny business: some rice and herbs, large pots and cooking utensils. Some were natural entrepreneurs who I knew would thrive with a little help. I hovered around them like a mother hen.

A young mother of two, Josephine—also known as Min Asama, mother of Asama—had arrived at the reception centre from Corner Kilak, an outpost on the road from Lira to Kitgum, just as the six-month catering program was starting. 'She's one to watch,' I had said to colleagues on the first day that Josephine joined the training. She had a stocky build and a serious manner that made her stand out in the crowd. I had sensed in her a formidable determination to succeed, and made a note to follow her progress.

Min Asama watched the teacher with the focus of an eagle eyeing prey as she mixed spices to make chicken and beans more flavoursome, or added ginger to beef, and bicarbonate to soften tough meat. She positioned herself close to the trainer in class and asked questions about how to keep customers happy and have them coming back for more.

'Min, did you learn to cook from your own mother?' I pried one day, as the class dispersed. The young woman lifted her chin and looked at me.

'No, madam. I was taken to the bush when I was thirteen, and when I returned with two children, my mother did not want to know me,' she replied, resolutely. It was clear that she was not looking for pity. 'I like business, and I like to cook.' Then she filed out of the room behind the other catering students.

'That girl, she is one of the smart ones who will never just sit in the village and say, "I have nothing to do." She is a good role model for the other girls,' I told my colleagues after this encounter. I had known other girls who had fallen into prostitution in their desperation to feed their children, and ended up with more mouths to feed. I felt confident that this girl would always be able to take care of herself.

It wasn't long before I saw Josephine in action in the sub-county market, busy greeting people at first light with milk tea from a flask, then rolling out and frying chapattis that were quickly snapped up and consumed by the ravenous villagers who had walked hours in darkness to be there. I lined up behind the other clients, some of whom came away with steaming bowls of millet porridge. Min Asama was too busy to notice the tall woman in the line until I stood at her low table.

'Good morning, Min Asama. Your stall is the busiest one of them all,' I announced, smiling with pride.

'Thank you, Madam Alice. That is because my food is the best. When this morning crowd moves on, I will start cooking chicken and rice for lunch. I sell out quickly, so I tell them,

"First in, first served." Sometimes when I move from market to market, I can make one hundred dollars in a single day.'

'That is very good. What will you do with all that money?' I knew her well enough to ask.

'Soon I will be able to afford my own store in Corner Kilak, where travellers will come for my food, and I will have a refrigerator for cold drinks. And my children will go to school.' I smiled and nodded my farewell, walking away to visit other stalls with a dripping chapatti in hand.

*

While elsewhere people debated the impact of climate change, I did not need scientific evidence to tell me that we were vulnerable; the security of our food supplies hung by a tenuous wisp of a thread that could break in any season. I had already seen the tyranny of climate in our isolated pocket of the African continent in September 2007, when the rains came with such force that they flooded the waterways and swept away the sweet green shoots of our crops. Then the following year, the rains had failed altogether, and I had watched young maize, millet and sorghum plants shrivel in the unrelenting sun.

The planting had been such a joyful event for the young girls. 'Let us go out into the field after our lessons,' Miss Anenna had directed them, and they gathered their spades and picks to peck at the mounds of clay until they yielded a hole for the seeds. They sang as they worked—songs of the bounty to come—at times stopping to laugh or chase each other, just as girls in their early teens would play anywhere. They worked contentedly until the sun fell in deep golden bands around their shadows and dew gathered on the strands of grass, then they traipsed back to their dormitory in the dying light.

When the rains of early 2009 failed as well, I knew that we were in trouble. The school's food supply was stored in a leftover shipping container, to keep it dry and free of mice and rats. Some of the grain had been held over from a surplus the previous year, between the floods and the drought, but when I nervously opened the container's rusty door each week and saw how quickly the food stocks were running down in feeding 150 girls—many of them mothers—I knew that we could not get through another barren season.

The school was a cocoon for the girls, who—in their routine of classes and chores, and lining up each evening with their plastic bowls by the huge pot of bubbling gruel—were unaware of the fragility of their situation. We often chastised them for wasting water from the taps as they washed their clothes and their babies. The whole of northern Uganda— and with it more than a million people—was heading into a famine, and no one could see a way out. The markets had emptied, and few had the shillings to travel outside the district.

I carried the burden and shared it with few around me for fear of creating anxiety. Yet even with a famine looming, I was not distressed. *Panicking will not bring more food,* I told myself. Instead, I held fast to my faith, which made me calmer and clearer than in times when I could see the source of our food. Deep down, I knew that we would all come through, and I intimated as much to Florence, who stood by me. 'God has given me sole responsibility for this number of children, and I am still confident that God will provide,' I shared.

As the end of term approached and the girls were due to return to their village homes, I had to act. 'We can't send these girls home,' I declared, as I mulled over our options with the teachers. 'There is no food in the villages, and already children and old people are starving. We must keep the girls here, or they may not come back after the break,' I announced to the staff.

'Why don't we ask the World Food Programme to help us?' someone asked.

'They are in Karamoja now, and the drought is even more severe there,' I replied. I had heard that almost all the Karimojong relied on food from the WFP to stay alive.

As food supplies diminished, I felt pressure from within my own extended family. Every day now I had a visit from a needy, distant relative. 'Alice, my child is sick, can you pay for the hospital?' or 'Can you please pay for the coffin and funeral for my child?'

The pressure intensified when the World Food Programme gave CCF Pader the task of distributing food to those in the community who were HIV-positive and needed food supplements to accompany their antiretroviral drugs. I could see that my half-sisters and their families were hungry and weak, and they knew that there was food at the school. Soon, even the little money I had could not help them, as there was no food in the market to buy. It distressed me so much that I set out one day to Lira to buy beans to bring them back to the village, but still some family members complained: 'You are feeding these strangers and not looking after your own.' That night I wept. Refusing to help family members went against the culture I held dear, but I knew my integrity was at stake.

Please God, let your grace be upon me, as I feel so divided,

I prayed through my tears, while my mind strained to find a way through this minefield beyond the war. *Please give me the strength and wisdom to manage this.*

When the burden of carrying so many grew too much for me, I resolved to ask my brothers what to do. Soon afterwards, I pulled my eldest brother aside at a family gathering. 'Gabriel, what am I do with requests from the clan? This is what they think: "This is Alice's organisation, surely she should help us, her family, first." I have given all I have to give from my salary, and I have run out. My bank account is empty. Don't they understand that it is not my money when it comes to CCF?' I threw my arms into the air, as if throwing away my responsibilities.

'I understand, Alice. You must be firm,' he replied, his voice reassuring. At this, I closed my eyes and let the relief flow like nectar through my veins. My brother's words released the invisible cord that had kept me so tightly bound through this ordeal. Finally, I felt strong enough to stand up to the requests. 'This food, it is not my property, and it would be wrong to give an able-bodied person these WFP supplies when there is a single mother with four children who are all HIV-positive,' I responded to the next request.

It cleared my head to think again about the girls in my care and how I could feed so many young mouths. 'I will ask our friends outside Uganda for help,' I announced, thinking of the visitors and others I'd met in various places, who had responded so generously to the needs of the girls over the past three years.

At the start of June 2009, I sent out a distress signal. 'We are in trouble here,' my email broadcast to my circle of friends outside Acholiland. The response was immediate and overwhelming. Some responded with money, others with food. Within a couple of weeks, CCF had raised US$40,000 and was able to send a truck to bring supplies from the markets in Kampala, where food was still plentiful. One family from the United States sent a gift of US$5000, while other money came from friends in Australia. The Crossroads Church in Canada immediately appeared on local television to appeal for food, and six weeks later a container of rice and dried vegetables—enough to see the school through many months—arrived on the back of a truck from Kampala.

With the newly arrived bounty, we could reach outside the school to help vulnerable households make it through the famine. That year, the girls stayed in the school right until the end of the year without their summer break.

One day, there was a tinkle on the tin roof of my mud-brick building during the early hours of the morning. I briefly stirred, and then dozed again for some minutes before my consciousness registered what I had heard: rain. How long had it been since I had heard that sound? I pulled on my cotton wrap, unlocked the door and was soon outside, my heart pounding at the thought of a reprieve. I breathed in the mushroom-like smell of wet soil and watched in the dawning light as the splotches of water painted the dry dust. Then I perched on the edge of the balcony and smiled the smile of a woman set free from a death sentence. I smiled for the girls, who could continue their quest to learn, and for the farmers, who could grow crops again. The rain pounded the ground, shooting pellets of mud onto my dangling legs, but I did not move. My heart could not contain the gratitude that I felt at that moment. *Thank you, Lord*, I breathed, lifting my eyes skyward.

24

The End of the Peace Talks

'It's finished,' Florence told me one day in November 2008, with tears in her eyes. As a community leader, she was often the first to hear and pass on government news. This time, I knew exactly what she was talking about: the peace talks, which had kept our hope afloat from day to day for the past two years, had failed.

Such was my disappointment, I quickly sat down to stop myself falling.

'They've retreated into the forests of north Congo. With the children,' she informed me. I dreaded going back to the reception centre, or into the camp, where the parents of those girls and boys would be in despair at this news. The forests of north-eastern Congo were impenetrable; Kony's remnants would soon disappear, and they were six hundred or more kilometres from Pader. What could I possibly say to make the families feel better?

Under an agreement with a government agency, CCF had agreed to accept all Pader girls returning from the LRA. The flow of girls had slowed with the LRA's retreat, but it seemed that the severity of the war's impact on them had grown. Within a few months, two young girls, each with a baby, had arrived at the school from the barracks, where they'd been held and questioned for several days. The other girls at the school went wild with excitement when they heard that these two had arrived from Congo. They whooped and danced, sang welcome songs and crowded them with their crushing hugs, some laughing and others crying. The new arrivals were swept up in a loving embrace, as though they'd come back from the dead, apparitions arriving through the school gates. It was a temporary salve for the pain of the new arrivals.

It took several weeks before one of the girls, Agnes, was ready to talk. Trust had to be built, and we had worked on this through counsellors, and by giving the two girls their own room.

We sat on hard wooden chairs in the privacy of my office, facing each other. 'Mine is a long story, Madam Alice,' Agnes said tearfully, lowering her eyes to settle on the baby suckling at her breast.

'It is okay, Agnes. I have time,' I replied, relaxing into my chair. The heat made the chair sticky against my skirt, and there was no breeze to cool the room. Children played loudly outside, and the girls laughed as they prepared the day's meal in the hut beside us, but for now we were aware only of each other.

'I was very young when they took me from the village,' Agnes started, in a story so familiar to me that I simply nodded without expression. Agnes spoke steadily, extracting any emotion from her voice that might slow her down. 'I won't tell you all the details, other than I escaped at the beginning of the peace talks, as the rebels were leaving our district for Congo.' I nodded again, willing her on.

'I was back with my family in the village when a government negotiator came to our home one day. He asked, "Can you please come with us as part of the peace-talk team? We are trying to build confidence between the LRA and the government. I'll bring you back after the talks are through," and I believed him.' Agnes tapped the ground with her sandal. 'I did not mind cooperating, as I thought it might help end the war. I did not know that the LRA commander had demanded me back as a condition of the peace talks.' Her face contorted into an angry scowl.

I clenched my fists and blew out a deep breath, expelling some of the anger that boiled inside me as I listened to Agnes's story.

'Madam Alice, I was not the only one. There were many of us who were taken back to the rebels after 2006. When the peace talks collapsed, they left us there. Forgotten.' Agnes let out a pained cry, her bony shoulders shaking. I took her hand and squeezed. I had to work hard to quell my own anger at the recklessness of leaders who could abandon so many innocent girls.

Over an hour, Agnes told me how she was left for a second time in the hands of the same commander who had sexually abused her before, and how again she was powerless against his daily violence. But this time, she was seventeen years old and at the peak of fertility. She had fallen pregnant to the commander once before and had brought his baby back to her family in the village, and now she fell pregnant a second time. 'Madam Alice, I cannot understand why they could not protect me from this man. I'm not able to care for two children,' she cried.

I leaned towards her. 'Agnes, we will help you with your children. We will see what we can do about getting them into care at the school. We will make sure that we find you a way of earning money to support your babies,' I told her, taking the girl's hands in mine.

I reflected on those two roller-coaster years. I had encountered the deepest despair in the IDP camps after the mass exodus of rebels to Congo. I had spent hour after hour with the mothers and fathers of these children, families who had never stopped pining, or asking questions I could not answer: Will they ever come back? How can a child survive walking hundreds of miles in such terrain? What will they eat if they are hiding from everyone who wants to kill them—from the rebels, the military and civilians? How will they ever return to a life in Pader after what they have seen and done?

Mothers and fathers waited anxiously as word filtered back about versions of peace treaties that were drafted, shredded and redrafted, only to eventually learn that the talks had once again broken down. The mood rose when the LRA sent its emissaries to Kampala to negotiate, and fell with a chorus of howls when it came to nothing. Some speculated that in prolonging the talks, the LRA leaders had seized the chance to regroup, while enjoying the food, clothes and medicines provided by the government.

Early on, I had heard through NGO networks that Joseph Kony was planning a mass release of children. The rumours were credible enough for Save the Children and UNICEF to scale up their operations in and around Juba in Sudan, and in 2007 CCF Pader dispatched a social worker to Bunia in the far north-east of Congo. Then, in October 2007, Kony killed Vincent Otti, his right-hand man, after accusing him of disloyalty and double-dealing by supporting the peace process.

'How did you come back here?' I gently probed, after a pensive break in our conversation. Agnes sat up, alert again.

'We ran when Kony killed Otti,' she answered, and I nodded. 'I was in Otti's camp, and we did not want to join Kony's group. There were nine of us, all Acholi girls. One was still twelve years old and had been with the LRA for three years. I ran with my baby.' I wondered if anyone outside the north would have heard about Kony killing his own second-in-command had it not sparked a battle between the two powerful groups of rebels. Kony's stronger force won, scattering Otti's rebels, along with the girls and their children.

Agnes's escape was sudden and opportunistic. The girls fled to the north, breaking a path through thick bush with their bare hands, not stopping to consider whether escape was a fanciful idea when the area was overrun with Kony's rebels, who would know immediately that they had come from Otti's camp.

'We just kept moving, so we could get far away from Kony's camp. We stayed together, as we had no one else we could trust. The Congolese hated us, too. None of us could speak Lingala or French to explain ourselves.' Agnes stared into the distance as she talked. 'We walked at night, and by day we hid in the bushes. It was so frightening in the national park.' Agnes stopped talking and closed her eyes at the memory. She rocked her body back and forth.

I could barely imagine it. Garamba was a vast national park in Congo, with predators such as lions, and other deadly beasts such as wild buffalo, rhinos and wild boar. Unarmed girls were surely prey. I closed my eyes, mirroring Agnes's pain. 'We lost two girls to the animals,' Agnes whispered.

'Ah, sorry,' was all I could muster in response.

'We walked north for four days to reach the edge of Garamba, then walked another four days.'

'Into Sudan?' I asked.

'Yes. It started to look like Uganda. We saw huts and people in a village, and I heard someone speaking English,' Agnes said, her voice lighter. I could tell that she enjoyed relating this part of her tale—the part about coming home to her family. 'We found a town with electricity, but did not dare enter. We waited all that night and the next day under the trees until we could get closer to the town. We hoped that they would speak our language and be kind to us.'

When the girls saw a convoy of UN peacekeepers, who were observers rather than participants in the wars of the LRA and the Sudan People's Liberation Army, they knew that they were close to safety. 'Please help us,' the girls had pleaded in unison, jumping into the air to flag down a UN truck full of blue-bereted soldiers.

'We come from Garamba,' Agnes explained in her rudimentary English. The soldiers looked at the girls' ripped clothes, their bare feet and their bleeding and swollen legs, and did not question their story. They scooped up the girls onto the back of the truck and rumbled down to the UNICEF camp, where nurses could dress their wounds and give them food and new clothes. The United Nations flew the girls to Bunia, where the CCF social worker was waiting to welcome them with open arms.

'I cried when I heard the social worker speak Lwo,' Agnes

said, looking into my eyes and smiling. 'I thought of my mother, and my brothers and sisters, and all I wanted to tell them.'

For the girls from Congo, the school in Pader was like heaven. No more walking for days or fear of dying in a battle or men forcing them into loveless sexual relations. Each morning, the girls gathered for chapel to sing songs of praise and to hear words of love and encouragement. The school matron, Santina Abalo, cared for them until they felt confident enough to face the world again. Santina was herself a mother, and she loved these girls as her own. She helped fill their empty shells until they could participate in the school. Then came the inevitable questioning from the other girls: Did you ever meet the group under this commander? Where were you fighting? Did you ever meet so-and-so? It was a secret society, a dark world that they had all survived, and whose language they all spoke.

I prowled the dirt pathways each morning, surveying the school of broken girls who were being pieced back together. *You are walking on sacred ground,* I whispered in a silent meditation. The small signs poked into the grass, with slogans such as 'Educate a Girl, Educate a Nation', were as much a reminder for me as anyone. I wanted never to forget why we had started CCF: to help the girls become whole again, to be able to learn and heal and reclaim their lives. With each step, I would absorb their anger and pain, and all the staff would as well. I would show understanding when a girl in her frustration screamed, 'Stupid baby, why are you sick?' I would fill the gap with love.

*

The act of putting lives back together was full of complexity, yet there were often divine connections and impossible reunions. These extraordinary moments seemed to come just when our team had reached a low point. When we were demoralised and starting to wonder whether our work was useful, a simple reunion could turn us around.

In April 2010, a young girl with a baby on her back came to the reception centre as one of a group who had escaped the LRA. The social worker, Esther, launched into the questions that were routinely asked during the documentation process. 'How many children did you have during the war?' she asked casually, and then followed up with an unusual question: 'Is this your first child?'

'No, it is my second child,' the girl, called Nancy, replied. She had a stern face and spoke quietly.

'What happened to your first child?' Esther probed. Over the past few years, she had learned to be businesslike in order to avoid being drawn deep into each story, and to guard her heart. She managed well, at least outwardly.

'My first baby is dead. There was a big attack on our rebel group, and we were caught in a battle just as I was having my baby,' Nancy said, with little emotion in her voice, as if she was describing leaving her *calabash* at the well. 'I threw the baby as I ran away, and it probably died in the bush.' Esther nodded her head, giving nothing away.

'What was your baby's name?' Esther asked, treading gently.

'My baby did not have a name. I passed through all the reception centres and asked about him, but he could not be found. He did not have a name.' Her voice trailed off as the memory of that day returned. She had carried this life within her as a silent companion for many tense months. She swallowed and lifted her head.

Esther kept her eyes on her clipboard, scratching at the paper until it was time for another question. Her training and experience told her that this was not the time to start the counselling process. She simply pressed for more information. 'Where is your village? Where is your family from?' she asked, trying to brighten the atmosphere.

'I don't remember the village very well. I was young,' came the stony answer.

'Let me see what we can do,' Esther replied, wrapping up the interview with a smile. Tracing the girl's family became her personal mission. She organised transport and visited village after village, running blind, with just a picture of the girl in her hand. Wherever she went, she asked, 'Do you recognise this girl?'

Finally, many weeks into her quest, she met a man who said, 'That girl died a long time ago. I'll take you to someone who will know where to find her parents.'

He led Esther to a group of huts in Kalongo, in the middle of which sat a weathered older couple with a small child playing at their feet. She pulled out the finger-marked picture and pushed it towards them, asking, 'Do you know this girl?' They crowded around Esther's outstretched hand, and then touched the photo.

'We were told that she was dead,' cried the woman, whose name was Mercy. 'Other girls told us that she died in the fighting.' Mercy took the photo in her hands and held it in front of her face, studying it for several minutes as tears flowed. 'She is so grown up. Can we see her with our own eyes?' she asked, her face now bright and younger-looking.

'Of course, come to the reception centre with me,' Esther replied, beaming with delight and holding back her own tears.

The couple arrived at the reception centre with gifts—a live chicken and groundnuts—and with a four-year-old boy. For all these years, Mercy had mourned her lost daughter and believed that she was raising an orphan. She wrapped her arms around her daughter and sobbed. Nothing in her hard life had prepared her for this happiness.

'Who is this?' Nancy asked, looking at the little boy.

'This is your son. We call him Emanuel Komigum,' her mother replied, and again there were tears of disbelief. 'They found him and brought him to us. He looks so much like you.' The child was the very same one found as a baby by a government soldier and brought to the reception centre in 2006.

We all watched and cried. Our most treasured reward was to reunite families. To bring together this mother, who never expected to see her daughter again, and the daughter, who never expected to see her baby son again, was a gift beyond our dreams.

Later, as I reflected on this moment of reconciliation, I thought about our measurement of success: it is seeing people lifted from nothing to something, and the restored hope of the mothers and children who arrive at our reception centre.

*

Around the time of the reunion, I visited Kampala with Polline, arranging for visas to visit the United Kingdom later in 2010. CCF's partners from War Child UK and Comic

Relief had invited the two of us to go to the United Kingdom to talk about the plight of girls in conflict, with Polline to be the main guest, speaking at schools and to the media. War Child UK had been a loyal partner from the earliest days of Pader Girls Academy, helping with reintegration and child protection, and now education, with Comic Relief. When their local director had raised the topic of a visit to London, I had jumped at it, and more so when Polline was invited to join me to address schools and parliamentarians.

After their dramatic retreat from northern Uganda into Congo and Sudan for the peace talks in 2006, the LRA had weakened its grip on us, and we had started to think about rebuilding our lives in peace. The rebels transferred their tactics of murder, rape and abduction onto the innocent people of our neighbour, the Democratic Republic of the Congo, and when they found opposition there, they moved further north-west to the Central African Republic. Reports of LRA activity caught the eye of parliamentarians in the United Kingdom, who had a broader concern about the Great Lakes region of Africa. The G8 summit meetings in Canada in June 2010 had refocused Britain's role in international affairs; at the same time, the UN Under-Secretary-General, Special Representative for Children and Armed Conflict, was in the United Kingdom. The groups wanted firsthand, evidence-based information, not a second-hand report from observers. The parliamentarians asked War Child UK to find someone to speak—someone who had been to Congo with the LRA and who had seen what was happening.

Soon afterwards, War Child UK sent a team from the United Kingdom to Pader to select the best candidate to bring to London. After interviews in the community and interviewing four girls from the school, Polline was chosen to speak on behalf of all the girls about the atrocities of the rebels and their impact on the girls' lives.

The room erupted with cheers and ululation when we announced the choice at the next assembly. I knew that Polline was our most powerful speaker, that when she articulated her own and other girls' experiences, her audience was spellbound. She could inspire and lift a group of people to believe that their situation was dire but not hopeless, despite the obstacles. She spoke from her heart, and with such a well of passion about educating girls, that I was confident our visit would bear fruit.

In Kampala, Polline's new passport came through in only two days, and the visa, too, with a letter of introduction from the British politicians who would host us. She and I were sharing a small hotel room, and away from the pressures of school—with the insulation of time and distance from the memory of war—Polline chose to reveal the next layer of her life and near death with the LRA. In other conversations, she had mentioned her pregnancy and the baby she did not even see, who now lay far away from her homeland, without so much as a cross to mark his burial place, but I had not felt comfortable asking for details. Now she said, 'I would like to tell you what happened to me in Congo,' and I made time to listen that evening.

We sat on the edges of our single beds, facing each other, the room cooled by the fan overhead. It felt secure, a safe space to dissolve the hierarchies of age and position. For this time, we were two young women sharing deep secrets. I took a deep breath as I prepared to listen without distraction.

'I tried so hard in the hut . . . for days I tried. At the start there were some women with me, but they grew tired of my long labour and left. They were called out to fight, and I was left in the hut on my own. It was more than a week, and I had no way to prepare food, so I could not eat much after they left me,' Polline said, staring at the floor. My body stiffened as I fought back a wave of emotion.

'Sorry,' I squeezed out, as my tears gathered.

'I knew the baby was gone, and I wanted to die, too. I was very sick.' Polline paused. Her chest heaved, and when she started speaking again, her words came quickly. 'The commander came after one week, and he was worried for me. I pleaded with him, "I have no use anymore. Please take me out into the bush and kill me now." But he refused.'

For that moment I was immersed in the loneliness of a dark hut in Congo with Polline, waiting to die. I looked at the young girl's lowered head, then stood up and moved across the room to sit with her, taking her shaking hand.

I could not even imagine the pain and brutality she had endured. I broke my own rule about staying strong for the girls, and together we wept.

It was some minutes before Polline sat up and, with a hint of a smile, said, 'The peace talks saved my life. I would have died, but the peace negotiators were near our camp, so they could airlift wounded rebels and their women to Nairobi. The LRA commanders were clever in this way. They sent minders with us, to make sure that we did not run, or tell secrets. But I ran, and now I am home.'

Back in Pader, Polline took it upon herself to care for the other girls. She stepped into the role of counsellor and friend to the young mother of Emanuel Komigum, listening to the girl's story as I had hers, and helping her manage two young children. 'It is a good thing that this child survived,' Polline convinced her, picking up the younger child with a wide-open smile.

25

The World Opens

By 2010, Pader Girls Academy had been running for almost two years, but the school still did not have an official licence to operate. There were many gaps to fill before it could reach the minimum standards for accreditation from the Ministry of Education in Kampala. I was aware of this every day. 'The Ministry could close us down any day,' I kept saying to Florence, who kept reassuring me that it would not happen.

'Why don't you explain how we are trying our best to meet their requirements?' she'd offered. 'Surely they will understand how hard it is.'

One of the most pressing needs was a simple one: having a secure fence around the perimeter of the school—rather than just the fences that enclosed the gaps between the buildings—so the girls could move freely around the school without worrying about uninvited outsiders. After speaking with Florence, I knew what to do. The next week I caught the crowded bus for the twelve-hour trip to Kampala. I had decided to speak directly to the bureaucrats. The Ministry of

Education is housed in one of the big, old postcolonial-era blocks opposite Parliament House in the centre of the city. I steeled myself to meet the men who controlled the girls' future.

I moved through the doors and down the length of the dark central corridor, with its uninviting warren of boxed-in timber offices and paper-stacked desks on either side, finally stopping at a name that I recognised on the lettered plaque above the door. The room smelled of musty bureaucracy, and of decades of youthful ambition buried under towers of paper. 'I'm Alice Achan, director of Pader Girls Academy. I'm here to talk about the accreditation of my school,' I announced to the humourless clerk, who was sitting behind a desk in his unblemished white shirt and narrow tie.

'Ah yes, Miss Achan, I have the report right here.' He looked at my application, then at the report, and then looked up at me, shaking his head. 'If the fence is not there, we don't allow the girls to be in a boarding school.'

Why couldn't these men understand? The school had so many other demands on funding that even feeding the girls from day to day had at times been a stretch. The conversation soon escalated, with me pressing the point that the school would be forced to close without the licence.

He was equally stubborn and not about to budge on this point. His stonewalling gaze told me that he was accustomed to saying 'no' to streams of requests. 'Until there is a fence around the perimeter of the school, the Ministry will not allow you to continue to operate. It's as plain as that,' he replied, unmoved.

I was determined not to leave empty-handed, even at the risk of being rude. Too many broken souls relied on me. I leaned across the desk, reached for one of the photos attached to the school report and thrust it before him. 'These are not just girls. These are girls who have seen a hard life, and now they only want an education like other children. They were under LRA captivity, and you people were not able to provide them with a facility. So we decided to open a school for them.'

He glared at me and then looked at the photo I had pushed under his nose. He paused to take in the smiling faces of the girls. His jaw softened, and he turned to look at me as if seeing me for the first time. 'Let us go to the next office,' he said in a kinder voice.

The man in the office next door sat at his big desk, holding a pen in his hand, which he put down as I approached him with my hand outstretched. I could see from the soft creases around his eyes that he was friendlier than the man who worked for him. Perhaps he was someone who would listen. I knew that he certainly had the power to make a decision about our licence.

'Sir, our school is not a perfect school, but it is a vital school,' I declared, as I met his eyes. 'Many of the girls in the north are pregnant and have babies, and it is not just their doing. These girls want to learn, too, and they have nowhere else to go.' He sat straight in his chair, watching me intently, nodding occasionally as I explained how hard I—and my colleagues—had worked to provide a good environment for the girls, with few resources and without assistance from his department.

'I see,' he said after a long pause. His mouth turned upwards into a fatherly smile. I could see that my words had made their mark, but I was still unsure of what would come next.

Finally he leaned towards me across his desk and looked me in the eye. 'Alice—thank you. You're right, we don't have facilities for girls with babies, so I am very happy with what you are doing.' I dropped my shoulders and allowed my body to relax for the first time since I left Pader. I had so longed to hear these words.

I mumbled, 'Thank you, sir.'

His voice took a sterner tone: 'As you know, according to our standards, there are a lot of things missing, but as long as you promise me that in one year you will have these things done, then we will give you the licence.'

'Yes, sir,' I said. 'Please give me the licence and also all the adjustments that you require.' I smiled, relieved that the long trip to Kampala had been rewarded.

I received the licence that very day, and went away with a list of recommendations. I knew some of them, such as the fence, involved the security of the girls, and others had to do with the quality of the facilities. They were all issues that we hadn't yet addressed due to a lack of funding, but I was emboldened by the licence in my hand—and the deadline— to approach the people who had already supported us.

A message to Mary Page at the MacArthur Foundation in Chicago soon came back with a positive response. 'You can do what you need to do,' Mary replied. I sighed with relief. I had the go-ahead to make the improvements we needed to comply.

The District Education Officer, the staff at the Ministry of Education and others wanted to help us, but so often they were simply caught up in policies and laws that did not allow for an unusual case like Pader Girls Academy. It was the girls' stories that eventually turned people around and garnered support for the school to succeed.

The long bus ride home to the north gave me many slow-moving hours to reflect on this triumphant moment in the life of the school. The government and NGOs were building new systems in the north after the war, but it seemed to me that there was no point in building new systems without building human beings. I was certain that the best way to build the capacity of human beings was through education and learning. Having access to information, income and knowledge would allow the girls to become self-reliant.

I smiled when I thought about a recent conversation I had had with a foreign friend. 'Look at my background,' I had said to my friend. 'I have just a diploma and cannot be considered well educated, yet with my little bit of education I can find information from around the world, and I am able to analyse and make informed decisions. The more the girls are exposed to the outside world and taught how to gather information, the further they will go.' I knew that if a girl had an education, she could think up strategies, make contacts and get things done.

Polline and I would be doing just that in London. We would be telling stories, and we would be showing that a woman with just a little education can make things happen.

We arrived in London on a Friday night at the end of June 2010, into clear, warm summer weather. 'You've come at a good time,' I heard several people say in those first few days, which made me wonder what it was like during other summers and in other seasons.

Though her passport was in the name of Polline Akello, at the first briefing with War Child UK, Polline was given a pseudonym: Juliet. They were taking no chances with her safety. Though we now lived in peaceful times, it was barely so, and there was such a lingering distrust of the LRA that no one could truly believe they had gone for good. A young woman with Polline's knowledge of the rebels and incriminating stories could become a target.

Travelling into central London on the Saturday morning—into the busiest part of one of the busiest cities in the world, a place where everyone rushed—left me disorientated and panicky. When I looked at our schedule, it all seemed tight, without space to learn the system or about the people. It was specific and ordered. Even walking on the street was orderly, with solemn-faced people moving past us on either side. Before the week was finished, I would be left standing on the platform of the London Underground as the train pulled out and my companions rushed on without me.

I could feel the weight of stress bearing down on me, crippling me. I found London bewildering: the fast-moving crowds, the constant rush and crush, and everywhere there were systems that I did not understand.

By the evening of our first day, as we returned to our hotel room, my head was pounding and chills shook my body. I knew these symptoms. Malaria was so common in the north of Uganda; only a minority had not endured its racking shakes and sweats, the headaches, the body aches, the vomiting. I sat on my bed, closed my eyes and prayed that the medication I had brought with me as a precaution would keep the next cycle of the sickness at bay. So many mothers in the IDP camps saw their children die from bouts of malaria that elsewhere could be treated with a simple drug. I wondered whether stress had accelerated the re-emergence of the benign malaria parasite living in my blood, but I could never know.

On Sunday morning, after a miserable night, I called my friend at War Child UK. 'I have malaria and will need to stay at the hotel today,' I told her, resting my head in my spare hand. I'd had only one bout of malaria, two years before, but it had been a serious one, the type of malaria that kills small children.

The illness sent our hosts into a tailspin, and I soon found myself in isolation at a leading university hospital not far from the War Child UK office. For a northern Ugandan, so accustomed to living communally—sharing huts with a dozen others, sharing food, sharing all I owned—being placed in quarantine in a cold, clinical room, wholly alone and without human touch, felt like punishment. I was concerned about how Polline would manage on her own in a foreign country, as she was so inexperienced with the ways of the Western world.

'It's just malaria,' I told the nurse. 'I've had it before, and the symptoms will go on for a day, two at the most.' But the doctors weren't so sure. Five times they came back for blood samples, saying that they thought it might be something more serious, such as Ebola.

'I'm afraid we can't release you until we've discounted all the more sinister possibilities,' the nurse told me. This allowed time for my worries to fester, planting the idea that my illness might be more serious than malaria and that I could die in this country I barely knew. At the end of a night and a full day, the doctors gave me medication that I did not recognise, and sent me back to the hotel.

I felt much better by then, but was unnerved by the experience. It made me disorganised—dull, tired and stressed—for the rest of the program. Without close connections in the United Kingdom, both Polline and I felt an underlying sense of loneliness. We were staying in a hotel, without a family, rising at six o'clock in the morning to prepare for a seven o'clock pick-up, having meetings and more meetings, and then being dropped back at the hotel at nine o'clock at night, exhausted and still lonely.

Polline excelled in expressing herself, as I expected. In the space of seven days, she had five interviews—two of them live—two visits to high schools, and a host of meetings with politicians and officials. As an enthusiastic young woman, she was able to cope easily with the public speaking and packed schedule. She was sharp, picking up things quickly, and adapted easily to her environment, even though she was a less experienced traveller than me. Her only time out of Uganda before this had been against her will as an LRA captive in Sudan and Congo, and then her recovery in Kenya. Importantly, Polline could skilfully present a model of education that was working for the girls of northern Uganda, and this opened doors.

We found our way into the halls of the Department for International Development (DFID), where Polline made a presentation, and Pader Girls Academy was cited as a model school. I stood alongside, watching her like a proud mother, ready to present more on the workings of the school, the challenges we faced within the Ugandan education system and the impact we were having in getting girls back into school. After our visit to the United Kingdom, Comic Relief became even more interested in CCF's work, and started to help with teachers' training and other programs.

The time we spent in the United Kingdom was invaluable, as it gave me the courage to believe that the international community might recognise Pader Girls Academy and other initiatives for the girls. We raised awareness, advocated for more action and strengthened the funding base, making it a successful visit. I watched Polline's confidence soar throughout this time as she realised the power of her stories of survival, of life with the rebels, of lost innocence and lost friends, and I saw how her stories touched people's hearts.

On this platform—media interviews and meetings with political leaders—she could speak for the many girls at home who lacked her confidence and access to outsiders. She shared her own long story, but also related that of another young girl, Alice, one of the many girls who were like ghosts arriving back from the bush when their parents had given them up for dead, to illustrate the struggle that the girls faced on their return from the LRA.

She wrote a letter to the British Prime Minister, David Cameron, containing an outline of her experiences with the LRA and how she had almost died in the bush, but escaped to Kenya. She wrote clearly of her ambitions. 'I want to be a lawyer, so I can defend girls who have been sexually abused and bring men who abuse to justice,' she wrote in her slanted writing. She then asked that Cameron lead his country in helping bring other girls back from the bush, and requested he bring the matter before the United Nations when it met in September 2010. Polline was bold and focused, yet she was still surprised when she received a positive reply not long afterwards, straight from Mr Cameron's office.

The printed letter acknowledged Polline's letter and outlined the steps that the UK government was taking to catch Joseph Kony and support education in Uganda. At the end, there was a handwritten note. In pale blue ink, written in a distinctively masculine and slightly unruly hand, were these words: 'I was very moved by your letter and your story—I admire your courage in wanting to stop this brutality happening to others. With best wishes, David Cameron.'

The visit cemented Polline's quietly held desire to fight back against the war and the circumstances that had robbed the girls of so much. Her personal aspirations were rising. In the bush she had wanted to become a nurse, so she could help her community. Then, when she came out of captivity she saw how journalists had a voice and wondered whether she could be more effective in this field. Now she resolved to become a human-rights lawyer, if she could just get through two more years of school.

Back in Pader, I noticed Polline stepping up in her leadership of the girls, unafraid of any situation presented to her, even if it meant being disliked. She was the first to welcome visitors and to take them around the school, and the first to step in to diffuse any conflict among the girls.

Every girl in the school came from a background of vulnerability, but there were clear categories. There were the formerly abducted girls, some with babies and some without; girls who came as orphans; and also girl mothers who had not been abducted. Some girls came from the bush surrounding Pader, others from Sudan and Congo, and most recently there had been the first two arrivals from the Central African Republic, girls who had been arrested as LRA spies after escaping, and were later brought back home by a child-advocacy group.

A potent dynamic began to form among the girls at the school. I did not notice it immediately myself, as my home was away from the school grounds, and even the teachers were on the sidelines. Still, we had all witnessed how the war had brought about a breakdown in the authority of parents, teachers and leaders. After all, who had protected the girls against the brutality of the LRA?

So until Polline brought it to my attention, I was not aware that the girls were starting to segregate themselves according to their recent past. Girls who had bonded in the bush as wives to rebels under one commander now set themselves up as a bloc against another group who came from a different commander. They formed distinct gangs that stood up to each other and bullied the girls who had not been abducted. The tension was escalating and the rivalries rising, but it had not yet percolated into physical violence.

One day, Polline found a young girl sitting alone, sobbing, behind the dormitory building. 'Why are you crying?' she asked, putting her arm around the girl.

'They hate me—they tell me I am worth nothing, and that I don't deserve to live,' she replied. It then came out that the other girls had surrounded her and threatened her on the basis of her LRA group in the bush.

'Ah, sorry. You know it is not true: you are very important,' she reassured the girl. 'Let me see what I can do,' she offered, walking the girl back into the dormitory. Polline then wandered around the school grounds on her own, pondering her next actions. She lamented how deep the scars of abuse ran and how they seemed to be immovable.

'I'd like to talk to the girls myself,' Polline requested when she took the news to the teachers. 'I know well what these girls have been through, and how they can be so divided. I think they will listen to me as someone who understands.' The teachers agreed. Most of the teachers knew the agonies of the war, but none had been abducted.

So Polline sent word around the school. 'We are meeting in the hall after dinner this evening. Please be there.'

With the entire school gathered, she stood boldly in front of them. 'Look at the girl next to you. Look at each other,' she said firmly, pausing as the girls sheepishly turned to take in the girls in the rows around them. 'We are all children of the one God, and we are all sisters. We have all been through trials. We have all suffered, but let us turn this around. We need to love one another as sisters and not have pride around this war. Let's not divide ourselves, but love each other,' she told them. Silence fell in the room as Polline's words cut through the tension and broke down the factional barriers.

From that time onwards, I saw a change in the way that the girls related to each other, and a growing trust in Polline's leadership among all the girls. I was so proud of Polline's strength and how she had dealt with a situation that she had never handled before. She had an innate leadership ability that I knew would take her far.

26

Facing Down Memories

In 2011 girls were still trickling back from the LRA, three years on from the rush of broken girls who came into our care after the peace talks were abandoned. Throughout this war, radio broadcasts had allowed even the most isolated in the north to stay connected. Community groups could reach out into camps.

I still learned something new from each arrival, and could still be shocked. When two young women with small children arrived at the school with a representative from the reception centre in Gulu, I was not expecting to hear how far they had come.

'These girls escaped from the Central African Republic,' the woman told me. It was rumoured that a remnant of Kony's group had left Congo and crossed into CAR, but I had never heard of anyone escaping. 'They are in a bad way. This one, Resty*, has bullets in her shoulder and is in constant pain.'

I could see it on her face. 'How are you, Resty?' I asked her, to open a dialogue.

'I'm fine,' she whispered, pushing herself against the wall, holding tightly to her son's hand. Resty had a strong build and a broad, open face, but she was as timid as any girl I had ever met. It was only later, when the girls and children had settled into a small side room in the dormitory block, that I could ask more questions.

'I was taken ten years ago,' Resty started in a soft monotone. 'When we heard that the LRA was near, I ran with my brothers and cousins to Kilak, but the rebels were already there. We were all taken together. Most of them were released three days later, but I was taken to a bigger camp. I tried so hard to escape.'

My mind ran quickly through the calculation of her age: she was now nineteen years old, so she must have been nine going on ten when she was taken. *Nine.*

'What happened to your shoulder?' I pried, after seeing her wince when she shifted in her chair.

'The soldiers attacked us from the air, and we could not hide in time. The bullets are deep. They cannot remove them.' I nodded, and my eyes slid to the raised scars on her legs. 'It was the *panga*. They cut us so we couldn't run,' Resty told me, before I could ask. 'And I had two hundred strikes of the cane when they learned that we planned to escape while we were near here. That was a few years ago.'

I'd often wondered about the bonds that formed between captors and captives in light of such brutality. In our social-work course, we'd learned about 'Stockholm Syndrome', where hostages develop feelings for their captors as a survival strategy, and how this can grow into genuine affection. In Resty's case, she had already been in captivity for four years before she reached puberty at thirteen and was given to a thirty-one-year-old commander as his 'wife'. She soon forgot her old way of life, and listened to her 'husband' when he told her that she'd be killed if she returned home. She'd run to the Central African Republic with a small group when the peace talks had failed, and, once there, the daily beatings had stopped.

'How was your life there?' I asked, as we sat in her dark room.

'Kony ordered that the women now be respected, because there were no more Acholi women to be captured,' Resty answered. 'He told them, "You should not cane Acholi women because they are the only ones who can stand and fight with us". But then he hurt the women from Congo and Central African Republic.'

'How did you come home?' Our conversation was filling in some of the missing pieces of this vast story, and I could not help asking.

'One day, I heard kind voices from home on the radio. They said that we were not to blame, and they wanted us back,' she replied, her head down and speaking in a whisper. 'I pleaded with the commander. "There is nothing here for my children. They will die from malaria or be killed by bullets. If I am killed in the bush, what happens to them? It is not a life for a child." But he would not listen to me. He cut me with his *panga* when I asked again.' She had then gone to her commander's brother, a lower-ranked rebel, who also refused to allow her to leave, and next to the youngest brother, who promised that he would help her. Finally, the men agreed that she could leave the camp in the Central African Republic, and the commander chose three young soldiers to accompany her as far as they could, with instructions that, if questioned, she must say that she had escaped. 'You know, I missed the commander when I left, as I had never been alone. I did not know how I would feed my children.'

I took a deep breath to dispel my confusion. I wondered how many of these girls had formed similar attachments, and how many had felt the pain of feeling unwanted in their home villages. I thanked God that the radio messages had got through, and some of those like Resty had returned.

*

That year, I had returned with my sister, Doreen, to Lira Palwo, to the childhood village I had rarely visited since fleeing the north with Gabriel more than twenty years ago. As peace unfolded, and I dared to consider a life ahead, I'd ached to be back, to see the gravesite of our father, Otto Zedekiah. So much had been left unresolved in our hasty retreat.

Late in the day, as the sun made skinny shadows in the bush, I stood alongside Doreen in solemn silence, our eyes cast down to a slab of rough concrete that was surrounded by a bed of straggly, straw-like grass. It was not far from where Baba's grass-thatch hut had stood before it was destroyed in a fire one night in the late 1990s.

The grave had no markings—no name or plaque that told the world this was the resting place of a chief, a great man known for his fairness to all those around him. It didn't seem right that his burial place had been lost for many years in the thick bush after his family moved away. My heart was heavy with regret that I had not been there to say goodbye when he died, and that he had endured the pain of cancer after all he had lost to the conflict.

'I am reminded of the goodness of our father,' I whispered to my sister.

'He was a very good man,' Doreen replied. She glanced towards me and then her gaze fell again to her feet.

I looked beyond the clearing and noticed the mechanical tractor, once my half-brother Peter's pride and joy, sitting like an artefact, abandoned and rusted in the field. I unravelled then, overcome by the loss with which I had not yet come to terms. The large thatch hut that I had shared with my mother and sisters was gone, and the newer square building, constructed from bricks laid to dry with my brothers' own hands, was rubble.

The rich soil that my mothers and sisters once cultivated and cared for had been dormant for many years, and the landholding was overrun with thick brush. I looked, but could not see the boundaries of our land. Nearby in the grass stood a tall, sandy ant hill with a halo of bush rising out of the centre of the mound on a slender trunk. I looked at the prickly shrub and shuddered, the memory of heart-stopping fear overwhelming me.

'I could not spend the night here in the village,' I spoke aloud. No, I could not bear to be here, with the ghosts of our father, our grandmother, our mothers, our aunts and uncles, and our cousins. The full, crushing weight of our lost way of life made my chest tighten, and I gulped for air.

I closed my eyes and breathed deeply, shifting my focus onto the chorus of crickets that surrounded us. It was a soothing sound, one that took me back to my early years, the days when we were free. It reminded me of other sounds and smells of that time: laughter, song, the mothers' chatter, aromatic smoke, the smell of crisp grass, the whirr of the wind in the tall trees. I remembered our evenings by the fire—the *wang oo* and the school of *ododo*—and smiled. *Those were good days,* I thought, glancing at Doreen. In this simple way, I had reclaimed some of what was lost. I wondered if she felt the same way.

*

At the end of school chapel one Sunday in March 2013, I called the older girls to my side. Sunday was my favourite day, the only time in the week when everyone in the school was relaxed and unhurried. In recent times, I had been saddened by the cultural void—the loss of the songs and traditional dances that had enlivened my childhood—and was determined to bring Acholi culture alive for our girls. Like a forager returning with food from the forest, I came back from the village with fragments of our shared heritage.

'We are going to learn a new song,' I announced. 'Please call all the members of the choir and all the dancers.' The girls came, and soon I was surrounded by expectant faces, their eyes, ears and spirits attuned and ready. I felt nervous—I was neither a confident singer nor a skilled dancer, as some of the students were—but I told myself that I would be good enough.

'Come, come, follow me,' I motioned with my hands, drawing the girls closer. 'I want to teach you a spiritual song from my childhood,' I said, smiling. I began to slowly shuffle my feet, dusty in my worn sandals, and hummed to warm up. Near the doorway the younger girls, who were looking after the toddlers, laughed as they watched.

'What have you defeated in your own life?' I asked the girls, who called out their answers in defiance of their struggles.

'Disease.'

'My poverty.'

'My school fees.'

'My life was saved.'

I closed my eyes and lifted my chin to the ceiling to open my throat and sing: *'Lalar Yesu ocer ki lyel ingeyo nino adel.'*

My words met with a resounding echo: *'Lalar Yesu ocer ki lyel ingeyo nino adel.'*

The words were a celebration of freedom from their brokenness. I continued.

> *Ocer ocango bala*
> *Ikwanya ki I can, col piny*
> *Ocer oyabo yoo nyima maleng.*

When I moved my feet, theirs moved in time. Soon, the group moved as one body, one spirit, one people, our actions so instinctive that they did not need words of instruction beyond the song.

I found the girls were sponges, soaking it all in: the words, the songs and the richness of connecting to their spiritual home once again.

When some girls faltered, others stopped to demonstrate, and laughter spilled out of the circle. Acholi had done this call and response forever, with resonant voices and sure rhythms. We moved in a circular motion, eyes closed, aware of the bodies nearby without seeing them.

Our voices rose together and filled the hall with praise. We finished with a mass exhalation, an afterglow of jubilance, as though the unity of our voices and movements had lifted the whole group. Then they giggled, while I beamed. I was silently aware that I was once again reclaiming some of what had been lost, and, in doing so, we might all move forward.

I was a guardian of their futures, and, like our songs, the rhythm of my own life rose and fell with theirs. I could see their futures with an education. I knew about the United Nation's Sustainable Development Goals (SDGs), and was aware that many of these issues—especially relating to disease—would not exist if girls and women were given a basic education.

An educated woman would make more far-reaching choices, such as having fewer children, based on her knowledge. She would know the importance of family planning. My heart soared to see the girls hungrily devouring lessons at school, then fell like a rock when I heard of rapes in the village, where they caused barely a raised eyebrow.

'How long will it be before girls can safely lead their lives without looking over their shoulders for men who are only interested in their own gratification?' I grizzled to my colleagues in the office. The teachers were doing all they could to change the idea that girls were of a lesser value than boys. We devised ways of inculcating values into the girls, inviting them to think about the privilege and importance of education, to build steel into their resolve, to bolster each girl to say a definitive 'no' to the older man in the village who might sweet-talk her into having sex. This was a well-trodden path: finding herself pregnant, then married and back in the village forever.

'Let's get the senior girls to debate the topic, then they'll have to think hard about it—and the other girls can listen,' the English teacher suggested, and the other teachers nodded their agreement. The teachers invited the senior girls to form teams, and helped as they worked hard in preparation for the debate, which would be in front of the whole school. When the girls filed into the hall several weeks later, they found a large sign in the centre of the stage with the deliberately provocative topic for debate: 'Education is Better than Marriage'.

The very act of discussing this in public, in front of other girls and teachers—and even visitors—broke down walls. One girl speaking for the negative team was so timid that her argument was inaudible. She stood before the assembled school, uncomfortably shuffling from foot to foot, clutching the crumpled piece of paper that was her speech, verging on tears. She was not looking like a victor as she struggled to put forward the negative argument. In this environment, a haven for the dreams of young girls, every teacher hoped that the affirmative would win in the life of each girl.

By this time, I had started accepting invitations to speak on talkback radio programs that were broadcast into the most remote of villages across northern Uganda. With evangelistic zeal, I did not hold back on my campaign to focus on the education of girls. 'The girls need a chance in life,' I told the audience—the men and women sitting and listening to the radio in their far-flung grass-thatch huts in villages around the district—before launching into details of the situation of girl mothers. I wished that the community radio could reach all the way to Kampala, where elements of the government remained deaf to the problems of girls in the north.

My passion was often met with vitriol from callers. 'It is the fault of the girl mothers. The girls are not well disciplined.

They are stubborn. The mothers of the girls are not taking responsibility for their daughters,' one caller told me.

'There are some parts of our culture that are dysfunctional, and we need to change,' I replied, feeling their judgement through the radio waves, and imagining them pointing their fingers in blame as they spat their anger back at me. 'We must value our girls and not see them as the property of men. They are not just there to fulfil a man's needs and to do the manual work,' I argued. Yet I knew that their anger was less about the girls and more about the frustration of the Acholi people, who now lived in a time of peace, but were struggling to pull themselves out of misery.

Dealing with the issues of young women in northern Uganda had been delegated to outsiders, and a few brave female politicians—groups working in the area of women's rights. They advocated for the right of inheritance for women, for the availability of HIV/AIDs drugs, for contraception, and for the removal of the bride price that made girls a commodity to be bought and sold like cattle, and kept families in poverty.

*

My home was a fifteen-minute walk from the school, along the main street of Pader and then a right turn onto a road that narrowed into a spider web of walking tracks and five-hut villages beyond. I enjoyed the walk early each morning, with the dampness still rising from the grass, the roosters strutting and crowing, the sleepy fathers stepping out of their huts, sloshing water on their faces to wake, and mothers bent over freshly lit fires.

'*Apwoyo!*' I greeted those I knew with a laughing smile, occasionally stopping to exchange pleasantries. It was the time of day I felt the lightest, before I stepped into a maze of problem-solving.

One day, I arrived at the school to find a father in his sixties standing with his daughter, waiting at the school gates to be allowed in by the security guard.

'Sir, it is good to see that you have accompanied your daughter to the school. You are most welcome to come and see what we are doing here,' I greeted him warmly, surprised that he would accompany his daughter to the school all the way from the village, when there was no need. The student's brothers had already delivered her mattress and a suitcase to the boarding school, and it was a full day's journey to accompany her and return home by public bus.

'Thank you, Madam Alice,' he replied. 'I didn't want to miss this opportunity to talk to the head teacher. I believe my girl should finish her studies now, and if she's sent home I want to know why. I want to give everything to that teacher so that my girl doesn't come home.'

I pushed back my shoulders and grinned at the man. I wanted to hug him. These were the moments that I lived for, when I saw glimpses of how girls, and their education, might be valued in the community. 'It is very good to see you and especially for your daughter to have your blessing on her education,' I told him quietly. For me, it was the school of restoration in action.

Epilogue

Scars on the Heart

Today I watch the girls grow stronger at school, and I have seen my own family pick up its broken shards to rebuild their lives. My mama, Lucie, moves often, an octogenarian nomad who is happy to fit into her children's lives.

She has lived for long stretches with Gabriel in Gulu, then for some months with me in Pader, and then moved to her birth village of Nyowa, where she could see her brother, nieces and nephews, and where she first met her husband so many years ago. For a time in 2013, she moved back to Lira Palwo, to an unfinished red-brick building in the village, surrounded by extended family.

In each place, she has her own jobs: in Gulu, she helps pound the groundnuts to a dun-coloured paste; in Pader, in my home, she spends her hours digging in the garden or sweeping the compound with the twig broom each morning before the heat of the sun drives her back under the verandah's cool shade.

'Mama, let me get you a chair,' I plead, but she is happier on the ground on her mat, a square of cloth that offers no padding for her bony frame. She sits for hours, listening to the chatter around her, until the light fades, the mosquitoes buzz around her ears and a blanket of coolness descends. Then it is time to retire for the night.

She no longer sees well, and survives on a diet of chicken and beef, and strong tea with sugar and milk. The years have brought me close to my mother, a far cry from village life when the lines were blurred between the co-wives. Mama Lucie is the last of the mothers. The others have long departed this life—some after drawn-out illness, some in violence, some in peace.

Only fifteen of the twenty-seven members of my family remained by the end of the conflict. War, disease and calamity took them, one by one. I do not dwell on this, just as others who have suffered great loss over twenty years of conflict now pick themselves up and limp into a different future.

Sometimes I feel the bile of resentment and anger well up inside me, choking my freedom. This is when I pray, 'Lord, help me to forgive.' I know that through Jesus I have received forgiveness, and I will only be released in my heart when I forgive with a free and unconditional spirit.

Now, more than ever, I am convinced that the future of the north is tied to the forgiveness of the past. This is a chain of forgiveness more powerful than all the evil I've seen and heard, one that can release us all from the bondage of bitterness. Some people confuse forgiving those who killed and maimed in our war with accepting bad behaviour, but it is not that simple. Without forgiveness, we will be left with only angry and powerless victims.

When I feel low, I go to my beloved village. It doesn't matter what time of year: it can be in the December dry season after the harvest, or in February when the shea blossoms cast the spell of their sweet scent. It can be in May when the ripe mangoes are so plentiful that they drop to the ground to rot, or in April when other wild fruits and roots are in abundance. These rhythms and seasons give me life.

*

In December 2013, the remaining members of the wider clan—a hundred people in all—gather in Lira Palwo from all over the district, under the shade of a borrowed tent. They come for the wedding of my brother, Charles, and Grace, who has been his partner since he lost his first wife, but the significance of the day runs even deeper. Finally, at the end of this trial called war, our family is recovering hope and moving beyond the hard journey started more than a quarter of a century before.

The wedding is a day of family thanksgiving. 'Let us place a stake in the ground about our future, let us thank God for the mercies we have experienced, let us honour our family members who did not make it through the war, and let us forgive those who have hurt us over these many years,' my oldest half-brother, Zebinia, says on behalf of the whole family. It is time to solemnly acknowledge the family's losses and move on.

Archbishop Henry Luke Orombi, head of Anglicans in Uganda—who has travelled from far away in West Nile to be with the family—prays that we'll have the strength to do so. Twenty-five clan leaders from the district and a crowd of a thousand others later join our family gathering. Afterwards, Mama Lucie dances like the young girl she was when she met our father at Murchison Falls seventy years before, so happy to be surrounded by those she loves—her children, in-laws, grandchildren, even family who have travelled from Canada.

After the ceremony, many sit by the fire until late in the evening. The flames are a mesmerising focal point as Mama Lucie relays stories to her grandchildren. I sit among them, content to soak up what I had missed as a young girl, inhaling the memories of my childhood before the war and remembering why I had been so happy. I watch the serious young faces around me—students sitting with their oral librarian: the school of *ododo*. As the children leave, I sidle closer to my mother. Soon we are sitting alone.

'What will happen when you go, Mama? How will we remember your stories?' I ask, genuinely concerned that the family history will soon be lost.

'Then it will be Zebinia who carries our traditions,' she replies, and I sigh with relief that my eldest half-brother has already been assigned this important role in the clan.

I stretch out my legs, my loose skirt falling to each side. My mama looks down to see the pale pink lines winding up my legs and pulls her head back as though slapped. When she leans forwards again, she moves her head slowly from side to side, her eyes soft with apology and watery with tears. She looks away towards the towering grass as though expecting to see her teenage daughter appear.

'I remember the day you came home—it was after many days. I remember picking the leaves to wrap around your legs, and how I worried that you might lose them and never

337

walk again.' She drifts into her own world—to a place only a mother goes.

'Yes, Mama.' I pick up my mother's slender hand, its creped folds so familiar. 'But they are just scars now. I can see them, too, but they cannot hurt me now,' I say, my voice subdued.

We sit in silence, each buried in the past. I think about the scars—those on my legs, and other, invisible scars. How my lost childhood is like a scar on my heart—a twisted, knotted scar that was once raw, with pinpricks, nerve endings, that stung me every day. I now feel the scars in a vague way— healed, but still there. We all bear these scars.

I pick up a stone from the ground near my feet and roll it slowly with my fingers in my left palm. Then I smile. *They cannot hurt me now.*

I've discovered that hope is more powerful than scars, and this will be my weapon. I will speak, and someone might listen, and in listening they may understand what it is like to be a girl growing into a woman in conflict.

Acknowledgements

The School of Restoration has been a long time in the making. It started in a dark restaurant in Pader on a March afternoon in 2010 when Alice said, 'It's time to tell my story. I feel it will help the girls.'

We'd like to thank those girls—there are many—for so bravely sharing their stories of gender-based violence, suffering, poverty and loss with us, at a personal cost of reliving their worst pain. Thank you to the CCF staff from the earliest days in 2002 until the present time: the social workers at the front line of receiving traumatised girls and reuniting them with their families; the board members who saw value in girl mothers when many in the community didn't; and the teachers, cooks, counsellors and drivers who were committed to rebuilding lives in the worst of circumstances. Thanks to David Livingstone for sharing images taken in IDP camps during the conflict and as the camps were dismantled.

Thank you to the visionary friends of CCF, who saw the need and supported the work with passion, time and finance.

The school, maternal and child health and community work only exist through your partnership. You are an important part of this story.

Heartfelt thanks to Alice's family, the respected Gule clan elders and siblings, for allowing us to see life during the war through their lens, and to Polline Akello, whose voice stands out in her community and beyond.

We are grateful to the gifted Nikki Denholm for the cover image and many of the beautiful shots of the girls in the school. Thank you for so generously volunteering your time and resources to travel to northern Uganda, and for taking us into the girls' souls through the lens.

Thanks to Alison Singh Gee in Los Angeles, whose friendship, advice and urgings to keep writing arrived at just the right time, and to Carol Major, whose insights helped move the manuscript to the next level.

The book may have languished without the steady hand and expertise of Catherine Drayton from Inkwell Management. Thank you—it's a delight to work with you.

A big thank you to Allen & Unwin's talented team—publishing director Tom Gilliatt, and senior editor Samantha Kent, plus freelance copyeditor Dannielle Viera and proofreader Aziza Kuypers—for their guidance and eagle eyes on dates and timing in a complex story. We're grateful to Deborah Parry for her striking cover design.

We appreciate the early readers of the manuscript, particularly Alice's brothers Gabriel Lajul and David Labeja, Charles Amone from Gulu University, Ron Burdock, Donna Ballantyne, Eric Stover, Mary Page, Allan Rock, Dr Briony Scott, Emma Dale, Anne McMullen, Imogen Tyndale, Penelope Tyndale, Merilyn Buckley and Andrew Tyndale.

We're grateful for a sisterhood of amazing women—too many to mention—who have surrounded us during this project. Big hugs to Chris Pringle and Bernie Kelsey, who led the way for a community of women—C3 Everywoman—around the world to mesh their hearts with Alice and the girls in her care.

Special thanks go to my husband, Andrew Tyndale, who as well as being my keenest fan and chief encourager, has also sacrificed time, finance and emotional energy to bring this book into being. To Andrew and our children, Tim, Liam and Imogen, who graciously endured an absent or distracted mother: thank you for your unending support and for sharing my burden to bring change to the poor and vulnerable.

Postscript

At the end of 2020, CCF changed its name to Te-Kworo Foundation. Te-Kworo means *under the kworo tree* in Lwo, the Acholi language, and it was under a kworo tree in an IDP camp where Alice first met with girls as they returned from captivity. The kworo tree is a place where Acholi meet, make decisions and reconcile disputes. The kworo fruit provides nourishment, while the tree's branches give shade in summer and provide shelter from storms. The kworo tree's roots are deep, and like the girls themselves, the tree grows shoots of new life and growth after hardship.

Te-Kworo seeks to fill a community void left when international humanitarian efforts moved on to more pressing crises in the region. Activities have expanded to meet many other areas of community need: maternal and child health, immunisation programs, health outreach to remote communities, social protection, and programs to prevent early marriage and teenage pregnancy. A sister school to Pader Girls opened in Nwoya district in 2014.

Fifteen years on from the northern Ugandan conflict, Acholi still struggle to regain their lost culture and livelihoods. Recovery is a long-term prospect, with ongoing challenges like the breakdown of families, loss of values and support structures, land disputes, a dearth of agricultural skills and knowledge, and some of the highest rates of rape, early marriage and teenage pregnancy in the country. The Covid-19 pandemic is a monumental setback. As a homegrown and locally staffed community group driven by community needs, Te-Kworo is a beacon to a broken community.

At Nwoya, there is a refuge for women affected by domestic abuse. A second guesthouse at Nwoya accommodates visitors to that district, right beside the Murchison Falls National Park, and provides hospitality training for the students. The original guesthouse beside the school in Pader has been updated and is open to host visitors and local groups.

In 2017, the Maternal and Child Health (MCH) centre opened in Pader on the site of the original reception centre for children returning from the LRA conflict. The facility serves a population of 300,000 people, with at times the only doctor in the area, half a dozen midwives and nurses, a laboratory, labour room, pharmacy, four wards and two consulting rooms all crowded onto one small plot. The gift of an ambulance in 2018 has been a game-changer, saving lives each day as it rushes locals with complicated births needing caesarean sections, children anaemic from malaria or men with motorcycle injuries to hospitals in Kalongo, Kitgum or Gulu. The staff members dream of having their own operating theatre and blood bank in the district.

In 2018, Te-Kworo launched its Labour of Love safe birth program, with the ambitious goal of providing 10,000 'mama kits' to expectant mothers across the region over three years.

Without a mama kit, women are unable to give birth in a hospital or clinic. A mama kit includes soap, plastic gloves, a cloth, a razor to cut the umbilical cord, a plastic sheet for the birth and string to tie the cord. A voucher system, where a pregnant woman contributes $2 to the overall cost of $45—for antenatal care, giving birth at the MCH centre and six months of care for the baby afterwards—has brought a flood of women into the centre for supervised births. Pregnant women will walk 20 kilometres from their villages to the centre for antenatal visits.

Te-Kworo started a second mobile maternal and child health clinic in the Nwoya district in 2018, with a second ambulance. Both districts provide local community health outreach, where hundreds of people from remote communities gather for immunisation, antenatal checks and treatment of their ailments.

Alice lives in Gulu, where she can move easily between Nwoya and Pader. She has supported her three adopted teenage daughters, all orphaned by the war, through boarding school, and has plans for them to go on to university.

She continues to devote herself to improving the lives of women and girls in northern Uganda.

To find out more or to support Te-Kworo go to: **https://te-kworofoundation.org** and **www.philippatyndale.com**

Royalties from the sale of this book support Te-Kworo's work with girls in northern Uganda.

Index

Printed in the USA
CPSIA information can be obtained
at www.ICGtesting.com
CBHW041200100424
6691CB00025B/2420